Arthur Edward Waite

FORGOTTEN ESSAYS

Book First

Darrell Jordan

Library of Congress Cataloging-in Publication Data
Names: Wait, Arthur | Jordan, Darrell
Title: Arthur Edward Waite - Forgotten Essays: Book First
Description: First U.S. edition. | Coeur D'Alene, Idaho: Athenaia [2024]
Identifiers: LCCN (pending) | ISBN 979-888556-049-8 (First Edition hardcover)
Subjects: OCC016000: BODY, MIND & SPIRIT / Occultism |
HI036000: PHILOSOPHY / Hermeneutics |
REL047000: RELIGION / Mysticism
LCCN record available at https://lccn. loc.gov

On the internet: Parallel47North.com/collections/esoteric-books
Managing Editor: Darrell Jordan
Original Author and Essay: Arthur Edward Waite
Executive Producer: Yuka Jordan
Book Cover Art and Illustrations: Jessica Naomi
Image Credits: Arthur Waite's and Darrell Jordan's personal collections

Printed and bound in the United States

Publisher: Athenaia, LLC
2370 N Merritt Crk Lp, Ste 1
Coeur D'Alene, ID 83814 , The United States
Enquiry@Athenaia.Co

Arthur Edward Waite
FORGOTTEN ESSAYS
Book First

Darrell Jordan

Dedication

To those who Search for Truth and
a Path with Heart.

Seat of Knowledge

An Inprint of Athenaia, LLC

Contents

FORWARD

Book First: THE MYSTICISM OF A. E. Waite

IT happens that when one seeks for the three writers of the most important and significant books on mysticism recently published in England, one immediately calls to mind Dean Inge, Miss Evelyn Underhill, and Mr. A. E. Waite. The first two have in common with one another more than either has with the third. Employing a loose classification, the attitude of Dean Inge towards mysticism may be termed philosophic, that of Miss Underhill scientific, and that of Mr. Waite sacramental. Both Dean Inge and Miss Underhill are associated with the Established Church, but Mr. Waite, while he stands apart from all formal religion, is avowedly sympathetic towards Roman Catholicism.

The importance of youthful influences may have been overstressed in recent years, but anyone who attempts to define Mr. Waite's position in the literature of mysticism and neglects to give due consideration to the early influences of this writer is willfully throwing away an important key. It cannot be denied that Dean Inge, although the severest critic of the modern age, with the possible exception of Mr. Chesterton, is nevertheless as much a product of it as Mr. Wells or Mr. Shaw; while of Miss Underhill, it can be said that she is perfectly at ease with current scientific and philosophic speculations. But Mr. Waite stands apart from the life of to-day. His spirit, inasmuch as it pertains to any historical period, unmistakably belongs to the Middle Ages.

A conception of the Middle Ages which assumes this period to have been wholly one of superstition and unreason is current. Such a false conception is not intended here. It is not contended that the mind of Mr. Waite lacks logic, nor that he is incapable of analytic and synthetic thought. Indeed, the purpose of this essay is to indicate that Mr. Waite's most important achievement is his acute analysis of the mystic's position. The contention is that, although the method of scientific thought is employed by Mr. Waite, the general outlook of modem man is undeniably foreign to him. His mind is calmer, more reposeful than that of the modem mind, and above all he has certitude and conviction.

We are told that Mr. Waite was scarcely out of his teens when one day, while browsing around a second-hand bookseller's, he came across a copy of Eliphas Levi's Dogme et Rituel de l'haute magie. No one who has read this amazing concoction of truth and charlatanism, written in a cunning and fascinating style, can doubt the nature of the impression which it made upon the sensitive mind of Arthur Waite. The glamour of magic is incomprehensible to those who have not sensed it, but to those others who have come under its spell, the very symbol suggests unseen worlds. There can be little speculation as to the effect which magic had upon Mr. Waite in these early days, but it is only necessary to study his writings to discover the extent to which his thought was bound up with ancient magic.

Mr. Waite is a voluminous writer and has produced many scholarly and illuminating books, but those which are the most significant and certainly the most relevant to my present purpose are two—The Occult Sciences and Lamps of Western Mysticism.

The Occult Sciences was published first in 1891, when Mr. Waite was just over thirty. A secondary title might well be The Magician's Vade-mecum. In the space of under three hundred pages, all phases of magic are discussed, and in so critical yet earnest a manner as must have startled the world when this book was first given to it. There is no other work on the subject of a corresponding size which is at the same time so exhaustive, complete, critical and serious.

Whatever truth there may be in magic, it is certain that romantic imaginings about it are most undesirable; and those who possess the greatest knowledge of the subject will agree that in this direction lies its greatest danger. In this way, magic can fascinate, confusing and eventually destroying the mind. Investigation undertaken in a critical and scientific spirit alone is the correct approach to this subject.

There is no doubt that, when he first published this book, Mr. Waite believed that in magic he had found the surest way to the stars; in fact, he declares in its pages that experimental magic is a valid means of attaining the mystic's end. There remains this difference, however, between Mr. Waite and almost any other modem practitioner of magic—it is difficult to believe that personal experience in practical magic is unknown to him—that, even in the early days of his investigations into magic, his sole aim was mystical, and not an attempt to extend his knowledge of worlds either natural or supernatural. But if it did happen that he came across secrets regarding the nature of the universe, this was accidental and merely incidental to his quest for God. It is in this respect that Mr. Waite differs from the majority of occultists, and it is because he has sought a divine Being by the path of magic that he differs from Dean Inge and Miss Underhill.

Only those who have passed through a similar schooling can realize the nature of the temptations which besiege those who adopt this method. It is one of the greatest tributes to Mr. Waite's sanity, and to the validity of his inspiration, that he has succeeded in emerging unscathed from his journeying in the realm of magic.

Many have found themselves called upon to lead the mystic's life at one period or another of their earthly existence, but few have received that call so early, or obeyed it so whole-heartedly, as Mr. Waite has done. No one who has studied his work even but slightly can doubt that the sole aim and illuminant of his life is his desire for divine union. Nor can they overlook the fact that with a richer experience his attitude towards magic has changed, and that method which he once considered the mystic way par excellence is now held by him not only as being invalid, but rather a way of illusion and self-deception.

"Mysticism," like most words descriptive of mental states and conditions, has received an undue amount of abuse and maltreatment. It is impossible to obtain a clear definition of the word from dictionaries, and most other books of reference are equally useless. It cannot be denied that this term has been employed by some to indicate vagueness of thought; but that these are as incorrect as those who regard it as a synonym for occult science or magic is demonstrated by the fact that mysticism definitely leads to a condition beyond thought. It dispenses with thought, and on this account is systematically opposed by those who maintain that, if reality can be comprehended, it is only by the normal faculties of the mind that this is possible. Mysticism does not solve world problems, does not give knowledge of other planes of existence. It does not claim to give knowledge—in the accepted sense of the word—of reality, unless by this phrase is implied Divine Union.

Mysticism from which the added superfluities of formal religion have been removed resolves itself into this: Mysticism is the attempt of the human mind to effect communication with God. From this desire to come in contact with Infinity, all religion has sprung, and on its realization, all religious truth depends.

Mysticism is not a creed, but an experience, and Mr. Waite is not propounding a theory, but speaking from experience, when he says that he who seeks out a Divine Being does not search in vain, but is rewarded by certitude and the knowledge of whence he has come and whither he is going. Mr. Waite has defined the mystic's position in the simplest terms; he has as clearly declared what it is not. He has sundered mysticism and occultism, and has indicated that, whatever truth there may be in spiritism, it has nothing to teach the mystic, for he knows that sooner or later he must return whence he came, and is therefore not concerned with intermediary stages of being. That there are various states of mystical experience is admitted, but all are experiences of joy. Whether the final experience can come to man while still in the flesh—that state of consciousness perhaps beyond consciousness in the accepted sense, which is termed divine union, and which is truly said to "pass all understanding"—is a question Mr. Waite is unable to answer.

The day has passed when competent psychologists can overlook the problems raised by the mystical experience; in fact, it is a subject which increasingly demands their attention. But psychology is still a young science, which has not yet fully emerged from its elementary stage: its methods are still uncertain and its conclusions tentative, while mysticism is the oldest art practiced by man. Psychology has shown, however, that the mystic's experience is one of a definite and unique kind, which cannot be confused with other experiences exhibiting similar, but superficial, resemblances. It is, however, in their interpretations of this experience that psychologist and mystic differ; for the psychologist maintains that "the still, small voice," the apparent divine response, the mystic senses, is nothing more than one section of the brain, the whole being in a condition of dissociation, responding to the other. But psychologists bear witness to the intense ecstasy of the experience, and are of the opinion that it is perhaps the most beneficial which one can participate in, for it appears to possess the power of re-establishing order and bringing harmony to the mind. The competent investigator realizes that mysticism cannot lightly be dismissed, and whether the mystic's experience is valid according to his interpretation or not, it seems probable that therein lies the solution of a large number of our modern mental problems.

Under many different symbols, and in a multitude of myths and legends, Mr. Waite has spoken of the mystic's experience. He has seen glimmerings of it in many unlikely places, and has discovered references to it in the legend of the Holy Graal, in Alchemy, in the Rosicrucian Order, in ancient Israel, and in Freemasonry. Whatever interpretation one may finally give to his experiences, one cannot deny their depth and intensity. One cannot doubt that he has passed far on the mystic's way, for he has spoken of it as clearly as words will avail him, and now that it would appear that he has passed to a deeper state beyond the power of normal language, he has been compelled to resort to symbolism and fable.

Pure mysticism is unconcerned with world problems, and those who seek in the writings of A.E. Waite a solution to the enigma of the universe must be disappointed. He is not interested in general religious problems. He is not a great moral teacher, for morals do not enter into his sphere. He does not speak of the future; he does not prophesy a spiritual revival, or the contrary. His sole concern is with the attainment of the mystic's goal. This does not imply coldness or selfishness on his part. In innumerable books, he has given the most valuable help which any man can give in these matters; while those who are favored with his friendship testify to his warmth and generosity of spirit. For him, the world is a symbol, and life a sacrament, "an outward and visible sign of an inward and spiritual grace." He is in the great tradition of mystics, and, like his great predecessors, he has borne witness to states of consciousness unknown to us who are less gifted, less spiritually refined. He has freed mysticism from the shackles of formal religion, and has given it to us in its pure form. He has set an example to be followed, and has indicated how this may be most easily achieved. He has found the Infinite, and if this be illusion, it is the Great Illusion.

Illusion or reality, the experience remains, and the testimony of Mr. Waite proves that it is one which may well be described as ecstatic. The path has been shown to us, and it depends on us whether we follow it or turn aside. It is only one possessed of great courage, sincerity, discernment and refinement who could have achieved what Mr. Waite has done, who could have followed the path of the mystics in these modern days, and who, avoiding illusion, can speak so lucidly and so fearlessly of his experiences.

Luis Trew

THE LIFE OF THE MYSTIC

January, 1905

THERE are certain conventional terms which, on the one hand, do not accurately represent the construction placed upon them along a given line, but that construction has been accepted so long and so generally that the defect in the application may be regarded as partially effaced; and, on the other hand, there are also conventional terms between which a distinction has come into existence, although it is not justified by their primary significance. As regards the first class, the very general use of the term "occult movement" may be taken as an example. It is inexact after two manners: in involves at once too much and too little—too much, because it has served to represent a good deal that is not at all of the occult order; and too little, because a slight change in the point of view would bring within the range of its meaning many things which nobody who now uses it would think of, including therein. The doings of more than one great secret political organization might, in the full sense of the words, require to be classed as part of the occult movement, though no one will need to be informed that the latter is not political; while certain events which have occurred and are occurring in the open day, and have all along challenged the verdict of public opinion, cannot strictly be included in occultism, as they betray none of its external characteristics.

I refer to the phenomena of animal magnetism, hypnotism, spiritualism and all that which is included in the field of psychical research. In respect of the second class, a very clear differentiation now exists between the term's "occult" and "mystic," and it is one also which it is necessary to recognize, though, fundamentally speaking, the two words are identical, differing only in the fact that one of them is of Latin and the other of Greek origin.

By the occultist, we have come to understand the disciple of one or all of the secret sciences; the student, that is to say, of alchemy, astrology, the forms and methods of divination, and of the mysteries which used to be included under the generic description of magical. The mystic is, at the first attempt, perhaps more difficult to describe, except in the terminology of some particular school of thought; he has no concern as such with the study of the secret sciences; he does not work on materials or investigate forces which exist outside himself; but he endeavors, by a certain training and the application of a defined rule of life to re-establish correspondence with the divine nature from which, in his belief, he originated, and to which his return is only a question of time, or what is commonly understood as evolution.

The distinction between the occultist and the mystic, however much the representative of physical science at the present day might be disposed to resent the imputation, is therefore, loosely speaking, and at least from one point of view, the distinction between the man of science and the man of introspection. The statement, as we shall see, is not exhaustive, and it is not indeed descriptive. It may be said more fully, in the words of the late Edward Maitland, that the occultist is concerned with "transcendental physics, and is of the intellectual, belonging to science," while the mystic "deals with transcendental metaphysics, and is of the spiritual, belonging to religion."

Expressed in modern terms, this is really the doctrine of Plotinus, which recognizes "the subsistence of another intellect, different from that which reasons, and which is denominated rational." Thus, on the one hand, there are the phenomena of the transcendental produced on the external plane, capable of verification and analysis, up to a certain point; and, on the other, there is the transcendental life. "That which is without corresponds with that which is within," says the most famous Hermetic maxim; indeed, the connection suggested is almost that of the circumference with the center; and if there is a secret of the soul expressed by the term mysticism, the phenomena of the soul manifesting on the external plane must be regarded as important; but these are the domain of occultism.

The importance must, of course, differ as the phenomena fall into higher and lower classes; the divinations of geomancy carry an appearance of triviality, while the design of ceremonial magic to establish communication with higher orders of extra-mundane intelligence wears a momentous aspect; but both are the exercise of seership, and this gift, as a testimony of the soul and her powers, is never trivial. Assuming therefore a relationship subsisting between occult practice and the transcendental life of the soul, it seems worthwhile to contrast for a moment the work of the mystic with that of the disciple of occult science; so as to realize as accurately as possible the points of correspondence and distinction between Ruysbroeck, St. John of the Cross and Saint-Martin, as types of the mystic school, and Arnoldus de Villanova and Martines de Pasqually, as representing the school of occult science.

The examples of such a contrast must naturally be sought in the past, because, although occult science is pursued at the present day, and by some ardently, it can scarcely be said to have votaries like those who were of old. The inquiry belongs also to the past in respect of the mystic, for, to speak plainly, the saint belongs to the past. So far as the life of the outside world is concerned, there is little opportunity amidst mundane distractions for the whole-hearted labors of the other centuries. The desire of the house is indeed among us, but the zeal of it is scarcely here, not, at least, in the sense of the past.

The distinction in question is more than that which is made between the man of action and the man of reflection; it is not that which we have come to regard as differentiating the man of science from the philosopher. There are many instances of synthetic occult philosophers—among them Cornelius Agrippa and Robert Fludd—who neither divined nor evoked—who were not alchemists, astrologers or theurgists—but rather interpreters and harmonizers; and yet these men were not mystics in the proper sense of the term. Nor is the distinction quite that which constitutes the essential difference between the saint and the specialist, though the occult student of the past was, in most cases a specialist who was faithful to his particular branch.

The activity and the strenuousness of the life was often greater with the mystic than in the case of the man who was dedicated to some particular division of occult knowledge, though alchemist and astrologer were both laborious men—men whose patience imbued them with something of the spirit which governs modern scientific research. The ground of the contrast is in the purpose which actuated the two schools of experience. The crucible in which metals are transmuted, on the assumption of alchemy, is still a crucible and the converted metal is still a metal; so also, the astrologer may trace the occult and imponderable influences of the stars, but the stars are material bodies.

The practical work of the mystic concerned, on the contrary, the soul's union with God, for, to state it briefly, this, and this only, is the end of mysticism. It is no study of psychic forces, nor, except incidentally, is it the story of the soul and her development, such as would be involved in the doctrine of reincarnation. It is essentially a religious experiment and is the one ultimate and real experiment designed by true religion. It is for this reason that, in citing examples of mystics; I have chosen two men who were eminent for sanctity in the annals of the Christian Church, for we are concerned only with the West; while the third, though technically out of sympathy, essentially belonged to the

Church. I must not, therefore, shrink from saying that the alternative name of the mystic is that of the saint when he has attained the end of his experiment. There are also other terms by which we may describe the occultist, but they refer to the science which he followed.

The life of the mystic was then, in a peculiar sense, the life of sanctity. It was not, of course, his exclusive vocation; if we are to accept the occult sciences at their own valuation, more than one of them exacted, and that not merely by implication, something more than the God-fearing, clean-living spirit, which is so desirable even in the ordinary business man. He who was in search of transmutation was counseled, in the first instance, to convert himself, and the device on the wall of his laboratory was Labora but also Ora.

The astrologer, who calculated the influences of the stars on man, was taught that, in the last resource, there was a law of grace by which the stars were ruled. Even the conventional magician, he who called and controlled spirits, knew that the first condition of success in his curious art was to be superior to the weakness of the inconstant creatures whose dwelling is amidst the flux of the elements. I have said that, in most cases, the occult student was, after his manner, a specialist—he was devoted to his particular branch.

Deep down in the heart of the alchemist there may have been frequently the belief that certain times and seasons were more favorable than others for his work, and that the concealed materials which he thought of symbolically as the Sun and Moon, as Mercury, Venus or Mars, were not wholly independent of star and planet in the sky; and hence no doubt he knew enough of elementary astrology to avoid afflicted aspects and malign influences. But, outside this, the alchemist was not an astrologer, and to be wise in the lore of the stars was an ambition that was sufficient for one life, without meddling in the experiments of alchemy.

On the other hand, the mystic, in common with all the members of his community, having only one object in view, and one method of pursuing it—by the inward way of contemplation—had nothing to differentiate and could not therefore specialize. Again, occult science justifies itself as the transmission of secret knowledge from the past, and the books which represent the several branches of this knowledge to bear upon them the outward marks that they are among the modes of this transmission, without which it is certain that there would be no secret sciences. The occult student was, therefore, an initiate in the conventional sense of the term—he was taught, even in astrology.

There were schools of Kabalism, schools of alchemy, schools of magic, in which the mystery of certain knowledge was imparted from adept to neophyte, from master to pupil. It is over this question of corporate union that we have at once an analogy and a distinction between the mystic and the occultist. The former, as we find him in the West, may in a sense be called an initiate because he was trained in the rule of the Church; but the historical traces of a secret association for mystic objects during the Christian centuries are very slight, whereas the traces of occult association are exceedingly strong.

The mysteries of pre-Christian times were no doubt schools of mystic experience. Plato and Plotinus were assuredly mystics who were initiated in these schools. Unfortunately, the nature of this experience has come down to us, for the most part, in a fragmentary and veiled manner. But, outside exoteric writings, it has in my belief come down, and it is possible to reconstruct it, at least intellectually and speculatively, for it is embedded in the symbolic modes of advancement practiced by certain secret societies which now exist among us.

A transmission of mystic knowledge has therefore taken place from the past, but the evidence is of an exceedingly complex nature and cannot be explained here. Nor is it necessary to our purpose, for western mysticism is almost exclusively the gift of the Church to the West, and the experiment of Christian mysticism, without any veils or evasions, is written at large in the literature of the Church. It may call to be re-expressed for our present requirements in less restricted language, but there is not really any need to go further. "The Ascent of Mount Carmel," "The Adornment of the Spiritual Marriage," and "The Castle of the Inward Man," contain the root-matter of the whole process.

I have also found it well and exhaustively described in obscure little French books, which might appear at first sight to be simply devotional manuals for the use of schools and seminaries. I have found it in books equally obscure, which a few decades ago would have been termed Protestant. There is the same independent unanimity of experience and purpose through all which the alchemists have claimed for their own literature, and I have no personal doubt that the true mystics of all times and countries constitute an unincorporated fellowship communicating continually together in the higher consciousness. They do not differ essentially in the East or the West, in Plotinus or in Gratry.

In its elementary presentation, the life of the mystic consists primarily in the detachment of the will from its normal condition of immersion in material things and in its redirection towards the goodwill which abides at the center. This center, according to the mystics, is everywhere and is hence, in a certain sense, to be found in all; but it is sought most readily, by contemplation, as at the center of the man himself, and this is the quest and finding of the soul. If there is not an open door—an entrance to the closed palace—within us, we are never likely to find it without us. The rest of the experiences are those of the life of sanctity leading to such a ground of divine union as is possible to humanity in this life. In the distinction—analogical, as already said—which I have here sought to establish, there lies the true way to study the lives of the mystics and of those who graduated in the schools of occult science.

The object of that study, and of all commentary arising out of such lives, is to lead those, and there are thousands, who are so constituted as to desire the light of mysticism, to an intellectual realization of that light. The life of the mystic belongs to the divine degree, and it would be difficult to say that it is attainable in the life of the world; but some of its joys and consolations—as indeed its trials and searching's—are not outside our daily ways. Apart from all the heroisms, and in the outer courts only of the greater ecstasies, there are many who would set their face towards Jerusalem if their feet were put upon the way—and would thus turn again home.

LESSER MYSTERIES OF THE LIFE OF LIFE

October, 1905

IT is possible to quote many names which belong to the literature of mysticism within the folds of the Christian Churches, and a few at least from which appeal would perhaps seem perilous. But we can almost calculate in legions the names of those who, in virtue of some limitation, either through a stricture in their surroundings or deficiency of faculty and grace, appear rather as dwellers on the borders of that which for every mystic is the life of life. They have left their memorials behind them, and these indicate that the threshold on which they remained had open doors through which they could and did behold not only the sacred rites celebrated in long cloisters, but something of the grand mysteries which are particular to the sanctuary itself. One of their characteristics is therefore an experience which, of its kind, is obtained at first hand and this has always its grade of value; while, seeing that so many of us, for whom the greater experience of the mystic has become the one thing desirable, are, by our callings and their environments, precluded from nearly everything that is outside the simple intellectual realization, it often happens that such memorials can offer us aids to reflection in ways that are comparatively easy, sometimes almost elementary. In this manner the "second best," though it enters into no comparison with the great good, brings to us precious gifts, as the Kings of the East brought gold, frankincense and myrrh—gifts which signify all that is beyond themselves and the givers. I propose some brief exclusion into these paths, now almost untrodden, taking as exemplars certain writings and their authors in which, I have personally found suggestions, and believe that they may prove of service to others.

One of these books has been known for many years past to a few collectors of the lesser curiosities of the soul, which no less lean towards greatness, under the title of, Le Mystère dr la Croix, affligeante et consolante, de Jésus Christ et de ses Membres, écrit au milieu de la Croix au dedans et au dehors. It has suffered from the neglect of centuries, and it has perhaps also suffered from the zeal of its rare admirers.

The Mystery of the Cross has a literary story which is at once unusual and not a little suggestive. It was finished, according to the original title page, on August 12, 1732, and it was published in the course of the same year without apparently attracting any marked attention. This notwithstanding, it appeared in a German translation at Leipsic in 1782, and it has been stated that in this form it was long read and highly prized by the philosophical circles of the period. It was also re-issued at Lausanne in 1786, or 1791, under the attributed editorship of Philippe du Toit de Mambrini, who, adopting a certain guise of Protestantism and an assumed name, published a number of volumes which are adaptations of Christian Mysticism conceived in an errantry of the spirit that is not less than bizarre. The first French issue had become very scarce in his day, and there is ground to think that it was misconceived by the alleged editor, who refers to it in his own works; but I have no record of its destiny under his fantastic hands. Probably it perished, almost without a sign, and was unheard of until it attracted attention from the anonymous author of a book called A Suggestive Enquiry into the Hermetic Mystery, of which a few copies were circulated prior to its destruction in the year 1850. Ten years later the French book was reprinted in London, under the auspices of Williams & Norgate as publishers, by an English editor, also anonymous, who neglected the obvious precaution of translating it, so that it is still under its first seals. A rendering in manuscript does, however, exist, though I am unable to speak of its claims. The author termed himself simply "A Disciple of the Cross of Jesus," and till 1877 it was known only in Germany that this pseudonym covered, or is said to have covered, the identity of a Mystic called Douze-Tems, described as a countryman and spiritual kinsman of Madame Guyon.

Dr. Otto Zoeckler, who furnishes this information, does not appear to speak with any firsthand knowledge; it seems probable from its form that the book was, as its writer hints, the work of a man experimenting in a language not wholly familiar to himself, and it is possible at least that he was a German of French descent. Dr. Zoeckler's work unfortunately errs in several ways on the side of imprudence, as its English translation in 1877 veers perilously towards the illiterate. There is no reason, in any case, to suppose that a name like Douze-Tems is itself anything better than a pseudonym. On the whole, we must rest content with the scanty particulars which have been transmitted by report concerning the writer, as follows:

1. That his ancestors were French Protestants of the Desert.

2. That he sought an asylum from persecution in the dominions of the Elector of Saxony.

3. Finally, that for some unknown reason, he was imprisoned at Sonnestein on the Elbe. The last statement rests on the authority of the book, and is the only certainty concerning the author, though, in spite of one whimsical remark, somewhat after the manner of Leibnitz, it is difficult to suppose that he was wholly unconnected with so much of the Rosicrucian movement as may have remained in secret at his period. The connexion is palpably to be assumed from a number of his allusions and generally from his affiliations in mysticism. On this subject it is scarcely possible, or indeed necessary, to enlarge in the present place, nor does it signify much about what was the author's private history or what his real patronymic. Perhaps, in the last resource, it would also not signify seriously to the mystic if the Fraternity mentioned had been itself, as Douze-Tems suggests, only a beautiful invention, though projected in good faith. It is possible, however, that the remark may call for a certain interpretation, and is an instance of the precaution concerning which the author has warned the correspondent whom he addresses, and readers generally through him, namely, that several matters have not been

fully treated, and that about others his prudence has counselled him to maintain a certain reserve. The various chapters are indeed sown with maxims extracted literally from published Rose Cross documents, and it is difficult to account for such uniform fidelity in citation if Douze-Tems did not possess affiliations which he informally disavows. However this may be, he has signal connexions in literature which are of the esoteric order outside anything that he may have derived from sources ascribed to the Fraternity. He recalls continually the later Kabalists, for one example, and he must have celebrated many unusual marriages in books before he wrote his own treatise.

I mention these points because they will interest people who are concerned rather with historical issues, and on this account, they are not less than important. I must perhaps confess to some personal predilection derived from strange ways of reading if I express the opinion that it is probably from the later Kabalists that Douze-Tems drew part at least of the intellectual generosity, which is one of his most attractive characteristics. There is nothing to show that he knew them at first hand, but there were many treasures of learning then available in Latin books which presented Jewish theosophy as an eirenicon between the Law of Moses and the Law of Christ, and which sought at once to lay the foundation of lasting peace in Israel and to heal the many dissensions of the several sects in Christendom.

From sectarian bitterness Douze-Terns was wholly free, and, though certainly not a Catholic, he speaks invariably with an enlightened indulgence towards the Latin Church and its mystery which, at his period, was exceedingly rare in those that did not belong to it. As the work is so little known and in no sense readily accessible, I must not permit it to be inferred that its Rosicrucian and Kabalistic connexions make The Mystery of the Cross beyond measure obscure and difficult. On the contrary, it is a manageable treatise which, supposing discrimination in the student, is full of wise guidance and ministries at the initial stages of the life within.

It has, in an unusual degree, that seal of conviction which I have already mentioned; in spite of certain limitations, that are sufficiently obvious, it is the work of a man who has been in those high places of which he discourses, and there will be no disposition to challenge his claim to the use of one daring statement which appears in his first lines: A bsque nube pro nobis. What was this darkness which for him had ceased to be clouded and of which he claims to have written both "within and without"—that is to say, with a plain external sense and yet with an inward meaning? Who was this pilgrim through eternity who could cite that other maxim: Dulcia non meruit qui non gustavit amara—which bitterness is actually the experience of that cross, the mystery of which he records? He says further, with the Rosicrucian Masters, who went before him:

In cruce sub sphcera

Venit sapientia vera.

Here there is no opportunity to discuss questions of symbolism, but the simple planetary figure of the star Venus represents, for those who used it after this concealed fashion, the crucifixion of love issuing in that wisdom which is not of this world. Those who are acquainted with symbolism may be disposed to regard the apparently obscure allusion as one of the keys which opens the closed entrance to the particular palace of Douze-Tems; for, in its final understanding, the work of the mystic can only present itself to the mind as a part of the work of that love which produced the whole universe in consequence of an infinite clemency. In this case, the bitterness which is inseparable from the Cross of advancement is the essential acerbity of election, whereby that which is gross is transmuted, and this realized, the darkness of all the Carmels is indeed no longer clouded.

The book is divided into fifteen tabulated considerations—on the origin of the Cross; its outward and inward providences; its use and misuse; its perpetuation after death; the supernatural experiences which it comprises; and in particular its lessons of humiliation and of victory in the passion and death of Christ. It is not a work which lends itself readily to quotation, or to any process of summarizing which will carry much light with it. A synopsis of its chapters would also suggest little, apart from the knowledge of its pages. To put the matter briefly, it is a story of the experience of a soul to which utter resignation has brought peace and knowledge by some firsthand contact with hidden truth.

If the afflictions and advancements of the Cross were those simply which are less or more with us along all our daily roads; if they were entirely identical with our common trials and were the common recompense of our resignations; there would be little probably between the leaves of this book which would make its notice seem necessary, for the literature of the lighter mysticism is almost as the sands of the sea. It provides the first spelling-books and readers of the spiritual life in all the churches and sects; and it is characterized by every convention and every form of insufficiency. On the surface, nevertheless, or at least for many people, this may well seem to be the simple limits of the message found in The Mystery of the Cross. It is certainly the rigid term for those unversed in the separation of the inward from the outward sense—for those to whom the spiritual expression intus et foris scriptus means something that is past finding out. But there are others who will understand readily enough, under what guise soever, that the Cross about which there is a mystery is no economy of catholic salvation, as it is no mere application of morality, and it is to these that the obscure mystic will come with another meaning in his message than that of light trials in life and the way to bear them. He will say that the knowledge of God is only to be obtained at the center, while this center must be sought, which is not by any means impossible in the present life, though no teacher can affirm that the path is easy. There can also be no question that it carries the seeker far away from those putative particular centers which are recognized and count for anything in the material world. It is often claimed that a certain knowledge of the divine, as at great distances and I know not under what veils, is obtainable by the testimony of things which are without; and it is indeed to furnish these evidences that is the chief purpose of the multiplicity which exists in Nature. The Mystery of the Cross has some of the sacramental kinships which come from the touch of Nature, but it makes wholly for that final end, of which its author truly says that there is none other conceivable as a term of the soul. It is married, as will be expected, to a doctrinal system which, within limits, is characteristic of the period, though for that period it is also liberal, in the laudable sense of the word. It is liberal, for example, in eschatology, not in the sentimental sense which sometimes draws a broad mark of cancellation over great principles of equity, but with a simplicity which is chaste, severe and conscious of the counterclaim, yet ends as reasonable eschatology can alone end, namely with God as all in all for all that lives and has its being in Him.

We are not so intellectually certain at the present day that the old divines and single-hearted seers of the past, clearly as they did discern and steadfastly as they were accustomed to look, are entirely indisputable guides upon specific doctrinal points. We may not be prepared to accept literally the particular interpretation offered by The Mystery of the Cross concerning, let us say, the descent of Christ into Hades; certain issues have entered into the mystic consciousness, which had scarcely been raised in the days of the early leaders; and this is why I have referred to a saving gift of discernment as desirable in the modem student. All this notwithstanding, the book remains, when it is taken in the larger sense, as one which will be helpful in the initial stages because it makes for that kind of righteousness which must be the first possession of the mystic, namely, the unswerving devotion to something which has got to be done with his might, constituting the origin of that general and catholic cross which he has to bear in the flesh,—and which is the common burden, as it is also the common support, of those who have resolved steadfastly to enter the true path. That it has its advantages is known early, as it is assuredly known fully. That for the world it must be always folly, because the world can judge only after discrimination of its own kind; and that it is at the same time the first step in wisdom; this he will also know; and it is indeed assumed beforehand. That it is a cross within as well as a cross without, he has to realize profoundly; and seeing that all mystics are acquainted with seasons of inhibition, he will in due course experience what our author terms, "the use and abuse of the Cross." But when he has overcome in this struggle, he will have entered already into a moderate familiarity with the designs of God in the Cross, and will be prepared to realize that, in so far as he falls short of his term, this Cross will follow him to the end of his days, even after death, at once his humiliation and his triumph.

I have perhaps intentionally presented what might be termed the metaphysical process of The Mystery of the Cross without guise or decoration. It proceeds entirely from the principle that it is impossible for God to do otherwise than love His children, however far they pass under the law of rebellion, and, so far as I am aware, it is to this extent the first professedly mystic thesis concerning that reintegration of man in God which became afterwards so famous in the school of Martines de Pasqually and his successors. The punishments of the Cross after death are therefore the free workings of the scheme of redemption, and humanity ends where it also began, in the Divinity which is its home. Some ways are short and keen and splendid; some are long and obscure, with the darkness of all suspension and desolation; but the term is still the same: and sweetened by patience and clemency the mystic who has sounded the depths, but at the same time can give us a scale plan professionally tabulated of many exalted altitudes, has come forth from the experience consoled, saying with a later adept, that God who alone is real and alone present everywhere, fills the limitless immensity with the splendors of the sovereign reason.

The lessons of the recluse of Sonnestein, though delivered with an accent which is individual and set apart almost wholly from the conventions and commonplaces of the purely devotional treatise, have their affiliations in mystic literature which not only deserve remark but have actually an aspect of importance, because they interlink men whose writings and lives were at the same time widely different. To simplify this point, I will mention six dates which represent the publication of as many books, the first of which is The Mystery of the Cross, in 1732. The second date is 1615, just prior to the Rosicrucian fervors, when the great name of Cardinal Bellarmine was attached to a title of the tract concerning "The Ascent of the Mind in God by the Grade of Natural Things." The third is 1677, when the works of a lesser but still illustrious prince of the Church, Cardinal John Bona, were collected at Antwerp, including his Manuductio ad Cælum and Via Compendii ad Deum. The fourth is the year 1738, which saw the appearance of the first volume of The Testimony of a Child of the Resurrection on several matters of the Interior Life, extending in all to nine volumes, which were the work of an unknown author, assisted by an anonymous editor, and were in their way a treasury of singular discourses. The fifth is 1784, when Louis Claude de Saint-Martin issued his Ecce Homo. The sixth and last book appeared in 1801 at Paris, as a translation from the Russian, under the title of Quelques traits de l'Eglise Intérieur. It connects, quite undesignedly, with The Cloud upon the Sanctuary, though it does not possess its authority, or indeed its convincing accent. I am unable to give any information concerning the ostensible author, the Chevalier Loupoukine, and I must dissuade my readers from supposing that I am simply making a short bibliographical list. The dates, if not exactly nothing, are of slender importance, and the only consanguinity between the persons is that of the spiritual order, on the principle, recognized by Saint-Martin, that all who have truly attained their spiritual majority use the same language since they come from the same country. Speaking generally, they owed nothing to one another, though the two Cardinals may have made acquaintance in the letter, even as they were united in the experience. Further, it may be true, as suggested by Mambrini, that Saint-Martin had once at least met with The Mystery of the Cross, but there is nothing to justify our expression of a bare possibility, from which very little would have followed, in the language of even tolerable certainty. I should say that the Chevalier Loupoukine had never heard of Eckartshausen, and it signifies less than little for the range of the documents that the unknown Child of the Resurrection, as well as his editor, had read quite widely the current French literature of mysticism. At the same time, as I have intimated, they are all kindred in the spirit, and the order in which I have cited them, though it violates chronology, is one which would serve to simplify the successive tabulation of their points of correspondence and divergence, as also after what manner one accounts for another, while he also extends another, each testifying signally to each, almost supposing each, after the tacit manner.

The truth is that such books, as also already indicated, are like doors which open successively, distance beyond distance, into certain great chambers of the soul. Their analogy is hereof, and hereof is also their importance. The works of Cardinal Bellarmine and Cardinal Bona, fully differentiated as they are between themselves, constitute an introduction to a spiritual life of the active and practical kind, while fully enforcing the true end of that life and the particular mastery of its experience. They have naturally many elements that have passed out of the region of necessity, and they are more valuable as intimations than as precise handbooks. Shall I say that they occupy, relatively speaking, much the same position as a Layman's Mass-book, reproduced from a rare manuscript by the Early English Text Society, when compared with a literal Missal containing all the local variations, all the propers of the saints and all the rubrics? I am speaking of course suggestively, not instituting a parallel. They contain what devotional treasuries term the Key of Heaven, but they do not always open exactly the kind of doors by which we, in these days, can most directly gain entrance into the House of the Father. On the other hand, the Ecce Homo, though it is much more profound, much more advanced, as one would say, calls for restatement and, as it stands, for some enlightened reserve, while The Mystery of the Cross is not without a certain fantastic spirit and the Testimony of a Child is a little hindered by its diffusive sentiment. Of The Characteristics of the Interior Church it is more difficult to speak; it is at once so much and so little—so much in its unconscious analogies with the far more important work of Eckartshausen and so little, since, from one point of view, it is purely a devotional treatise, one among many thousands, and not especially distinctive.

It is impossible within the limits of a single article to make an express summary of points of correspondence, and the bare affirmation must suffice, at least for the moment. To myself it comes with a certain quality of illumination. The different actuating influences, modes of thought and even of point of view, on the part of mystics who were at heart really one and tended to the same term, are assuredly of considerable importance. Those of whom we are speaking were all after their manner remarkable; they also lie beyond the habitual wake of knowledge for those who are themselves professed mystics at the present day and are exploring one or other of the same paths, unconscious perhaps how far they have been preceded.

The analogies, which are much more intimate and naturally much more easy to recognize, have one advantage which makes for simplicity of treatment; on the one hand, we are dealing with men who had attained their convictions by means of firsthand experience; but, on the other, they had not passed into those heights of the spiritual life which spell extreme difficulty for the aspirant who is seeking to follow them. The evidences of such attainment do not at least appear in the books, which are therefore serviceable manuals, well adapted for the school of the novices. The indoctrination differs, in other words, from that of St. John of the Cross, Ruysbroeck and Jacob Boehme, who are rather for adepts than for neophytes. Let me say, in conclusion, that it is better, in one sense at least, to read books that are imperfect, so only that the aim which they propose is the one undeniable and true end of all things, than the reputed masterpieces which do not make for eternity; and, this being granted, it is not only desirable but necessary that we should be proficient in the nature of their imperfections.

This is why theses like The Mystery of the Cross are so much more valuable than any technical criticism can realize, because they teach as much in their deficiencies as they teach in their fulness, though it is true that this quality of their ministration is more strictly for the doctors than the scholars. I do not mean that The Mystery of the Cross would tempt even a tyro to become a protestant of the desert, if such a vocation were possible in these days; but, its inward message notwithstanding, it might dispose him to believe that some of the great things are outside rather than within him, and that the indefectible gospel has been written elsewhere than in the soul.

I would therefore counsel the few persons who may fall across a work which the inscrutable star workings have contrived again to make rare, that they should avoid above all being scandalized at its occasional touch of the grotesque and its leaning towards issues which deflect from the path of the wise. On these accounts, it is the more rather than the less of importance; most of the great books of the soul call for re-writing, and one might have some ground to feel doubtful of any which offered no weak point to the strictures of its brethren.

There are amazing fatuities in Ruysbroeck, though he had sailed over trackless seas, and St. John of the Cross on Carmel seems occasionally like the ingenious gentleman of La Mancha rather than Galahad at the Graal Castle; but it is chiefly for this reason that, being that which they were, they can yet extend helping hands.

SOME ASPECTS OF THE GRAAL LEGEND

March, 1907
The Intimations and Suggestions of Subsurface Meaning

THE study of a great literature should begin like the preparation for a royal banquet, not without some solicitude for right conduct in the King's palace—which is the consecration of motive—and not without a recollection of that source from which the most excellent gifts derive in their season to us all. Surely the things of earth are profitable only in so far as they assist us towards the things which are eternal. In this respect, there are many helpers, even as the sands of the sea. The old books help us, perhaps above most things, and among them the old chronicles and the great antique legends. If the hand of God is in history, it is also in folklore. We can scarcely fail of our term, since lights, both close at hand and in the unlooked-for places, kindle everywhere about us. It is difficult to say any longer that we walk in the Shadow of Death when the darkness is sown with stars.

Now, there are a few legends which may be said to stand forth among the innumerable traditions of humanity, wearing upon them the external signs and characters of some secret or mystery within them which belongs, as it would seem, rather to eternity than to time. They are in no sense connected with one another—unless indeed by certain roots which are scarcely in time and place—and yet, by a suggestion which is deeper than any suggestion of the senses, it would appear as if each were appealing to each, one bearing testimony to another, and all recalling all. They might be broken fragments of some primitive revelation which, except in these legends, has passed out of written records and far from the memory of man. The fullness of their original design may be, and sometimes is, reconstructed from age to age, but the result bears always, and that of necessity, the tincture of its particular period, reflecting the first intention sometimes in a glass darkly and sometimes in a crystal brightly, so that it is less or more, according to the mind of the age. To the class of which I am speaking belongs the Graal Legend, which in all its higher aspects may be included among the legends of the soul. Perhaps I should say rather that, when it is properly understood, the Graal is not a legend, but a personal history.

It will be intelligible from this one statement that I am not putting forward a thesis for the instruction of scholarship, which is otherwise and fully equipped, and it may be desirable to make it plain from the beginning that my offering to the consideration of the literature is intended for those who have either found then placed within the sanctuary of the mystic life or are at least in the outer circles. I take up the subject where it has been left by the students of folklore and by all that which might term itself authorized scholarship. Ut adeptis appareat me illis parem et fratrem, I have made myself acquainted with the criticism of the cycle and I am familiar with the cycle itself. It is with the texts, however, that we shall be concerned, or at least more especially, and I approach them from a new standpoint. As to this, it will be better to specify from the outset its various particulars as follows: (1) The appropriation of certain myths and legends which are held to be pre-Christian in the root-matter, and their penetration by an advanced form of Christian Symbolism carried to a particular term; (2) the evidence of three fairly distinct sections or schools, the diversity of which is less, however, in the fundamental part of their subject than in the extent and mode of its development; (3) the connexion of this mode and of that form with other schools of symbolism, the evolution of which was going on at the same period as that of the Graal literature; (4) the close analogy in respect of the root-matter between the catholic literature of the Holy Graal and that which is connoted by the term Mysticism; (5) the traces through Graal romance and other coincident literatures of a hidden school in Christianity which, because it is an expression that has been used for over a century, I shall continue to call the Secret Church, though it predicates an instituted office that, I think, scarcely belongs to the unmanifested company with which it will be seen that I am concerned. Perhaps, within the admitted forms of expression, the idea corresponds more closely with that which is understood by the school of the prophets, though the term only describes a certain highly advanced state by one of the gifts which may be taken to belong thereto. This, I should add, is on an express assumption that the gift has little connexion with the external meaning of prophecy; it is not the power of seeing forward, but rather of sight within. In subjects of this kind, as in other subjects, the greater naturally includes the lesser, it being of minor importance to discern, for example, the coming of Christ in a glass of vision than to understand, either before or after, the vital significance of that coming. I mention this instance because it enables me to say, on the authority of my precursors, that it was out of the secret school, or company which had secured its election, that the Christ came at His season.

The Graal romances are not documents of this school put forward by the external way, but are its rumors at a distance. They are not authorized, nor are they stolen; they have arisen, or the consideration of the Hidden Church follows from their consideration as something in the intellectual order connected therewith. From this point of view, it is possible to collect out of the general body of the literature what I should term its intimations of subsurface meaning into a brief schedule, as follows: (a) The existence of a clouded sanctuary; (b) a great mystery; (c) a desirable communication which, except under certain circumstances, cannot take place; (d) suffering within and sorcery without; (e) supernatural grace which does not possess efficacy on the external side; (f) healing, which comes from without, carrying in most cases all the signs of insufficiency and even of inhibition; (g) in fine, that which is without entering within and takes over the charge of the mystery, but it is either removed altogether or goes into deeper concealment—the outer world profits only by the removal of a vague enchantment. The unversed reader may not at the moment follow the specifics of this schedule, but if the allusions awaken his interest, I can promise that they shall be made plain as we proceed.

II
The Literature which Embodies the Legend

The mystery of the Graal is a word which came forth out of Galilee. The literature which enshrines this mystery, setting forth the several quests which were instituted on account of it, the circumstances under which it was from time to time discovered and, in fine, its imputed removal, with all involved thereby, is one of such considerable dimensions that it may be properly described as large. This notwithstanding, there is no difficulty in presenting its broad outlines so briefly that if there be anyone who is new to the subject, he can be instructed sufficiently for my purpose even I from the beginning. It is to be understood, therefore, that the Holy Graal is, except in the German version of the legend, represented invariably as that vessel in which Christ celebrated the Last Supper and consecrated for the first time the elements of the Eucharist. According to the legend, its next use was to receive the blood from the wounds of Christ when His body was taken down from the Cross, or alternatively, from the side, which was pierced by the spear of Longas. Under circumstances which are variously recounted, this vessel, its content included, was carried westward under safe guardianship, coming in fine to Britain and there remaining in the hands of successive keepers. In the days of King Arthur, the prophet and magician Merlin assumed the responsibility of carrying the legend to its term, with which object he brought about the institution of the Round Table, and the flower of Arthurian chivalry set out to find the sacred vessel. In the quests which followed, the knighthood depicted in the greater romances has become a mystery of ideality, and nothing save its feeble reflection could have been found on earth. The quests were, to some extent, preconceived in the mind of the legend, and although a few of them were successful, that which followed was the removal of the Holy Graal. The companions of the quest asked, as one may say, for bread, and to those who were unworthy there was given the stone of their proper offence, but to others the spiritual meat which passes all understanding. That this account instructs the uninitiated person most imperfectly will be obvious to anyone who is acquainted with the great body of the literature, but within the limits to which I have restricted it intentionally, I do not know that if it were put differently, it would be put better or more in harmony with the general sense of the romances.

The places of the legend, its reflections and its rumors, are France, England, Germany, Holland, Italy, Spain and Wales. France and England were united in respect of their literature during the Anglo-Norman period, and when this period was over, England contributed nothing to the Graal cycle except renderings of French texts and one compilation therefrom. It should be further remembered that, according to the mind of scholarship, several of the Anglo-Norman texts are not extant in their original form, but have been edited and harmonized. Germany had an indigenous version of the legend, combined by its own evidence, with a French source which is now unknown. The Dutch version is comparatively an old compilation, also from French sources; Italy is represented only by translations from the French, and these were the work of Rusticien de Pise; the inclusion of Spain is really a question of liberality, for there is no Spanish version of the Graal legend as such, or it exists only in the rare allusions of a certain romance of Merlin, which again was originally in French. As regards Wales, there is also no indigenous literature of the Graal legend, as it was understood by the French romancers, but there are certain primeval traditions and bardic remanents which are held to be the root-matter of the whole cycle, and two at least of the questing knights are found among the Mabinogion heroes. In the thirteenth century and later, the legend, as we now have it, was carried across the Marches, but it is represented by translations only. It follows that the Graal literature, as I understand the term, belongs solely to France and Germany. To these restrictions of place may be added a restriction of time, for nothing which is now extant can be dated prior to 1175, and after circa 1230 we have only translations and digests. The allocation of individual texts to particular dates within this period is, in certain cases, inferential and in some entirely speculative. It will be understood, therefore, that in presenting the subjoined tabulation, I am not concerned with rigid priority in time, but rather with affinities of intention, by which certain texts fall into defined groups. The literature may in this manner be classified into sections as follows:

(A) The Lesser Histories or Chronicles of the Holy Graal, otherwise, the Cycle of Robert de Borron, in which is comprised: (1) The Metrical Romance of Joseph of Arimathea; (2) the Lesser Holy Graal, which is a prose version of the metrical romance as above; (3) the Early Prose Merlin, which represents a lost metrical romance, or more accurately a poem of which 500 lines alone remain extant; (4) the Didot Perceval, so called after the designation of the only manuscript by which it is known; it presents one version of the search after the Holy Graal, as distinguished from its legendary history and the connexions thereof.

The characteristics in common of these four romances, by which they are grouped into a cycle, are: (1) The idea that certain secret words were transmitted from Apostolic times and were carried from East to West; (2) the succession of Brons as Keeper of the Holy Graal immediately after Joseph of Arimathea.

(B) The Greater Chronicles of the Holy Graal, comprising: (1) The Saint Graal, or Joseph of Arimathea, called also the first branch of the Romances of the Round Table and the Grand or Greater Holy Graal; (2) the later prose romances of Merlin, being that which, because it is more widely diffused, has been sometimes termed the Vulgate, and that which is known as the Huth Merlin, following the designation of the only extant manuscript; (3) the great prose Lancelot; (4) the great prose Perceval le Gallois, an alternative version of the quest, known also in English as the High History of the Holy Graal; (5) the Quest of the Holy Graal, called also the last book of the Round Table, containing the search and achievement of Galahad. From my standpoint, this is the quest par excellence.

It should be understood that the great prose Perceval and the great quest of Galahad exclude one another, so that they stand as alternatives in the tabulation. The characteristics of this cycle are: (1) The succession of a second Joseph as Keeper of the Holy Graal immediately after his father, Joseph of Arimathea, and during the latter's lifetime, this dignity not being conferred upon Brons, either then or later; (2) the substitution of a claim in respect of apostolical succession for that of a secret verbal formula.

(C) The Conte del Graal, otherwise, the Perceval le Gallois of Chrétien de Troyes, being the metrical romance, which comprises the quests of Perceval and Gawain. It was successively continued by several later poets, some of whose versions are alternative and exclusive of one another. The Conte del Graal is the largest document of the Anglo-Norman cycle. (D) The German cycle, comprising: (1) The Parsifal of Wolfram von Eschenbach; (2) the Titurel of Albrecht von Schaffenberg; (3) Diu Cróne ly Henrich von dem Turlin; (4) the Lancelot of Ulrich du Zazikhoven.

The dominant text of the German cycle is that of Wolfram, which is almost generically distinct from the histories and quests offered by the Anglo-Norman versions. At the moment it will be sufficient to say that it represents the Holy Graal as in the custody of a knightly company which, both expressly and by inference, recalls the order of the Knights Templar. As a final consideration in respect of all the cycles, it may be added that the romantic literature of chivalry diminishes in consequence and interest in proportion as it is removed from the Arthurian motive and period. It does not matter how remote the connexion may be, there is still the particular atmosphere. The Carlovingian cycle, in comparison, is mere indiscrimination and violence. There are no books in the manner of chivalry to compare with The Morte d' Arthur, The history of Perceval and the quest of the Haut Prince Galahad after the Holy Graal.

III
The Implicits of the Mysteries

There are several literatures which exhibit with various degrees of plainness the presence of that subsurface meaning to which I have referred in respect of the Graal legends; but there as here, so far as the outward text is concerned, it is suggested rather than affirmed. This additional sense may underlie the entire body of a literature, or it may be merely some concealed intention, or a claim put forward evasively. The subsurface significance of the Graal legends belongs mainly to the second class. It is from this point of view that my departure is here made, and if it is a warrantable assumption, some at least of the literature will, expressly or otherwise, be found to contain these elements in no uncertain manner.

As a matter of fact, we shall find them, though it is rather by the way of things which are implied, or which follow as inferences, but they are not for this reason less clear or less demonstrable. The implicits of the Graal literature are indeed more numerous than we should expect to meet with at the period in books of the western world. I believe them to exceed, for example, those which are discoverable in the alchemical writings of the late twelfth or early thirteenth century, though antecedently we might have been prepared to find them more numerous in the avowedly secret books of Hermetic adepts.

In a single section of a paper which is short of necessity, I can deal only with those which are most important, leaving to a later period any additional examples which may transpire as the inquiry proceeds. The explicit in chief of that cycle which I have termed the Lesser Histories or Chronicles of the Holy Graal is that certain secret words were communicated to Joseph of Arimathea by Christ Himself, and that these must remain in reserve, being committed from Keeper to Keeper by the oral method only. On the other hand, the implicit of Robert de Borron's poem resides in the question as to what he understood by their office. In the Lesser Holy Graal the implicit of the metrical romance passes into actual expression, and it becomes more clear in this manner that the secret words were those used by the custodians of the Holy Graal in the consecration of the elements of the Eucharist.

When the Greater Holy Graal was produced as an imputed branch of Arthurian literature, there is no need to say that the Roman Pontiff was then as now, at least in respect of his claim, the first bishop of Christendom, and, by the evidence of tradition at least, he derived from St. Peter, who was episcopus primus et pontifex primordialis.

This notwithstanding, the romance attributes the same title to a son of Joseph of Arimathea, who is called the Second Joseph, and here is the first suggestion of a concealed motive therein. The Greater Holy Graal and the metrical romance of De Borron are the texts in chief of their particular cycles, and it does not follow, or at least in all cases, that their several continuations or derivatives are extensions of the implicits which I have mentioned. In the first case, the early prose Merlin has an implied motive of its own which need not at the moment detain us, and the Didot Perceval is manifestly unauthentic as a sequel, by which I mean that it does not represent the mind of the earlier texts, though it has an importance of its own and also its own implicits. On the other hand, in what I have termed the Greater Chronicles of the Holy Graal there is, if possible, a more complete divergence in respect of the final document, and I can best explain it by saying that if we can suppose for a moment that the Grand Saint Graal was produced in the interests of a Pan-Britannic Church, or alternatively of some secret school of religion, then the Great Prose Quest, or Chronicle of Galahad, would represent an interposition on the part of the orthodox church to take over the literature. At the same time, the several parts of each cycle under consideration belong thereto and cannot be located otherwise.

The further divisions under which I have scheduled the body general of the literature, and especially the German cycle, will be considered at some length in their proper place, when their explicit and implied motives will be specified; for the present it will be sufficient to say that they do not put forward the claims with which I am now dealing, namely, the secret formula in respect of the De Borron cycle and a super-apostolical succession in respect of the Greater Holy Graal, with that which derives therefrom.

As regards both claims, we must remember that although we are dealing with a department of romantic literature, their content does not belong to romance; the faculty of invention in stories is one thing, and I think that modern criticism has made insufficient allowance for its spontaneity, yet through all the tales of chivalry it worked within certain lines. It would not devise secret Eucharistic words or put forward strange claims which almost make void the Christian apostolate in favor of some unheard of succession communicated directly from Christ after Pentecost. We know absolutely that this kind of machinery belongs to another order.

If it does not, then the apocryphal gospels were imbued with the romantic spirit, and the explanation of Manichean heresy may be sought in a flight of verse. I suppose that what follows from the claims has not entered into the consciousness of official scholarship, because it is otherwise concerned, but it may have entered already into the thought of those among my readers whose preoccupations are similar to my own, and I will now state it in a summary manner.

As the secret words of consecration, the true words which have to be pronounced over the sacramental elements so that they may be converted into the true Eucharist, have, by the hypothesis, never been expressed in writing, it follows that since the Graal was withdrawn from the world, together with its custodians, the Christian Church has had to be content with what it has, namely, a substituted sacrament. And as the super-apostolical succession, also by the hypothesis, must have ceased from the world when the last Keeper of the Graal followed his vessel into heaven, the Christian Church has again been reduced to the ministration of some other and apparently lesser succession.

If I were asked to adjudicate on the value of such claims, I should say that the doctrine is the body of the Lord and its right understanding is the spirit. Whosoever therefore puts forward a claim on behalf of secret formulae in connexion with the Eucharistic rite has forgotten the one thing needful—that there are valid consecrations everywhere. The question of apostolical succession is in the same position, because the truly valid transmissions are those of grace itself, which communicates from the source of grace direct to the soul; and the essence of the sacerdotal office is that those who have received supernatural life should assist others so to prepare their ground that they may also in due season, but always from the same source, become spiritually alive. It remains, however, that the implicits with which I have been dealing are actually the implicits in chief of the Graal books, and that they do not make for harmony with the teaching of the orthodox churches does not need stating. From whence therefore and with what intention were they imported into the body of romance? Before this question can be answered we shall have to proceed much further in the consideration of the literature, but my next section can deal only with a preliminary clearance of the ground.

As a conclusion to the present part, let me add that any scheme of interpretation which fails to account for the claim to a super-efficacious

Eucharistic consecration and a super-apostolical succession accounts for very little that is important in the last resource. It is in this sense that I take up the subject at the point where it has been left by scholarship, considering these problems in the light of all that can be gathered from the texts themselves, from certain coincident literatures, and from the theological and historical position of the Celtic Church, as a preliminary to the consideration in fine which I have already indicated by my reference to a secret school existing within the Church, or at least to be approached intellectually more readily from this direction.

IV
Some Antecedents in Folklore

The beginnings of literature are like the beginnings of life—questions of antecedents which are past finding out, and perhaps they do not signify vitally on either side, because the keys of all mysteries are to be sought in the comprehension of their term, rather than in their initial stages. Modem scholarship lays great and indeed exclusive stress on the old Celtic antecedents of the Graal literature, and on certain Welsh and other prototypes of the Perceval Quest in which the sacred vessel does not appear at all. As regards these affiliations, whether Welsh, English, or Irish, I do not think that sufficient allowance has been made for the following facts: (a) That every fiction and legend depends, as already suggested, from prior legend and fiction; (b) that the antecedents are both explicit and implicit, intentional or unconscious, just as in these days we have willful and undesigned imitation; (c) that the persistence of legends is by the way of their transfiguration.

We have done nothing to explain the ascension of the Graal to heaven and the assumption of Galahad when we have ascertained that some centuries before there were myths about the Cauldron of Ceridwen or that of the Dagda, any more than we have accounted for Christianity if we have ascertained, and this even indubitably, that some ecclesiastical ceremonial is an adaptation of pre-Christian rites. Here, as in so many other instances, the essence of everything resides in the intention. If I possess the true apostolical succession, then, ex hypothesi at least, I do not the less consecrate the Eucharist if I use the Latin rite, which expresses the act of Christ in the past tense, or some archaic oriental rite, which expressed it in the present.

There is in any case no question as to the Graal antecedents in folklore, and I should be the last to minimize their importance after their own kind, just as I should not abandon the official Church because I had been received into the greater Church which is within. I believe personally that the importance has been unduly magnified because it has been taken by scholarship for the all in all of its research. But there is plenty of room for every one of the interests, and as that which I represent does not interfere with anything, which has become so far vested, I ask for tolerance regarding it. My position is that the old myths were taken over for the purposes of Christian symbolism, under the influence of a particular but not an expressed motive, and it was subsequently to this appropriation that they assumed importance. It is, therefore, as I may say, simply to clear the issues that I place those of my readers who may feel concerned with the subject in possession of the bare elements which were carried from pre-Christian time into the Graal mythos, as follows:

1. We hear of an Irish legend concerning the Cauldron of the Dagda, from which no company ever went away unsatisfied. It was one of the four talismans which a certain godlike race brought with them when they first came into Ireland. As the particular talisman in question, though magical, was not spiritual, it is useless to our purpose; but it connects with the palmary hallow of the Graal mystery, because that also was food-giving, though this property was the least of its great virtues, just as the stone of transmutation by alchemy was classed among the least possessions of the Rosicrucian Fraternity.

2. There is the Cauldron of Bendigeid Vran, the son of Llyr, in one of the old Welsh Mabinogion, the property of which, says one story, is that if a man be slain to-day and cast therein, tomorrow he will be as well as he ever was at the best, except that he will not regain his speech. He remains, therefore, in the condition of Perceval, when that hero of the Graal stood in the presence of the mystery with a spell of silence upon him. Except in so far as the Cup of the Graal legend concerns a mystery of speech and its suppression, it is difficult to trace its correspondence with this cauldron, which I should mention, however, came into Wales from Ireland. It so happens that institutions of analogy are made sometimes by scholarship on warrants which they would be the first to repudiate if the object, let us say, were to establish some point advanced by a mystic. I do not reject them, and I do not intend to use similar comparisons on evidence which appears so slight; but I must place on record that the derivation, if true, is unimportant, even as it is also unimportant that Adam, who received the breath of life from the Divine Spirit, had elements of red earth which entered into his material composition. The

lights which shine upon the altar are not less sacramental lights because they are also earthly wax; and though the externals are bread and wine, the Eucharist is still the Eucharist.

In addition to analogies like those which I have just cited, there are two versions of the quest or mission of Perceval into which the mystery of the Graal does not enter as a part. In their extant forms, they are much later than any of the Graal literature. One is the story of Peredur the son of Evrawc in the Welsh Mabinogion, and the other is the English metrical romance of Syr Percyvelle. The Welsh Mabinogi is like the wild world before the institution of the sacraments, and from any literary standpoint it is confused and disconcerting. Scholars have compared it to the Lay of the Great Fool, and I think that the analogy obtains, not only in the Welsh fable, but also in such masterpieces of nature-born poetry as that of Chrétien de Troyes. On the other hand, the English poem is a thing of no importance except in respect of its connections, and as to these it will be sufficient to say that even scholarship values it only for its doubtful traces of some early prototype which is lost.

The antecedents of the Graal legend in folklore have been a wide field for patient research, nor is that field exhausted; it has also offered an opportunity for great speculations which go to show that the worlds of enchantment are not worlds which have past like the Edomite kings; but as I know that there was a king afterwards in Israel, I have concluded at this point to abandon those quests, which for myself and those whom I represent are without term or effect, and to hold only to the matter in hand, which is the development of a sacramental and mystical cosmos in literature out of the wild elements which strove one with another, as in the time of chaos so also in pre-Christian Celtic folklore.

MYSTERIES OF THE HOLY GRAAL IN MANIFESTA-TION AND REMOVAL

April 1907
The Institution of the Hallows

I T is a very curious heaven which stands around the infancy of romance-literature, and more than one warrant is required to constitute a full title for the interpretation of the strange signs and portents which are seen in some of its zones. The academies of official learning are consecrated places, and those who have graduated in other schools, and know well that they hold the higher authority, must be the first to recognize and respect the unsleeping vigilance and patience of students who are their colleagues and brothers in a different sphere. In the study of archaic literature, the external history of the texts and the criticism thereto belonging are in the hands of official scholarship, and its authority is usually final; but the inward spirit of the literature is sometimes an essence which escapes the academical process. For example, the implicits of certain books belonging to the cycle of the Holy Graal, as I have endeavored to express them, would seem to have eluded learning; but any school of criticism which decides that these books do not put forward extraordinary claims of the evasive kind, and do not so far contain the suggestion of an interior meaning, are comparable to those who should say that the effect does not presuppose a cause, and this of necessity. According to those Lesser Histories which I have connected with the name of Robert de Borron, the secret of the Graal, signifying the super-substantial nourishment of man, was communicated by Christ to His chosen disciple Joseph of Arimathea, who, by preserving the body of the Master after the Crucifixion, became an instrument of the Resurrection. He laid it in the sepulcher, and thus sowed the seed whence issued the arch natural body.

On Ascension Day this was removed from the world, but there remained the Holy Vessel, into which the blood of the natural body had been received by Joseph; strangely endued with the virtues of the risen Christ and the power of the Holy Ghost, it sustained him, both spiritually and physically, during forty years of imprisonment; and it was a sign of saving grace, instruction and all wonder to the great company which he led subsequently westward. He committed it in fine to another keeper, by whom it was brought into Britain, and there, or otherwhere, certain lesser hallows were added to the hallow-in-chief, and were held with it in the places of concealment. Those which we meet with more frequently are four in number, but the mystery is really one, since it is all assumed into the Cup. It is understood that for us at least this Cup is a symbol, seeing that the most precious of all vessels are not made with hands. It is in such sense that the true soul of philosophy is a cup which contains the universe. We shall understand also the ministry of material sustenance, sometimes attributed to the Holy Graal, after another manner than can be presumed within the offices of folklore. It is for this reason that the old fable concerning the Bowl of Plenty, as incorporated by the Graal Mystery, assumes a profound meaning. Some things are taken externally; some are received within; but the food of the body has analogies with that of the soul. So much may be said at the moment of certain aspects which encompass the literature of the Graal, as the hills stand round Jerusalem. The four Hallows are the Cup, the Lance, the Sword and the Dish, paten or patella—these four, and the greatest of these is the Cup.

As all the hallows are therefore, in a certain sense, reducible to a single hallow, so there are four epochs in the history of the Sacred Vessel, and about these there is one question into which they are resolved. The first epoch in the history is concerned with the origin of the Vessel; the second gives us the place and circumstances of its partial manifestation; the third tells us of things within and without which led to its removal or recession; and the fourth epoch deals ostensibly with its departure. The texts therefore purport to provide the complete history of the Graal, including whence it came and whither it has gone. In the present article I shall deal with these four epochs, regarded as the institution of the Hallows, the hereditary keepers of the Graal, the enchantments of Britain in connexion with a wounded keeper; and, lastly, the close of those times which the texts term adventurous, since when there has been silence on earth in respect of the Holy Vessel. If there is a secret intention pervading the entire literature, it must be held to reside in these epochs; their consideration should manifest it in part, and should enable us to deal, at the close of the whole research, with the final problem, being that which is really signified by the departure of the Graal.

Each of the Hallows has its implied mystery, besides that which appears openly in its express nature, and as we know that the mysteries of God are mysteries of patience and compassion, we shall be prepared to find in those of the Graal legend that even their offices of judgment are formularies of concealed mercy. They are therefore both declared and undeclared, that is to say, understood; and as there are certain Hallows which only appear occasionally, so there are suggestions and inferences concerning others which do not appear at all. The Lance, as I have said, is that which was used by the Roman soldier Longis to pierce the side of Christ at the Crucifixion, or it is this, at least according to the general tradition. Of the Sword there are various stories: it is (a) that which was used to behead St. John the Baptist, in which case we can understand its place as a sacred object; (b) that of the King and Prophet David, committed by Solomon to a wonderful ship which went voyaging and voyaging throughout the ages, till it should be seen by Galahad, the last scion of the Royal House of Israel; or (c) it is simply an instrument preserved in connexion with a legend of vengeance, in which case it was brought over from folklore and is nothing to the purpose of the Graal.

The Dish is more difficult to specify, because it's almost invariable appearance in the pageant of the high procession is accompanied by no intelligible explanation concerning it, and although it has also its antecedents in folklore, its mystic explanation, if any, must be sought very far away. Like the rest of the Hallows, it is described with many variations in the different books. It may be a salver of gold and precious stones, set on a silver cloth and carried by two maidens, a goodly plate of silver, or a little golden vessel, and this simply, except in the great prose Perceval which, as it multiplies the Hallows so it divides their ministry; but here, as elsewhere, the Dish does not apparently embody the feeding properties, which are one aspect of the mystery. As to these, in speaking of everything shortly, which I am compelled to do, I can state only that what was filled was the heart of man and what was refected was the entire soul. At the close of our studies, we shall find a better explanation concerning it than that of antecedents in folklore, though it will acknowledge these antecedents.

II
The Hereditary Keepers of the Hallows

The true legitimacies are for the most part in exile, or otherwise, with their rights in abeyance. The real canons of literature can be uttered only behind doors, or in the secrecy of taverns. The secrets of the great orthodoxies are very seldom communicated, even to epopts on their advancement. The highest claims of all are not so much wanting in warrant as wanting those spokesmen who are willing to utter them. We shall not be surprised therefore to find that the custodians of the Holy Graal, which was a mystery of all secrecy, "there were no sinner can be," despite the kingly titles ascribed to them, abode in the utmost seclusion.

Let us seek in the first instance to realize the nature and place of that castle or temple which, according to the legend, was for a period of centimes the sanctuary of the Sacred Vessel and of the other hallowed objects connected therewith. We have seen that the Vessel itself was brought from Salem to Britain, and it follows from the historical texts that the transit had a special purpose, one explanation of which will be found ready to our hand when the time comes for its consideration.

The castle is described after several manners, the later romances being naturally the more specific, and we get in fine a geographical location. In some of the earlier legends, the place is so withdrawn that it is neither named nor described. Even the late Merlin texts say merely that the Holy Vessel is in the west, that is, in the land of Vortigem, or that it abides in Northumbria. On the other hand, the temple in the German cycle is completely spiritualized; it has almost ceased to be a house made with hands, though the description on the external side is almost severe in its simplicity. In the Chrétien portion of the Conte del Graal, Perceval discovers the castle in a valley, wherein it is well and beautifully situated, having a four-square tower with a principal hall in front of it, while a bridge leads up to the chief entrance. The section, which is referable to Gautier de Doulens, describes it as situated on a causeway tormented by the sea. The building is of vast extent and is inhabited by a great folk. In a word, we are already in the region of imaginative development and adornment. The prose Lancelot is in better correspondence with Chrétien, representing the castle as situated at the far end of a great valley, with water encircling it. The most decorative account is, however, in the great prose Perceval, where the castle is reached by means of three bridges which are horrible to cross. The true legitimacies are, for the most part in exile, or otherwise, with their rights in abeyance. The real canons of literature can be uttered only behind doors, or in the secrecy of taverns. The secrets of the great orthodoxies are very seldom communicated, even to epopts on their advancement. The highest claims of all are not so much wanting in warrant as wanting those spokesmen who are willing to utter them. We shall not be surprised therefore to find that the custodians of the Holy Graal, which was a mystery of all secrecy, "there were no sinner can be," despite the kingly titles ascribed to them, abode in the utmost seclusion.

Let us seek in the first instance to realize the nature and place of that castle or temple which, according to the legend, was for a period of centimes the sanctuary of the Sacred Vessel and of the other hallowed objects connected therewith. We have seen that the Vessel itself was brought from Salem to Britain, and it follows from the historical texts that the transit had a special purpose, one explanation of which will be found ready to our hand when the time comes for its consideration. The castle is described after several manners, the later romances being naturally the more specific, and we get in fine a geographical location. In some of the earlier legends, the place is so withdrawn that it is neither named nor described. Even the late Merlin texts say merely that the Holy Vessel is in the west, that is, in the land of Vortigem, or that it abides in Northumbria. On the other hand, the temple in the German cycle is completely spiritualized; it has almost ceased to be a house made with hands, though the description on the external side is almost severe in its simplicity. In the Chrétien portion of the Conte del Graal, Perceval discovers the castle in a valley, wherein it is well and beautifully situated, having a four-square tower with a principal hall in front of it, while a bridge leads up to the chief entrance. The section, which is referable to Gautier de Doulens, describes it as situated on a causeway tormented by the sea.

The building is of vast extent and is inhabited by a great folk. In a word, we are already in the region of imaginative development and adornment. The prose Lancelot is in better correspondence with Chrétien, representing the castle as situated at the far end of a great valley, with water encircling it. The most decorative account is, however, in the great prose Perceval, where the castle is reached by means of three bridges which are horrible to cross. Three great waters run below them, the first bridge being a bow-shot in length and not more than a foot in width. This is the Bridge of the Eel; but it proved wide and a fair, thorough way in the act of crossing. The second bridge is of ice, feeble and thin, and is arched high above the water. It is transformed on passing into the richest and strangest ever seen, and its abutments are full of images. The third and last bridge stands on columns of marble. Beyond it there is a sculptured gate, giving upon a flight of steps, which leads to a spacious hall painted with figures in gold. When Perceval visited the castle a second time, he found it encompassed by a river, which came from the Earthly Paradise; it proceeded through the forest beyond as far as the hold of a hermit, where it found peace in the earth. To the castle itself there were three names attributed: The Castle of Eden, the Castle of Joy and the Castle of Souls. In conclusion, as to this matter, the location, in fine, is Corbenic, which our late redaction of the Grand St. Graal mentions specifically, and which, all doubtful clouds of enchantment notwithstanding, looms almost as a landmark in the Lancelot and the Quest of Galahad. So did the place of the mysteries, from a dim and vague allusion, become;

A wilderness of building, sinking far

And self-withdrawn into a wondrous depth

Far sinking into splendor.

We can scarcely say whether that which had begun on earth was assumed into the spiritual place, or whether the powers and virtues from above descended to brood thereon.

I have left over from this consideration all reference to another spiritual place, in Sarras on the confines of Egypt, where the Graal, upon its outward journey, dwelt for a period and whither, after generations and centuries, it also returned for a period. As this was not the point of its origin, so it was not that of its rest; it was a stage in the passage from Salem and a stage in the transit to heaven. What was meant by this infidelity, which was yet so strangely consecrated, is hard to determine, but its consideration belongs to a later stage. It is too early again to ask what are the implicits of the great prose Perceval when it identifies the Castle of the Graal with the Earthly Paradise and the Place of Souls, but we may note it as a sign of intention, and we shall meet with it in another connexion where no one has thought to look for it.

Such was the abode of the Hallows; and those who dwelt therein, the succession of Graal Keepers, belong to that order which we should expect in such precincts. Joseph of Arimathaea, the first guardian of the Vessel, passes from the scene before it has found its sanctuary. According to the Lesser Chronicles, he was succeeded by his son-in-law Brons; but according to the Greater Chronicles, as I have termed them, he was succeeded by his own son, the second Joseph, who is unknown to the other cycle. The Lesser Chronicles bridge the centuries between that generation which saw the Ascension of Christ and that which was to behold the flower of chivalry in Arthur, by means of a single keeper, who was to remain on earth till he had seen his grandson Perceval and had communicated to him the secret words pronounced at the sacrament of the Graal, which he had learned from Joseph. Perceval is the third who counts in the line of election to complete the human trinity of Graal guardians, reflecting, after their own mystic manner, those Three who bear witness in Heaven, namely, The Divine Trinity. To accomplish the hero's geniture, Alain, the son of Brons, although he had accepted celibacy, married in some undeclared manner, and it was as his issue that Perceval was born in the fullness of the adventurous times.

From one point of view, the succession in respect of the Greater Chronicles involves fewer difficulties, because it exhibits a rudimentary sense of chronology and develop in consequence, a long line of successive custodians. They are, however, quite shadowy and exist only to bridge the gulf of time. It serves no purpose to enumerate them, and I will speak therefore only of the alternative keepers who were in evidence during the days of the quest. We have thus passed at one step all that period represented by the Lesser and Greater Holy Graal, by the Early History of Merlin and by the reign of Vortigem. Nor shall we be retarded by the later Merlin, according to either recension, after which there are only the quests, including the romance of Lancelot, but so far only as it enters into the time of the quests. On the one side, there is Brons, to whom succeeded Perceval, at the close of a life of search; on the other, there is the King Pelles, lord of the Castle Corbenic, whose daughter Helayne gave Galahad as issue to Lancelot, himself a lineal descendant of the King reigning at Sarras in the days of Joseph of Arimathæa and the first flight of the Graal. Galahad was the last keeper recognized by this cycle, and he seems to have been appointed only for the purpose of removing the Vessel. It was: Ite, missa est, and est consummatum, when he died and rose to the stars.

III
The Enchantments of Britain and the King's Wounding

We have seen that, according to the High History of Perceval, the great and secret sanctuary gave upon the Earthly Paradise, even as the visible world gives upon the world unseen; and there will be no question for us that its external splendor signifies the soul within, even as the outward beauties of Nature are the vestures of the high graces which communicate under indefectible warrants to those instituted sacraments which exceed Nature. This manner of doctrine, put forward evasively in story-books, while the Orthodox Church stood aloof but vigilant and dubious, is enough in the way of wonders; but we have now to consider how a horror fell upon the Secret House of God and a subtle work of sorcery on the world which encompassed it. No one knew better than the old makers of romance that the places of enchantment are places of high seeming and not of realities situated in time and space; they were not therefore dealing in common legendary lore, but were plying, if I may so express it, some secret trade, which may perhaps disclose its nature in the light of events externally, or, this failing, in that more obscure light which shines about the precincts of other coincident mysteries—a possibility which bears the greater aspect of likelihood because the fact that the Graal, throughout the romances, is uniformly described as a mystery must render it a tolerable thesis that it can be explained by other mysteries, if any such were prevalent at the same time in the same countries of Europe.

The nature of the horror within, which I have termed already a certain cloud upon the sanctuary, is described after several manners. In one cycle, the flesh, which at no time profits anything, has smitten deeply into the life of the Keeper; in another, he is unable to die till he has seen the last scion of his house and has communicated to him certain secret words; in yet another, which on the surface is void of meaning, he is suffering more, especially from his great age; he has alternatively received a dolorous stroke from a sword-thrust; and as a final explanation there is that of a mystic question which should have been asked and was not for a period of many years. These things are reflected upon the order without, sometimes, as it would seem, only in the immediate neighborhood of the castle; more generally on the whole of Britain; while in rare instances, the world itself is involved, at least by imputation. The quality of the enchantment is sometimes a suspension of Nature in her common operations; sometimes it approaches a frenzy which leads knights to destroy each other, which rifles maids and matrons, and so forth. In the legends of Perceval and Gawain, the healing depends on the asking, in fine, of the question, which restores Nature to her proper course and the sense of sanity to chivalry. In the great quest of Galahad, owing to continuous editing, there is some confusion regarding the King's wounding; the enchantment without is replaced by the notion of certain times of adventure; and there is no interrogation which can be identified with that of the other traditions. There is, however, a dual healing, that of the Keeper of the Graal in those versions of the text which show clearly that he was wounded, and that of another personage, whose sin dates back to the first times of the legend, being one of unprepared intrusion into the most secret mysteries of the Graal.

We have otherwise the whole process of the Quest lifted into a high spiritual region, the implicits of which will provide us at a later stage with the master-key of the mystery.

IV
The Removal of the Hallows

A distinction in the Graal literature between Quest versions and versions of Early History is known to scholarship in England, and though it is not quite definite in itself, it can be adapted in our interest. Speaking of the first class, the keynote of the Perceval quest is the suppression of a certain word and this, as we shall see, at first causes dire misery, postponing the advancement of the hero; but in the end it makes perhaps for his further recognition and ensures his more perfect calling, so that he is crowned in fine as he would not have been crowned at first. On the other hand, the keynote of the historical series, to make use of the expression in a sense that is not usually attached to it, is: A, the suppression or concealment of that potent sacramental formula, in the absence of which, as we have seen already, the office of the Christian ministry is not indeed abrogated but is foreshortened or substituted, so that there is something of an extra-valid character wanting to the external sanctuaries; B, the removal, cessation, or assumption of a certain school of ordination which held from heaven the highest warrants, but itself ordained no one; and the substitution thereafter of some other mode of succession, venerable enough in its way and the next surviving best after the abrogation of the old, but not the high actuality of all, not the evidence of things unseen made physically and spiritually manifest as the term of faith.

Seeing now that the great sacraments do not pass away, it must follow that in the removal of the Holy Graal, as it is narrated in the texts, we are in the presence of another mystery of intention which appears the most obscure of all. The cloud that dwelt on the sanctuary, the inhibition which was on the world without, the hurt almost past healing which overtook the hereditary keeper, are ample evidence in themselves that evil had entered into the holy place, despite all the warrants which it held and all the graces and hallows which dwelt therein. With one curious exception, the keeper was, in fine, healed; the enchantment was also removed; and the achievement of the last Warden, at least in some instances, must have been designed, after a certain manner and within a certain measure, to substitute a greater glory for the cloud on the secret sanctuary. All this notwithstanding, the end of the great quests, the term of the whole mystery, was simply the removal thereof. It occurs in each romance under different circumstances, and it was not, as we shall learn, always of an absolute kind. In the Conte del Graal, it is said that it was taken away, possibly to heaven, a statement which also obtains in respect of the alternative ending supplied by Gerbert; in the Didot Perceval, it was seen no more; in the great prose Perceval it was distributed, so far as we can tell, with the other Hallows, to certain hermits, and it ceased simply to manifest; in Wolfram, the whole question is left open in perpetuity, for at the close of the poem, the keeper remains alive; in the Titurel of Albert von Schaffenberg, the Vessel was carried eastward into the dubious realm of Prester John, and there apparently it remains;

in the quest of Galahad it is assumed by Heaven itself, and the last keeper followed; but, in spite of this, the lost recension, as represented, faithfully or otherwise, by the Welsh Quest, says that though it was not seen so openly, it was seen once by Sir Gawain, the least prepared and least warranted of all the Graal seekers, whose quest, moreover, was for the most part rather accidental than intended.

Speaking now from the mystic standpoint, the removal of the Holy Graal has, in a certain sense, the characteristics of an obscure vengeance. The destruction of the external order would appear to have been decreed. The Graal is carried away and its custodians are translated. The removal certifies the withdrawal of an object which we know, mystically speaking, is never taken away. In respect of its imputed removal, it is taken thither where it belongs; it is the same story as that of the Lost Word in Masonry. It is that which in departing hence draws after it all that belongs thereto. In other words, it goes before the cohort of election as the Pillars of Fire and Cloud before Israel in the Wilderness. The root and essence of the matter can be put shortly in these words:

The Graal was not taken away, but it went to its own place, which is that of every man. The Galahad Quest closes the canon of the literature. Other romances have said that the Sacred Vessel was not seen so openly, or that it was heard of no more, or that it had passed into concealment, and so forth; but this crowning legend carries it into complete transcendence, amidst appropriate ceremonial, though otherwise it leaves the Arthurian sacrament sufficiently unfinished. That is to say, it is still to be communicated for the last time to the whole world on the return of Arthur. The Graal is in hiding, like Arthur; but the Graal is, like Arthur, to return. Meanwhile, the chivalry of the world is broken, and the kingdom is destroyed. The master of all chivalry has received in his turn a dolorous stroke and is removed through a mist of enchantment, under dubious wardens, to the land of the setting sun, even into an exile of the ages. But he also is to be in fine healed and to return, though at what time we know not, for centuries pass as days, within the certain knowledge of Ogier the Dane. So much as this may perhaps be hazarded on the point of time, namely, that the King's rendering shall be when the King's dark barge, sailing westward, like the lighter craft of Hiawatha, shall meet with the Graal, which set forth eastward, since the Graal must heal the King, and these shall meet truly when justice and mercy kiss. The Graal is not therefore lost, but gone before.

THE CHRONICLES OF THE HOLY QUEST

May, 1907
The Prolegomena Thereof

AS there is no one towards whom I should wish to exercise more frankness than the readers to whom I appeal, it will be a counsel of courtesy to inform them, at this stage of the research, that scholarship has once at least commented on the amount of mystic non-sense which has been written upon the subject of the Graal. Who are the mystic people and what is the quality of their nonsense does not appear in the pleadings; and as, entirely outside mysticism, there has been assuredly an abundance of unwise speculation, I incline to think that the one has been confused with the other by certain learned people who were unfamiliar with the limits of the term to which they have had recourse so lightly. After precisely the same manner, scholarship still speaks of the ascetic element of the Graal literature, almost as if it were a term implying reproach; and again, it is not justified by reasonable exactitude in the use of words. Both impeachments, the indirect equally with the overt, stand for what they are worth, which is less than the so-lar mythology applied to the interpretation of the literature. My object in mentioning these grave trifles is that no one at a later stage may say that he has been deceived.

Now, seeing that all subjects bring us back to the one subject, that in spite, for example, of any scandalous histories, every official congre-gation returns us to the one official Church; so, at whatever point we may begin, all the great quests take us ultimately to the Galahad quest; it would seem, therefore, that this is the crown of all, and we can affirm the position as follows: There are three that give testimony on earth con-cerning the Mystery of the Holy Graal—Perceval, Bors and Galahad—and the greatest of these is Galahad. This notwithstanding, as there are persons who, by a certain mental deviation, turn aside from the high-ways of Christendom and look for better paths out of the beaten track in the issues of obscure heresies, so it has happened that scholarship, without repudiating the great heroes of research, has discovered some vague preference for the adventurous and courtly Sir Gawain. They have even been led to regard him as the typical and popular hero of the Graal quest. If the evidence can be held as sufficient—and in some directions it is strong—I suppose that I should waste my time by saying that it does not really signify, any more than the preference of Jewry for Barabbas in the place of Christ could accredit that liberated robber with any reasonable titles. In order to strengthen their case, scholarship has proposed certain speculative versions, now more lost than regrettable, which present Gawain more completely as the Quest hero than any document which is extant. Assuming that they ever existed, these versions were like the poem of Chrétien, according to the poem of Wolfram—that is to say, they told the wrong story. The intention of Chrétien can scarcely be gathered from his unfinished narrative, but of those who follow him, more than one certainly regarded Gawain as a personage who was destined to have a distinct part in the mystery of the whole experiment. Even the German cycle, as represented by the romance of Heinrich, has shown him to be a hero of the achievement. There are also, as we shall see, certain respects in which the legend of Perceval is not, symbolically or otherwise, at a demonstrably higher level than is that of Gawain. It will be, I assume, unnecessary to inform my readers that the disqualification of Gawain must be referred to by his indiscriminate life of passion and occasionally of gross indulgence. At the same time, he was exactly the kind of character who would be disposed to suggest and to begin all manner of quests, high and low. That he was a popular Graal hero may mean that some of his historians did not exactly see why his methods and mode of life should create a barrier. For the purposes, moreover, of the greater mysteries, it is sometimes possible that the merely continent man, who is of moderate life in all things, may require a more express preparation than will sometimes be one who is rather of the opposite tendencies. I think also that the old romancers had in their minds a distinction between the continuity of the sin in Lancelot and the more sporadic misdemeanors of Gawain, as also between the essential gravity of the particular offences in each case. There is the fullest evidence of this in respect of Guinevere, when considered side by side with some other heroines of the cycle. We are, in fact, dealing with a period when the natural passions were condoned rather easily, but when the Church had stepped in to consecrate the rite of marriage in an especial manner. It was no stigma for a hero of chivalry to be born out of lawful wedlock, but the infidelity of a wife placed her almost outside the pale of social forgiveness. The ideal of virginity remained, all this notwithstanding; in which respect, the makers of romance knew well enough where the counsels of perfection lay, but they rendered implicitly to nature the things which belong to nature. It is comparatively late in the cycle that the ascetic purity of the hero became an indefectible title to success in the quest of the Holy Graal, about which time Gawain and Lancelot were relegated to their proper places—ridicule and confusion in the one case, and complete, though not irreverent, disqualification in the other.

Before proceeding to a brief outline of the quests in their order, as I conceive it here, it may seem pertinent to say a few words concerning the order itself which I have adopted for these studies, because at first sight it is calculated to incur those strictures on the part of scholarship which, on the whole, I rather think that I should prefer to disarm. I must in any case justify myself, and towards this, in the first place, it should be indicated that the arrangement depends entirely from the proper sequence of the texts, and secondly, by an exercise of implicit faith, from the findings of scholarship itself. There are certain texts which arise out of one another, and it is a matter of logic to group them in their proper classes. There is, however, some ground of criticism because of a certain apparent sacrifice of chronology. It might be difficult to show that the Greater Holy Graal is precedent in time to the later Merlin, which my arrangement causes to follow therefrom. Outside this, I do not know that there is any apparent offence, but there is one of the implied kinds, because scholarship has concluded that there are lost early forms of certain texts, as, for example, of the Galahad Quest, which in all probability antedated the Greater Holy Graal. We seem to possess the latter approximately in the form of its first draft. But it is really out of this fact that the order properly arises. The Greater Holy Graal was intended to create a complete sequence and harmony between those parts of the cycle with which it was more especially concerned, and the Galahad Quest, as we have it, may represent the form of that document which it intended to harmonize. The alternative is that there was another version of this Quest which arose out of the later Merlin, or that such a version was intended. I believe in fine that my order is true and right, but the exact chronological arrangement, in so tinkered a cycle of literature as that of the Holy Graal, is perhaps scarcely possible, nor is it my concern exactly.

I come now more directly to the matter in hand. There are two cycles of the Quest which alone signify anything. Of one—which is that of Perceval—there are several phases; but this is the lesser Quest. Of the other there is one phase only, led up to by many romances, but represented in fine by a single transcendent text. This text is the quintessence and transmutation of everything, allocating all seekers—Perceval, Bors, Lancelot, Gawain—to their proper spheres, over whom shines Galahad as the exalted horn of a great pentagram of chivalry. Of the Perceval Quest there are two great versions; one of them, as I have already noted, is an alternative conclusion to the cycle of the greater chronicles; and one—which is the German Parsifal—all antecedents notwithstanding, is something set apart by itself in a peculiar house of mystery. It is the story of the natural man taken gradually to the heights. There is also a third quest, that of the Didot Perceval, which, amidst many insufficiencies, is important for several reasons after its own manner, that is to say, because of its genealogy. The fourth is the Conte del Graal, and this is of no importance symbolically, but it is a great and powerful talisman of archaic poetry. The truth is that for all the high things there are many substitutes, after the manner of colorable pretenses, and many transcripts, as out of the languages of the angels into that of man, after the same way that the great external Churches have expressed the mysteries of doctrine in words of one syllable for children who are learning to read. But it sometimes happens also that as from any comer of the veil the prepared eyes can look through and perceive something of the immeasurable region which lies beyond the common faculties of sense, so there are mysteries of books which are in no way sufficient in themselves, but they contain the elements and portents of all those great things of which it is given the heart to conceive. Of these are the Graal books in the forms which present the legend at its highest.

II
The Quests of Perceval le Gallois

At this point, the reader will do well to remember that the chronicles which I have connected with the name of Robert de Borron are those which put forward a mystic formula of consecration, committed from Keeper to Keeper; and that those which, under all reserve, I have connected tentatively with the name of Walter Map, put forward a certain claim in respect of super apostolical succession. From the first there follows the Didot Perceval, making three texts in all, corresponding, in this series, to the earthly witnesses of the Holy Graal—Joseph, Brons, Perceval—that is, the metrical romance of Joseph, the early prose Merlin, corresponding to the keepership of Brons, and the Didot Perceval, in which Brons is still the Keeper but in that state of inanition which prepares the way for his successor. From the second there follows the great Prose Perceval, called otherwise the High History of the Holy Graal, as an alternative to the Galahad Quest.

The outlines of the general story, taking the Didot MS. as an example, are sufficiently simple to state them within comparatively a small space. It is only necessary to premise that Alain, sometimes represented as Perceval's father, is dead at the opening of the story. Brons is the existing guardian of the Graal, holding from Joseph of Arimathea, and he cannot depart from this life till he has communicated to his successor those secret words pronounced at the sacrament of the Graal which were learned by himself from Joseph. Perceval, to outward seeming, has no title whatever to a participation in the mystery, except that of his geniture. He is brave, savage, and imperious; he is also chivalrous, but he is without the spiritual chivalry which we find in the great Quest. Further, the exigencies of the story make him, in certain respects, a little short of a fool. Brons, who, under circumstances which I have not the space to specify, is called also the Rich Fisherman, is said to be in great infirmity, an old man and full of maladies, nor will his health be restored until the office of the Quest has been fulfilled in all perfection. It follows that he is not suffering, as in other cases, from any curse or enchantment, but simply from old age. Perceval, after certain episodes which explain why he was reared in seclusion, a widow's son, under the care of his mother, in obedience to a Divine Voice, repairs to the Court of King Arthur, where he is armed as a knight. He is proclaimed the best knight of the world, after vanquishing Lancelot and other peers of the Round Table at a joust. He becomes to some extent exalted and desires to occupy the Siege Perilous, that is to say, a chair left vacant at the Round Table for the predestined third custodian of the Holy Graal. A tremendous confusion ensues, and it is thought that Perceval will share the fate of others who had made the same dangerous experiment. He survives, however, the ordeal, and the voice of an invisible speaker bears witness that the Sacred Vessel is at the castle of the Rich Fisher, whose heading can only be performed when the best knight of the world visits him and asks the secrets of the service of the Graal. By the instructions which will follow a period will be put to the enchantments of Britain. Perceval undertakes this quest. After many adventures, one of which is referable to the terrestrial paradise, he reaches the castle of his grandfather, the Rich Fisher, or Brons. He beholds the Graal and its marvels, but, in spite of what the voice told him in the presence of the knightly company, he asks nothing concerning it, for the odd reason that his instructor in chivalry taught him to avoid unbecoming curiosity. It is around this episode that the Perceval quests may be said in each case to turn. He awakes on the morning, which follows to find the castle deserted. As soon as he leaves it, the whole building disappears, and he wanders for seven years in search of it. Through distress at being unable to find the Fisher King, he loses all memory of God, until he meets with a band of pilgrims on Good Friday. He is asked by these why he goes armed for purposes of destruction on a day so sacred as this. His better nature then returns, and after a meeting with Merlin, who reproaches him for neglecting the Quest, he does in fine reach the Graal castle for a second time. He sees the Holy Vessel and the procession thereof, asks the required question, at which the King is cured, and all changes. He is led before the Graal and its mysteries are explained to him. A voice tells Brons to communicate the secret words. Perceval remains with his grandfather, practicing wisdom, and there is an end to the enchantments of Britain. The hermit Blaise, who was the scribe of Merlin and produced under the latter's direction the long chronicle of the Graal, becomes his assistant in the custody of the Sacred Vessel, and Merlin also abides with him. Merlin finally goes away, and neither he nor the Graal are heard of subsequently.

This is the story in its outline, but the variations of the several texts are almost innumerable. Some contain no reference to the episode of the Siege Perilous; some narrate the death of the hero and some leave him alive. For the one instance in which he is made the companion of Blaise and Merlin, all others are silent concerning these personages, and it is obvious from the general literature that the authorized version is that which, like Malory's book, puts Merlin into permanent seclusion, through high offices of enchantment, long before the quests begin. The Conte del Graal intercalates great episodes connecting Gawain with the Graal between the visits of Perceval to the castle. Its alternative ending by Gerbert preserves the hero's virginity even on his marriage night; Wolfram ensures his chastity by introducing his marriage at an early stage; the High History is like Heaven, knowing neither marriage nor giving in marriage, while it never supposes that the Quest could be achieved in full by one who was not a virgin. The rest of the romances show little conscience on the subject, the deportment of the hero being simply a question of opportunity.

One feature of the prose Percevals and of the poetical romance also is the termination of the enchantments of Britain; its correspondence in the Galahad Quest is the sealing up of the adventurous times. One of the questions is in both cycles: Who is the Keeper of the Graal? It is one also which is always answered with variations. In the Didot Perceval, it is Brons, as we know already; and in the Conte del Graal he is only termed the Rich Fisher, from which it does not really follow that here, also he is Brons. This is, however, specified in the pseudo-Gautier intercalation, which is found in a single MS. at Berne. In the alternative version of Gerbert, he appears to be the King Mordrains, who was never an instituted Keeper. In Wolfram the name give is Amfortas, of the dynasty of Titurel, and in the Quest of Galahad he is subject to certain confusions on the part of editors, the maimed King Pelles, whose genealogy is provided in the Greater Holy Graal.

There is, however, a much more important distinction between the two cycles, but to this I have already made some reference, both here and in a previous paper. The essential and predominant characteristic of the Perceval literature is the asking and answering of a question which bears on its surface every aspect of triviality, but is yet the pivot on which the whole circle of these romances may be said to revolve. On the other hand, the question is absent from the Galahad story, and in place of it we have a stately pageant of chivalry moving through the world of Logres, to find the high mystery of secrecy which is destined only to dismember the Arthurian empire and to pass in fine, leaving no trace behind it, except the sporadic vision of a rejected knight which is mentioned but not described and occurs under circumstances that justify grave doubts as to its existence in the original texts.

Now, the entire literature of the Graal may be searched in vain for any serious explanation as to the actuating motive, in or out of folklore, concerning the Graal question. On the part of the folklore authorities there have been naturally attempts to refer it to something antecedent within the scope of their subject, but the analogies have been no analogies, and as much nonsense has been talked as we have yet heard of in the connexion which scholars have vaguely termed mysticism. The symbolical and sacramental value of the Graal Quest, outside all issues in folklore, is from my standpoint paramount, as it is this indeed without any reference to the opinions which are founded in folklore or to the speculations thereout arising; and the fact remains that the palmary importance of the mystic question lapses with the pre-eminence of the Perceval Quest. Initiation, like folklore, knows many offices of silence but few of asking; and after many researches, I conclude—or at least tentatively—that in this respect, the Graal romances stand practically alone. It is therefore useful to know that it is not the highest term of the literature.

III
The Quest of the High Prince

Having passed through many initiations, I can say with the sincerity which comes of full knowledge that the Graal legend, ritually and ceremonially presented, is the greatest of all which lies beyond the known borders of the instituted mysteries. But it is exalted in a place of understanding of which no one can speak in public, not only because of certain seals placed upon the sanctuary, but more especially, in the last resource, because there are no listeners. I know, however, and can say that the Cup appears; I know that it is the Graal cup; and the wonders of its manifestation in romance are not so far removed from the high things which it symbolizes, whence it follows that the same story is told everywhere. It is in this way that on these subjects we may make up our minds to say new things, but we say only those which are old, because it would seem that there are no others. If Guiot de Provence ever said that the Graal legend was first written in the starry heavens, he said that which is the shadow of the truth, or more properly, its bright reflection.

Let us now set before our minds the image of the Graal castle, having a local habitation and a name on the mountain-side of Corbenic. The inhabitant in chief of this sanctuary is the Keeper of the Hallows, holding by lineal descent from the first times of the mystery. This is the maimed King Pelles, whose hurt has to be healed by Galahad. The maiden who carries the Sacred Vessel in the pageant of the ceremonial rite is his daughter, the pure maiden Helayne. To the castle on a certain occasion there comes the Knight Lancelot, who is the son of King Ban of Benwick, while his mother Helen is issued from the race of Joseph of Arimathea, and through him is of the line of King David. It is known by the Keeper Pelles that to bring to its final term the mystery of the Holy Graal, his daughter must bear a child to Lancelot, and this is accomplished under circumstances of enchantment which seem to have eliminated from the maiden all sense of earthly passion. It cannot be said that this was the state of Lancelot, who believed that his partner in the mystery of union was the consort of Arthur the King, and to this extent, the sacramental imagery offers the signs of failure. In the case of Helayne, the symbolism only fails of perfection at a single point, which is that of a second meeting with Lancelot under almost similar circumstances. I must not specify them here, except in so far as to say that there was a certain incursion of common motive into that which belongs otherwise to the sacramental side of things, so far as she was concerned. I can imagine nothing in the whole course of literature to compare with the renunciation of this maiden, on whom the whole light of the Graal had fallen for seasons and years, and who was called upon by the exigencies of the quest to make that sacrifice which is indicated by the great romance. It is at this point that the book of the knight Lancelot sets finally aside all sense of triviality and is assumed into the Kingdom of the Mysteries.

So, therefore, Galahad is begotten in the fullness of time, and overall connected therewith falls suddenly under the veil of concealment. We do not know certainly where he was born or by whom nurtured, but if we are guided by the sequel, as it follows in the great Quest, it was probably away from the Graal castle and with mystic nurses. When we first meet him, he is among the pageants and holy places of the mysteries of official religion. Subsequently he is led towards his term by one who seems a steward of other mysteries, and when the Quest begins, he passes at once into the world of metaphrase and symbol, having firstly been consecrated as a knight by his own father, who does not apparently know him, who acts under the direction of the stewards, while Galahad dissembles any knowledge that he might be assumed to possess. He has come, so far as we can say, out of the hidden places of the King. In the quests which he undertakes, although there is nominally one castle in which the Graal has its normal abode, it is yet a moving wonder, and a studied comparison might show that it is more closely connected with the Eucharistic mystery than it is according to the other romances, the great prose Perceval excepted. Still, an efficacious mass is being said everywhere in the world. The Graal is more especially the secret of high sanctity. Galahad himself is the mystery of spiritual chivalry exemplified in human form; his history is one of initiation, and his term is to see God. As contrasted with the rest of the literature, we enter in his legend upon new ground, and are on the eminence of Mont Salvatch rather than among the normal offices of chivalry. It is more especially this legend, which is regarded by scholarship as the last outcome of the ascetic element introduced into the Graal cycle; but it is not understood that throughout the period of the Middle Ages the mystic life manifested only under an ascetic aspect, or with an environment of that kind. The Galahad romance is not ascetic after the ordinary way, as the term is commonly accepted; it has an interior quality which places it above that degree, and this quality is the sense of the mystic life. Now, the gate of the mystic life is assuredly the ascetic gate, in the same manner that the normal life of religion has morality as the door thereof. Those who have talked of asceticism meant in reality to speak of the supernatural life, of which the Galahad romance is a kind of archetypal picture. Though Wolfram, on the authority of Guiot, may have told what he called the true story, that story was never recited till the creation of the Galahad legend. The atmosphere of the romance gives up Galahad as the natural air gives up the vision from beyond. It is the story of the arch-natural man who comes to those who will receive him. He issues from the place of the mystery, as Lancelot came from fairyland, or at least a world of enchantment. The atmosphere is that of great mysteries, the odor that of the sanctuary withdrawn behind the Hallows of the outward Holy Places. Galahad's entire life is bound up so completely with the quest to which he is dedicated that apart therefrom he can scarcely be said to live. The desire of a certain house not made with hands has so eaten him up that he has never entered the precincts of the halls of passion. He is indeed faithful and true, but earthly attraction is foreign to him, even in its exaltation. Even his meetings with his father are shadowy and not of this world—a characteristic which seems the more prominent when he is, the better fulfilling what would be understood by his filial duty. It is not that he is explicitly outside the sphere of sense and its temptations, but that his actuating motives are of the transmuted kind. In proportion, his quest is of the unrealized order; it is the working of a mystery within the place of a mystery; and it is in comparison therewith that we may understand the deep foreboding which fell upon the heart of Arthur when the flower of his wonderful court went forth to seek the Graal. In this respect, the old legend illustrates the fact that many are called, but few are chosen; and even in the latter class, it is only the rarest flower of the mystic chivalry which can be thought of as chosen among thousands. So are the peers of the Round Table a great company, but Galahad is one. So also, of the high kings and princes, there are some who come again, and of such is the royal Arthur; but there are some who return no more, and of these is Galahad.

We have, however, to account as we can for the great disaster of the whole experiment. The earthly knighthood undertakes, in despite of the high earthly king, a quest to which it is in a sense perhaps called but for which it is in no sense chosen. The result is that the chivalry of the world is broken and the kingdom is destroyed, while the object of all research is taken away. In a certain sense, it is the mystery of the Graal itself which gives forth Galahad as its own manifestation, in the order of the visible body, and sends him on designed offices of heading, with a warrant to close a specific cycle of times. When the Graal romances say that the Sacred Vessel was seen no more, or was carried up to heaven, they do not mean that it was taken away, in the sense that it had become unattainable, but that it was—as some of them say also—in concealment. It is certain that the great things are always in concealment, and are perhaps the more hidden in proportion to their more apparently open manifestation. In this respect, the distinction between the natural and supernatural Graal, which is made by the prose Lancelot, has a side of highest value. Let us reserve for the moment the consideration of the hallows as mere relics, and in so far as the Cup is concerned, let us remember the two forms of sustenance which it offered—in correspondence closely enough with the ideas of Nature and Grace. It should be understood, however, that between the mysteries themselves there is a certain superincession, and so also there is in the romances what the light heart of criticism regards as un peu confus, namely, some disposition to talk of the one office in the terms of the other. At the same time, some romances give prominence to the greater and others to the lesser office.

THE HOLY GRAAL IN THE LIGHT OF THE CELTIC CHURCH

June, 1907
Statement of a Possible Implicit Accounting for all Claims

AMONG all external institutions there is one—and there is one only—which by the way of analogy offers exactly those signs and warrants that we should naturally expect in a society, a sodality, a body—let me say, at once, in a church—which on any other consideration might be connected with the idea of the Holy Graal—as something nearest to its source, if not indeed that center from which the entire mystery originated.

The early history of the Holy Graal, as distinguished from the several quests undertaken for the discovery of that sacred object, is one of Christianity colonizing. We know already that it was a mystery which was brought into Britain, and seeing that the legend, as a whole, is presumably of Celtic origin, its religious elements, in the absence of any special and extrinsic claims, must be accounted for most readily by the characteristics of the Celtic Church. This is much closer to our hands than anything which has been so far suggested alternatively, and it was unquestionably that environment in which the legends, whatever their roots, developed into their present form.

Those who have previously recognized, in their imperfect and dubious way, that these legends have a mystic aspect, and that hence they are probably referable to something in instituted mysticism, have put forward some bare possibilities and, independently of these, scholarship has itself gone much further afield. It has thought of the far East as the home of the Holy Graal, and those who are more than mystics by a predisposition on the surface, know certainly—though it is in a certain sense only—that there is a country deep in Asia.

Now, although the limits of our evidence concerning the Celtic Church are somewhat narrowly circumscribed there seems no doubt that it bore distinct traces of eastern influence—by which I mean something much stronger and plainer than resides in the common fact that Christianity itself came to us from the oriental world. If, therefore, the Holy Graal has any marks and spirit of the East, it might be accounted for in this manner by the way of most colorable inference. If, however, we appeal to the veiled suggestion of pre-eminence in the Graal priesthood in respect of an extra-valid form of consecrating the Eucharistic elements and of a super-apostolical succession, it may be advanced that this is simply an exaggerated reflection of that which was actually claimed by the Celtic Church and more especially by this Church in Britain. That is to say, it had a title to existence independently of Rome, Christianity having been established in these islands for a long period prior to the arrival of St. Augustine, which, from this point of view, was an incursion upon territory already conquered and held to a certain extent, rather than a sacred endeavor to spread the gospel of Christ, and it brought spiritual war rather than the light of truth. I have classed these two points together—that is to say, (1) the Oriental marks, and (2) the Celtic development—not because I regard the first as important in comparison with the second, but because, as a fact, the Celtic Church had a particular claim upon an origin independent of Rome long before the legend of Joseph of Arimathea had been devised in the local interests of Glastonbury. I propose now to set forth some other specific analogies, from which we shall be enabled in fine to draw a general conclusion whether we can be satisfied with the evidence as it so stands, or whether we must go further, more especially if we are to account for the claims which are found as implicits in the literature. Let us remember, in the first place, that Oriental traces in the literature, if they can be taken apart from similar traces in the Celtic Church, would probably mean an origin for the Holy Graal independent of Celtic environment, like that of some eastern heretical sects which passed into southern France, or alternatively a derivation through Spain. But if we abandon the earlier and are compelled to have recourse, or this mainly, to the latter point, then the legend of the Holy Graal belongs to that class of fable which has grown up in an external interest, and though it is not in the position of forged decretals, nor even of a decretal in literature, it would be useless to look therein for any secret intention beyond that of the particular pretense which it was designed to support. With the merits and defects of Celtic Christianity in Britain, we are sufficiently acquainted to deal rather summarily with the value of any mystical suggestions that are discernible in the cycles or remanents of literature which must be regarded as thereto belonging. The suggested implicit with which I am dealing, if found to obtain, would signify, therefore, the closing of the whole inquiry.

II
The Formulae of the Hypothesis Scheduled

There are traces in the Anglo-Norman romances of a certain fluidic sense in which Britain and its immediate connexions, according to the sub-surface mind of their writers, stood typically for the world. They were familiar enough with the names of other regions—with Syria, Egypt, Rome; but their world was the Celtic world, comprised, let us say, by Scotland, Ireland, Wales and Brittany. This region came, I think, to signify symbolically, and so we hear that the failure to ask "one little question" involved the destruction of Kingdoms, while the belated interrogation seems to have lifted the veil of enchantment from the world itself. The cloud upon the sanctuary was a cloud over that world; its lifting was a glory restored everywhere. But as the enchantment, except within very narrow limits, was only of the imputed order, so the combined restoration of Nature in common with Grace was but imputed also; the woe and inhibition were removed as secretly as they were imposed. The whole position reminds one of that chapter in the Apocalypse, which presents a sheaf of instructions to the Seven Churches of Asia. No one knew better than the Jews concerning Rome, Greece and

Alexandria, but when the great book of the secret Christian mystery was written, the world of Christendom was confined within narrow limits in Asia, and this was the world of the Apocalypse. It was actually all Assiah of Kabalism, though the few who have dared to institute a philological connexion between the one name and the other have gone, as usual, astray. Recurring to the fact from which this analogy arises, let me add, out of justice to the hypothesis which I seek to present adequately, that within this Celtic world the first and most natural sympathies in the religious order would be indubitably with its own aspirations. The chief points of the hypothesis may be collected into a schedule as follows:

1. It is certain that the Graal Legend is of Celtic origin and making, because of the Celtic attributions of the romances and their Celtic mise-en-scene and characters; because of the Celtic names, disguised and otherwise, which are found in the romances, even in those which belong to the Teutonic cycle; and because of the undoubted derivations in the Graal Legend from Welsh folklore. This is agreed on all hands and will therefore call for no extension or comment in this place.

2. The romance of the Holy Graal, regarding the cycle synthetically, is a glorified ecclesiastical legend of Celtic origin; there are other ecclesiastical legends, referable to the same source, which suggest the Graal atmosphere. The "Graal Church" was in its earlier stages, the Celtic Church contrasted with the Saxo-Roman.

3. The nucleus is to be found in the story of St. David and his miraculous altar. The apostle of South Wales, with other saints, made a pilgrimage to Jerusalem, where the patriarch consecrated him archbishop and gave him "a consecrated altar in which the body of our Lord had lain."

It performed innumerable miracles, and after the death of St. David, it was covered with skins and was never seen by anyone. According to one legend, this altar, and possibly some other hallows, was carried through the air to Britain, and hence was often described as e cælo veniens. Though apparently it was the rock-hewn sepulcher mentioned in the New Testament, no man could specify its shape, its color, or of what material it was fashioned; in addition to its other wonders, it gave oracles, that is to say, a voice spoke therein, as it did, according to the romances, in the Graal itself. St. David died about A.D. 601; he gave the Mass to Britain; he was of the lineage of Our Lady; and his birth having been foretold by the finding of a great fish, he was termed the Waterman, which recalls the Rich Fisherman of the later legends.

4. The secret words of the Robert de Borron cycle refer to the Epiclesis of the Celtic Rite. The act of Eucharistic consecration in the Latin rite is actually the words of Institution, that is to say, the New Testament's account of the Last Supper. In the East, however, consecration is affected by Epiclesis, that is, the invocation of the Holy Spirit, the change in the substance of the elements being referred to as the work of the Paraclete. The liturgy of St. John Chrysostom may be consulted on this point. The priest prays, after the Epiclesis, that the gifts, which have been changed by the Holy Spirit, may be to the participants for the "purification of soul, forgiveness of sins, communion of the Holy Ghost, fulfillment of the Kingdom of Heaven," etc. The evidence is, however, confessedly somewhat indirect, as no Gallican or other Celtic liturgy gives the words of institution, but they are found in full in a North Italian, perhaps a Milanese, work, and elsewhere, as we shall see shortly. Between A.D. 750 and 820, the Celtic rite vanished, and was replaced by the Saxon.

5. The hereditary Graal Keepers, so strongly emphasized in the romances, are derived from the Hereditary Relic Keepers of the Celtic Church. Mr. J. Romilly Allen, in his Monumental History of the Early British Church, has said: "The vicissitudes through which the relics passed in the course of centuries were often of a most romantic description. The story was generally the same. The book, bell or crozier, belonging to the founder of the Church, was supposed to have acquired peculiar sanctity and even supernatural properties by association with him; and after his death, it was often enclosed in a costly metal shrine of exquisite workmanship. Each relic had its hereditary custodian, who was responsible for its safe keeping and who in return received certain privileges, such as . . . the title to inherit certain land, of which the relic constituted the tenure." The preservation of relics under hereditary guardianship seems to have been common among Welsh families. So also, the relics of certain saints belonging to the Scoto-Irish Church were placed in the care of families of hereditary keepers; they were consecrated objects, not human remains, and they were regarded as of great virtue when borne in battle by a person who was free from any deadly sin. The general characteristics of the Celtic relic may be enumerated as follows, but it is not intended to say that every sacred object possessed all the qualities: (a) It came from heaven, like the Graal; (b) it was of mysterious and incomprehensible matter; (c) it was oracular; (d) like the Graal, it had the power of speech; (e) it healed the sick, as the Graal did also occasionally, though this was not its specific office; (f) like the

Graal, it must not be seen by unqualified persons; (g) it had the power of miraculous self-transportation, and the Holy Cup, in certain romances, was also a wandering vessel; (h) it acted as a guide; (i) it was a palladium; (j) it executed judgment on the wicked and profane, which is the characteristic in chief of the Graal in the metrical romance of De Borron.

6. In the Panegyric of St. Columba, a document ascribed to the last years of the eleventh century, it is recorded among his other good works that he provided a Mass Chalice for every Church in the Western Hebrides. Readers of the great prose Perceval Le Gallois will remember that chalices were so uncommon in Arthurian days that the King, during a certain quest, seems to have met with one, and that miraculously, for the first time in his life. It is possible that wooden bowls were used for purposes of consecration. It is only at the close of the Graal cycle, that is to say, in the romance which I have just mentioned and in the Galahad quest, that, in spite of all claims, the sacred vessel is expressly connected with the administration of the Eucharist, though it is not the vessel of communion except in the quest itself.

7. There are historical memorials of mystic and holy cups, possessing great virtues and preserved in old Welsh families. Among these is the Holy Cup of Tregaron, which was made of the wood of the true cross, and its healing virtues were manifested so recently as the year 1901. The curious thing in the romances is that the Holy Graal heals everyone except the Keeper himself, who in the Perceval cycle can only be cured by a question, and in the Galahad legend by the magnetic touch of his last lineal descendant.

8. In England during the Middle Ages, the Eucharist was reserved in a Columbarium, or Dove-House, being a vessel shaped like a dove. This was the Tabernacle of its period, and it recalls (a) archaic pictures of a Cup over which a dove broods; (b) the descent of a dove on the Graal stone in Wolfram's poem; (c) the passage of symbolic doves in connexion with the Graal procession, as told by several romances, but especially in the Quest of Galahad; and (d) the office of the Holy Spirit in the Graal legend.

9. The vanishing of the Graal refers (a) to the actual disappearance of St. David's altar; (b) to the disappearance of the Celtic Church before the Roman; and (c) to the subjugation of the British by the Saxons. The Welsh Church was pre-eminently a monastic church and, in spite of the existence of Bishops, its government was in the hands of monks. The claim of the ancient British Church generally, with its final evolution in

the eleventh century into a legend that the first Church of Glastonbury was consecrated by our Lord Himself, may help us to explain the undertone of dissent from Rome which may be noted in the subsurface of so much of the Graal literature, but especially in the great prose Perceval. To appreciate the position fully, we have to remember that the Latin rite gained ground and influence with the Norman conquest, but independently of that rite there were monasteries in remote valleys where the ancient form of consecration may have been still used and where also the ancient wisdom of the Druids was preserved, though it was never considered consistent for a man to be a mystic Druid and also a Christian. The druidic secret was symbolized by the term Afalon, which means the Apple Orchard. The last Welsh Archbishop of St. David's died in 1115, and his successor gave allegiance to Canterbury, which right had not been established previously.

10. Cadwaladr is Galahad. This chieftain, who loomed so largely in the Welsh imagination, who, like Bran of pre-Christian legend, was termed the Blessed, was regarded as of the royal line of David; he is thought to have been the custodian of holy relics belonging to his family before him, and when he died of the Yellow Sickness in 664 his return was confidently expected. So many legends grew up around him that he seems to have gathered up in himself all the aspirations of Celtdom. His return is associated with the second manifestation of his relics and with the final felicity of the Celts. I may note here that a great Welsh revival began in the year A.D. 1077 with the return of Rhysap-Tewdwr from Britanny. Bards and Druids were at white heat, and Rhys himself was a descendant traditionally of Cadwaladr the Blessed, who was to return and restore all things. He even claimed identity with that departed hero. He assumed the sovereignty of South Wales and has been said to have brought with him the system of the Round Table, "as it is with regard to minstrels and bards." In this connexion we may remember that Cadwaladr and not King Arthur was the mystic hero of Wales. Paulin Paris was the first who sought to identify him with Galahad of the Great Quest.

III
In what Sense the Plea must be Held to Fail

If this hypothesis can be taken with such high seriousness as to suppose that it is put forward—shall I say?—as an equivalent by analogy of that which has offered St. Dominic and the enchanting fable of a question which should have been put to the Pope as a real explanation of the

Perceval-Graal myth, we may be forgiven for dealing with it along some of the following lines. Let us put aside in the first place all that part, which is purely in the region of supposition and take the actual facts as things for valuation in the schedule. As regards the Epiclesis, it is obvious that the oriental terms of consecration, when those prevailed in the West, were the secret of no particular sanctuary as distinguished from all other holy places in Brittany, Britain and Wales. They were catholic to these countries and also to a great part of that which we understand by Scotia, Ireland and Gaul. They connect in themselves with no keepership and with no hallows. We know that the Roman rite colonized all these countries and that in the course of time it prevailed. But the period between the public use of these words and their final abrogation was one of centuries, and although during a portion thereof they may have been perpetuated in concealment, there is no doubt that they had fallen practically into desuetude long before the third quarter of the twelfth century. It is impossible to suppose that there was at that time anyone concerned in them sufficiently to put them forward as a great mystery of sanctity inherent in the heart of Christianity. They do not appear in the metrical romance of Joseph as in any sense the material of romance; they appear with all the marks of a particular claim put forward for a special reason and maintained through more than one generation by the successive production, firstly of a prose version of the early metrical Merlin, and secondly, or in all probability, by the independent invention of the Didot prose Perceval, which carried on the same tradition, though it is left unfinished both from the standpoint of narrative and of the term of its intention. In the second place, two concurrent claims appear, and the second, which is stronger than the first, abandons the claim in respect of secret words. It does this so explicitly that it makes public the words of consecration, by which we are enabled to see at once how little they could have ever signified, if these indeed are the lost words of Graal literature. In their place, as we know so well already, we have the claim to a super-apostolical succession—as I have said, a much stronger claim, and one for which there is no precedent in the dubious history of the Celtic Church. It is out of this claim that the Galahad quest arises, though at a period when the claim itself appears to have lapsed. We are agreed that so far as there is a true story at all; it is that of Galahad, and the question of secret words never entered into the heart thereof. It is, therefore, useless to put forward the assumed fact of their existence in the Celtic Rite of Institution as something which is explanatory of the literature. In this connexion, it is of importance to remember (a) that the only prose Perceval, which is of any importance mystically, is that which depends from the Greater Holy Graal, not from Robert de Borron; and (b) that the only metrical romance of Perceval, which mystically is also important, is that of Wolfram. The first has abandoned the words and the second all Eucharistic connexion. The first puts the Roman dogma of transubstantiation in its most materialized possible form. It will be seen, therefore, that the Celtic hypothesis fails along what must be regarded as the most important line. I submit, therefore, again that which I have stated from the beginning—that the pretension to a super-apostolical warrant is part of a scheme for pre-eminence, the details and motives of which are wanting on the historical side of things; and, this being the case, if we can supply them from certain hidden sources we shall be in possession for the time being at least of a provisional explanation concerning things which are most important in the literature and—donec de medio fiat—it must be allowed to hold.

The distinctive note of the Latin Eucharistic Rite is that, like the gospels of St. Matthew and St. Mark, it gives the first words of institution thus: Accipite et manducate ex hoc omnes. Hoc est enim corpus meum; "Take and eat ye all of this. For this is My body." Hereto certain oriental rites added other words, which would read in Latin; quod pro multis confrangetur—"which shall be broken for many." The Greater Holy Graal gives: venés, si mangiés et chou est li miens cors qui pour vous et pour maintes autres gens sera livrés à martire et à torment—the substantial equivalent of pro multis confrangetur. Compare the gospel of St. Luke in the Latin Vulgate, which uses the present tense: quod pro vobis datur. But there is no direct evidence nor presumption that the Epiclesis ever entered into the Celtic liturgy.

The truth is that analogies and possibilities of the kind with which we have been dealing are a little taking and they are caught at rather readily, but they seize upon a single point, where they can be made to apply, and all the other issues in a long sequence are ignored. The name Cadwaladr naturally suggests that of Galahad, and on the appeal to certain laws of permutation, it seems, for a moment, justified; but it is not justified in the legends. The last King of the Britons had the hallows of his family by the right of inheritance; there was no antecedent keeper whom he was required to heal; there was no quest to undertake in order that he might secure his own. But this healing and this quest inhere in the Graal legend and are manifestly at the root of the design, so that there is no comparison possible between the two cases. The same remarks will apply to all the traceable instances of hereditary Keepership in Celtic families, whatever the object reserved. It is even more certain that any comparison of St. David the Waterman with the Rich Fisherman who is wounded is the highest fantasy, though it is curious to note the connexion which apparently existed in Celtic minds between sanctity, fishing and fish; neither physically nor symbolically did the Saint suffer any hurt, but, again, one of the foremost Graal intentions resides in the King's wounding. The Lesser Holy Graal may create a comparison between the sacred vessel and the sepulcher in which Christ was laid, but it does not for this reason institute any analogy between that vessel and St. David's altar, nor is the appeal to Wolfram useful except in the opposite sense, for the Graal stone of the Parsifal which was once in the crown of Lucifer can tolerate still less the institution of its likeness to "a sepulcher that was hewn in stone, wherein never man before was laid."

It remains, therefore, that in this literature we are shown how evil fell upon the House of the Doctrine; how it overtook also the Keeper of secret knowledge; after what manner he was at length healed; how the hidden treasures passed under the care of his savior; and how at the term of all they were removed because of a fell and faithless time. That would be a very pleasant scheme of interpretation which could say that the House of Doctrine was the Celtic Church and that the wounded Keeper signified that Church in desolation, but it remains that we must go further in our search for a key to these mysteries.

If the legend of the Holy Graal were the last light of the Celtic Church before it expired in proscription, one would say that it was glorious in its death. But the most that we can actually say is that it left elements which in fine served a better purpose. The great prose Perceval, the great poem of Wolfram, and the sacred and beautiful quest of Galahad, these are three records which bear witness on earth of the secret things which are declared only in the heavens. They are three tabernacles wherein transfiguration takes place.

In the extrinsic Celtic remains, the only substitute which offers for the great legend of the holy and sacramental cup is an obscure and nameless vessel which is subject in its latest history to the irreverence of a pedlar, and this it was deemed worthwhile to avenge. From such inefficiencies and trifles, it is certain that we must have recourse, even if for a moment only, to the Glastonbury legend, which did invent high fictions to glorify the British Church. This resource must, however, in its turn fail us, because Glastonbury knows nothing of the Second Joseph and there is no need to add that, so far as the Greater Holy Graal is concerned, it seems to know little of Glastonbury. The legend was for the praise and exaltation of a particular monastery. It represented Joseph of Arimathæa as the chief among twelve apostles sent by St. Philip to Britain, and the first church built on the spot is said to have been dedicated by Christ Himself. While it is thought that Henry II was gratified by the general tradition, it is suggested that it was a weapon which could be used against St. David's and the Welsh as well as against the Pope. But of the Joseph claim, as we have it in the Graal romances, there is no trace in William of Malmesbury or any of the other authorities. We have indeed the alleged burial of Joseph at Glastonbury, against which the Greater Holy Graal represents it as taking place in the north of England, and the Abbey of Noirmoutier in France laid claim to its original possession, but it disappeared or was stolen, as some say, by the monks of Glastonbury. We have also in William of Malmesbury the story of a phial containing the blood of Christ and said to have been brought over by Joseph. This may have been the source of the Graal Cup, as it appears in the romances, which in this case began to be invented deliberately about 1150, or a little earlier. De Borron, the putative Map and all the quest versions are a generation at least later. It may be said that the second Joseph, who is a creation of the Greater Holy Graal, signifies some move in the strange ecclesiastical game which was played by Henry II, but the evidence is in the opposite direction, so far as it can be said to exist: it is obvious that any game would have worked better with the original apostolical Joseph than with his imaginary son.

I do not much care about what materials the makers of the Graal romances may be agreed to have worked, since it is clear that they imported therein a new spirit. If anyone should like still to think that Cadwaladr, who went to Rome or Jerusalem (as the eighth century equivalent of Rome), is to be identified with Galahad, who went to heaven, they can have it that way, since they so please, understanding that, on my part, I may reserve my judgment. I know that the one has suffered a high change before he has passed into the other. I know that every literature has its antecedents in some other literature, and that every religion owes something to a religion that preceded it. Sometimes the consanguinity is close and sometimes it is very far away. Only those who affirm that the one accounts for the other, and this simply and only, seem to be a little unwise. Christianity arose within Jewry and doctrinally out of Jewry, but this fact only brings their generic difference into greater relief. So also, the Graal literature, whether or not it rose up in the Celtic church, has its analogies therein, but there are also many ways in which the one as we know it does not account for the other as we actually have it.

The Celtic Church has, however, assisted us to see one thing more plainly, though we know it on other considerations, namely, that in fine there is but a single quest, which is that of Galahad. We must make every allowance for the honest findings of scholarship, to whom the Holy Graal, as it was, and it is, has never spoken, for whom it is only a feeding dish under a light cloud of imagery, and by whom it is thought in their hearts that the intervention of Christianity in the wild old pagan myth is on the whole rather regrettable. They turn naturally to those quarters whence issue the voices of purely natural life, and therefore they prefer Gawain and Perceval in his cruder forms, because these speak their own language. It is to be trusted, and this devoutly, that they will find more and more evidences for the maintenance of their particular view. Unmanifested now but still discerned darkly, if the true proto-Perceval should be at length found, that which went before the Peredur and the English metrical romance, and if, as there is no doubt, it should be devoid of all elements belonging to Graal or quester, our case will be the better proved which is (1) the natural succession of the Galahad quest after the Graal history in its longer recension; (2) the succession of Perceval in the sequence of Robert de Borron, but rather as the scion of a false legitimacy; (3) the introduction of the late prose Perceval le Gallois as a final act of transmutation in the Anglo-Norman cycle concerned with this hero, which introduction so far assists our case that it manifests the unfitness, realized at that period, of Perceval as he was known by the earlier texts; (4) the derivation of the Wolfram Parsifal in part from Celtic elements, in part from some which are or may have been Teutonic, but also with derivatives through Provence from Spain.

It follows, in fine, that we must go further, and in the next section I feel that, as one who has been in exile among disjecta membra, like Marius among the ruins of Carthage, I shall re-enter into my own patrimony. To my old friend, Arthur Machen, himself of Caerleon-upon-Usk, I owe most of the materials which have been collated for the presentation of the hypothesis concerning the Graal and the Celtic Church.

MYSTIC ASPECTS OF THE GRAAL LEGEND

July, 1907

I

The Victory of the Latin Rite

IN the last paper, there was put forward the hypothesis of the Celtic Church as it has never been expressed previously; nothing was diminished, and any contrary inferences were offered so far temperately; but the issues are not entirely those of the Graal legend, and, in view of that which comes after, a few words in conclusion of the previous part may perhaps be said more expressly. It should be on record, for those who have ears, that the Welsh Church, with its phantom and figurehead bishops, its hereditary priesthood, and its profession of sanctity as others profess trades, seems a very good case for those who insist that the first Christianity of Britain was independent of St. Augustine, which it was, and very much indeed, but on the whole, we may prefer Rome. When we have considered all the crazes and heresies, all the pure, primitive and unadulterated Christianity's, being only human and therefore disposed to gratitude, it is difficult not to thank God for Popery. But it would also be difficult to be so thankful, that is to say, with the same measure of sincerity, if we were still in the school courses, and belonged officially thereto. I mean to say, although under all reserves, that there is invariably some disposition to hold a fluidic and decorative brief for Rome in the presence of the other assemblies. Let therefore those who will strive with those who can over the dismembered relics of apostolical Christianity; but so far as we are concerned, the dead can bury their dead. We have left the Celtic Church as we have left the carved gods. A pan-Britannic Church may have been the dream of one period, and if so, seeing that it never came to fulfillment, we can understand why it is that in several respects the Graal literature has now the aspect of a legend of loss and now of a legend of to-morrow. The Anglican Church seems under the present aspect to recall for a moment that perverse generation which asked for a sign and was given the sign of Jonah. It has demanded apostolical evidences to enforce its own claim, and it has been given the Celtic Church. Let us therefore surrender thereto the full fruition thereof. There may be insufficiencies and imperfect warrants in the great orthodox assemblies, but in the Celtic Church there is nothing which we can regret. The Latin rite prevailed because it was bound to prevail, because the greater absorbs the lesser. On the other hand, but now only in respect of the legends, let it be said lastly that the ascension of Galahad is, symbolically speaking, without prejudice to the second coming of Cadwaladr. It does not signify for our purpose whether Arthur ever lived, and if so, whether he was merely a petty British prince. The Graal is still the Graal and the mystery of the Round Table is still the sweet and secret spirit of universal knighthood.

Seeing, therefore, that we have not found in the Celtic Church anything that suffices to account for the great implicits of the literature and that the watchwords call us forward, it is desirable at this point to consider the position of our research at the stage which it has now reached. I have to justify my statements that (a) the Graal is a legend of the soul, and is, in some respects, a history which is personal, namely, to all souls at a certain epoch of their experience; (b) its root-matter is analogous with that of mysticism; (c) the chalice, to speak of that only which is the hallow-in-chief, is from the mystic standpoint, a symbol; (d) a better explanation must be found for its feeding properties than has been so far offered by the folk-fore; (e) the four epochs of the legend—being (1) institution, (2) the Keepership, (3) the enchantments and wounding, (4) the close of the adventurous times—must be held to manifest in part the secret intention; (5) the remanents of the Graal mystery must be sought not in a castle of the Pyrenees, not in a Spanish church, though there is one in that country which claims to have been its last custodian; nor in respect of its traces at Sarras, that is to say, at Cesarea, or elsewhere, but in certain instituted mysteries, the reflection of which remains to the present day. Before entering into the consideration of these matters, there is a word in fine to be said about official scholarship.

How admirable is the life of the scholar, how zealous the devotion which impels him, and how sorrowful it seems that it enters so seldom into his heart to have concern for the great subjects! Yet there is one respect in which he does excellent service towards things that are really important; he is, in some cases devoted with great seriousness and all-ruling honesty to the elucidation of old literatures. The work is often final, or tends in the direction of finality, when these literatures have no consanguinity—absit omen, in the name of all folklore societies!—with the decried mazes of mystic thought. With such possibilities on the hill-tops, the work on the lower ground is still precious, but it is necessary at times and seasons to dissent from the official conclusions and the official attitude, because it is not to be expected that scholarship—crowned with "the simple senses" and saying: "Omega, thou art Lord," to many phantoms which for us are mere idols—should be in touch with these possibilities, or should deal with them fully and justly. May it exercise in the present instance a certain reasoning tolerance towards an investigation which, in differing from its own, offers a grateful recognition of all that has been so far accomplished!

II
The Mystery of Initiation

Like those who said in expectation of an imminent onslaught: "Gentlemen of the guard, fire first!" I will now make what must be certainly considered a fatal admission, as follows: The great literatures and the great individual books are often at this day to the mystic as so many counters, or heaps of letters, which he interprets after this own manner and so imparts to them that light which, at least intellectually, abides in himself. We know in our hearts that eternity is the sole thing which ultimately matters and true literatures should confess to no narrower horizon. It happens sometimes that they begin by proposing a lesser term, but are afterwards exalted, and this was the case with the Graal books, which were given the Perceval legend according to the office of Nature and afterwards the legend of Galahad according to the law of Grace.

Recurring now to the brief schedule of points which call to be dealt with and may be preferably taken at this, rather than at a later stage, I will make a beginning with that which comes last in the enumeration itself, because it is obvious that I can be concerned—for what it is worth—with simple affirmation only, and not with evidence. There is behind the great quests a Mystery of Initiation and Advancement, to the nature of which I can approximate only in reviews and in printed books, but that which it is possible to say will be expressed, under proper veils, at the close of the present paper. The warrant of it is in the secret fraternities which lie behind the surface-pageant of mystic literature. At this day, and for many generations backward, the great secret rites have been like the Rich King Fisherman, either wounded or in a condition of languishment, and it is for the same symbolic reason, namely, that there are few prepared to come forward and ask the required question, on account of the external stress and disillusion. At the same time, they have been saying, after their own manner, for many centuries: Ask, and ye shall receive. If these statements can be tolerated on the faith of one who, from the writer's standpoint, has perhaps more to lose than to gain by making them, it will follow that the mystic element in the Graal literature cannot be understood at first hand by those who are unacquainted with the interior working of those secret societies of which the Masonic experiment, let us say, is a part only, and elementary at that. The important lights are not in printed books, but in the catholic motive which characterizes secret schools that have never entered into the knowledge of the outside world, and in the secret body of doctrine communicated by these. It is there only that the student can learn why that sacred and mysterious object which is termed Graal is (1) A stone which is not a stone, and, like that of alchemy, at once a medicine and an elixir; (2) a cup of knowledge and a cup of memory; (3) a symbolic vessel or lamp, wherein is the light of the world and from which that light is transmitted. These memorials have been always in the world and their rumor has been heard always; in so far as the Graal literature can be called a concealed literature, there were other concurrent and more express witnesses, each of them claiming to draw from high authority in the past, in the main always oral but in part also written.

III
The Lost Book of the Graal

Now, if there is one thing which is clear from the whole literature, it is that the Graal romances claimed to follow some book which has not come down to us, and those who are concerned with such matters might, from the sole consideration of the texts, reconstruct in respect of its accidents the kind of apocryphal gospel which could have served as the proto-Graal book of the whole literature. It would have comprised many curious elements, a few of which may be hazarded in this place: A, power of words, reflected perhaps through Gnosticism from the old mysteries of Chaldea; B, Magical elements brought over by nomadic tribes deriving from Egypt; C, an eschatology with a motive akin to that of Origen; D, a special legendary interest in Pontius Pilate and Judas Iscariot; E, an expectation of the final redemption of Jewry symbolized by the deliverance of an unfaithful disciple named Moses, who appears in the metrical Joseph and in the texts which follow therefrom. This apocryphal gospel-book would, however, and above all, have included the particular great implicits which constitute the Graal literature. It may have been a manifesto of some secret sanctuary or school within the Church, of some hidden sect in Christendom, or some illustration of the Greater Mysteries of Initiation in Christian times. On this assumption, it contained materials and put forth warrants which, falling into the hands of romancers, or being heard of indirectly and by rumor, were gravely misconstrued. Indeed, this Sanctum Graal, this Vas insigne electionis, Calix inebrians, in a word, this Liber Gradalis was as much a mythical object to the putative hermit who wrote the Grand St. Graal as it was to Robert de Borron, who specifies his dependence upon this book but who may even have owed his acquaintance with its story to Walter Montbeliard, in whose service he tells us that he was. At what distance therefore he drew, whether, in the speculative case mentioned, his patron was clerk enough to read it in the Latin tongue, whether he, too, knew it by report only, as a tradition communicated in some order of chivalry, are things which we shall never know. Walter Montbeliard was possibly a Knight Templar; he took the cross, as a consequence of which he died in the Holy Land, and it was subsequent to this that De Borron wrote his poem, or at least its concluding part. On his metrical romance there follows the early history of Merlin, and we can assume that its prose version is a moderately fair presentation of the lost poem. It has brought the mystery of all sanctity into a wild kingdom of the west and many centuries have elapsed, during all which period the Keeper of the Holy Graal has continued alive in the flesh, but serving absolutely no purpose, so far as any official church or the claims thereof are concerned. From his secret place, he exercises no pontificate; he ordains no one; he teaches nothing. His undeclared asylum is one of uttermost refuge, and the scribe of the enchanter and prophet is promised repose therein when he has completed his records. In the meantime, the only consequence following from the presence of the Graal in Northumbria is that it enables Merlin to appropriate it in an obscure manner to his own use and to connect himself with it in every possible way. What was to have depended from this we do not know, for the tertium quid of De Borron's trilogy is represented by a forged conclusion, or perhaps I should rather say, by an unauthorized transcript in prose, which reduced the whole cycle to complete nullity. Alternatively, if De Borron never produced his pars tertia et ultima, then the Didot Perceval is an attempt to fill the gap. Therein the secret words are indeed communicated to the questing hero, but the Graal is taken from his custody; no one knows what becomes of it; no one hears of his own fate; all the offices are voided. This, therefore, is the history of the Lost Book in the Lesser Chronicles—one doubtless of long and grievous misconstruction—from which one thing only arises—that there was a secret office of the Eucharist, but outside its custodians no one knew what it was. On this cycle there follows that which begins with the Grand St. Graal, a work which, whoever was its author, recalls in so many ways the treatise De Nugis Curialium, written by Henry the II's archdeacon, Walter Map. It presents to us great fictions to account for its origin, but it confesses in fine that it depends from a Latin source, or the hermit of the prologue rendered what he saw miraculously into that tongue. This is only another way of saying that the author spoke as he could of that which he had read or seen as little as Robert De Borron. Now, either a stream of continuations followed from this document or alternatively it constituted an introduction to these. In the first case, the continuations do not present conclusions which conclude, and in the second, the limits of the existing texts are exceeded. Alternatively, there is a lost quest of Galahad which may have embodied so much of the Lancelot story as was necessary to its purpose, and no more. In any case, after all the stories have been told, all the adventures achieved, and "the dragon of the great Pendragonship" has been plunged in a sea of blood, we are left with the chief implicit of the cycle, allocated, as it must be irresistibly, to the Lost Book, still undeclared as to purpose. We have indeed the Galahad legend as presented in the Great Quest, forgetting all about Secret Words, all about Apostolical Succession, reverting apparently into the hands of the orthodox church, and thereby re-expressed as a great mystery of sanctity. We must therefore set aside for the moment the question of implicits and see what we can make of this simply as a sacramental legend, having insufficiencies of its own kind, but still offering the second sense of the Eucharist amidst the decorations of allegory, the glory of spiritual chivalry and the enchantments of romance.

IV
The Mystery of Faith

Now the mystery of faith in Christianity is above all things the Eucharist, in virtue of which the Divine Master is ever present in his church and is always communicated to the soul; but the Graal mystery is the declared pageant of the Eucharist which, in virtue of certain powers set forth under the veil of consecrating words, is in some way a higher mystery than that of the external church. We have only to remember a few passages in the Grand St. Graal, in the great prose Perceval and in the quest of Galahad, to understand the imputed distinction as:—(A) the Communication in the Eucharist of the whole knowledge of the universe, from Aleph to Tau; (B) the communication of the Living Christ in the dissolution of the veils of Bread and Wine; (C) the communication of the secret process by which the soul passes under divine guidance from the pageants of this world to heaven, the keynote being that the soul is taken when it asks into the great transcendence. This is the implied question of the Galahad legend, as distinguished from the Perceval question. There are those who are called but not chosen at all, like Gawain. There are those who get near to the great mystery but have not given up all things for it, and of these is Lancelot. There is the great cohort, like the apocalyptic multitude which no man can number—called, elected and redeemed in the lesser ways by the offices of the external Church—and of these is the great chivalry of the Round Table. There are those who go up into the Mountain of the Lord and return again, like Bors; they have received the high degrees, but their office is in this world. In fine, there are those who follow at a long distance in the steep path, and of these is the transmuted Perceval of the Galahad legend. It is in this sense that, exalted above all and more than all things rarefied into a great and high quintessence, the history of the Holy Graal becomes the soul's history, moving through a profound symbolism of inward being, wherein we follow as we can, but the vistas are prolonged for ever, and it well seems that there is neither a beginning to the story, nor a descried ending.

We find also the shadows and tokens of secret orders which have not been declared in the external, and by the strange things which are hinted, we seem to see that the temple of the Graal on Mont Salvatch is not otherwise than as the three tabernacles which it was proposed to build on Mount Tabor. Among indications of this kind, there are two only that I can mention. As in the prologue to the Grand St. Graal, the anonymous but not unknown hermit met on a memorable occasion with one who recognized him by certain signs which he carried, giving thus the unmistakable token of some instituted mystery in which both shared: as in the great prose Perceval we have an account of five changes in the Graal which took place at the altar, being five transfigurations, the last of which assumed the seeming of a chalice, but at the same time, instead of a chalice, was some undeclared mystery: so the general as well as the particular elements of the legend in its highest form, offer a mystery the nature of which is recognized by the mystic through certain signs which it carries on its person; yet it is declared in part only and what remains, which is the greater part, is not more than suggested. It is that, I believe, which was seen by another maimed King when he looked into the sacred cup and beheld the secret of all things, the beginning even and the end. In this sense, the five changes of the Graal are analogous to the five natures of man, as these in their turn correspond to the four aspects of the Cosmos and that which rules all things within and from without the Cosmos. I conclude therefore that the antecedents of the Cup Legend are (1) Calix meus quam inebrians est; (2) The Cup which does not pass away; (3) The vas insigne electionis. The antecedent of the Graal question is: Ask, and ye shall receive. The antecedent of the enchantment of Britain is the swoon of the sensitive life, and that of the adventurous times is: I bring not peace, but a sword; I come to cast fire upon the earth, and what will I but that it should be enkindled?—The closing of these times is taken when the Epopt turns at the altar, saying Pax Dei tecum. But this is the peace which passes understanding, and it supervenes upon the Mors osculi—the mystic Thomas Vaughan's "death of the kiss"—after which it is exclaimed truly: Blessed are the dead which die in the Lord, from henceforth and for ever. It follows therefore that the formula of the Supernatural Graal is: Panem cælestem accipiam; that of the Natural Graal, namely, the Feeding Dish, is: Panem nostrum quotidianum da nobis hodie; and the middle term: Man doth not live by bread alone. I should add: These three are one; but this is in virtue of great and high transmutations.

V
The Declared Mystery of Quest

And now, as the sum total of these mystical aspects, the desire of the eyes in the seeking and finding of the Holy Graal may, I think, be re-expressed as follows:

Temple or Palace or Castle—Mont Salvatch or Corbenic—wherever located, and whether described as a wilderness of building, crowded burg or simple hermit's hold—there is one characteristic concerning the Graal tabernacle which, amidst all its variations in the accidents, is essentially the same; the Keeper of the great hallows has fallen upon evil days; the means of restoration and of healing are, as one would say, all around him, yet the help must come from without; it is that of his predestined successor, whose office is to remove the vessel, so that it is henceforth never seen so openly. Taking the quest of Galahad as that which has the highest significance spiritually, I think that we may speak of it thus:—We know that in the last analysis it is the inward man who is really the Wounded Keeper. The mysteries are his; on him the woe has fallen; it is he who expects healing and redemption. His body is the

Graal Castle, which is also the castle of Souls, and behind it is the Earth-ly Paradise as a vague and latent memory. We may not be able to trans-late the matter of the romance entirely into mystical symbolism, since it is only a rumor at a distance of life in the spirit and its great secrets. But, I think, we can see that it all works together for the one end of all. He who enters into the consideration of this secret and immemorial house under fitting guidance shall know why it is that the Graal is served by a pure maiden, and why that maiden is ultimately dispossessed. Helayne is the soul, and the soul is in exile because all the high unions have been declared voided—the crown has been separated from the kingdom, and experience from the higher knowledge. So long as she remained a pure virgin, she was the thyrsis-bearer in the mysteries, but the morganatic marriage of mortal life is part of her doom.

This is still a high destiny, for the soul out of earthly experience brings forth spiritual desire, which is the quest of the return journey, and this is Galahad. It is therefore within the law and the order that she has to conceive and bring him forth. Galahad represents the highest spiritu-al aspirations and desires passing into full consciousness, and so into attainment. But he is not reared by his mother, because Eros, which is the higher knowledge, has dedicated the true desire to the proper ends thereof. It will be seen also what must be understood by Lancelot in secret communication with Helayne, though he has taken her through-out for another. The reason is that it is impossible to marry even in hell without marrying that seed which is of heaven. As she is the psychic woman, so is he the natural man, or rather the natural intelligence, which is not without its consecrations, not without its term in the great transcendence. Helayne believes that her desire is only for Lancelot, but this is because she takes him for Eros, and it is by such a misconception that the lesser Heaven stoops to the earth; herein also there is a sacred dispensation, because so is the earth assumed. I have said that Lancelot is the natural man, but he is such nearly at the highest; he is born in great sorrow, and she who has conceived him saves her soul alive amidst the offices of external religion. He is carried into the lesser land of Fa-erie, as into a garden of childhood. When he draws towards manhood, he comes forth from the first places of enchantment and is clothed upon by the active duties of life, as by the vestures of chivalry. He enters also into the unsanctified life of sense, into an union against the consecrated life and order. But his redeeming quality is that he is faithful and true, because of which, and because of his genealogy, he is chosen to beget

Galahad, of whom he is otherwise unworthy, even as we all, in our daily life, fall short of the higher aspirations of the soul. As regards the Keeper, it is certain that he must die and be replaced by another Keeper before the true man can be raised, with the holy things to him belonging, which hallows are indeed withdrawn, but it is with and in respect of him only, for the keepers are a great multitude, though it is certain that the Graal is one. The path of quest is the path of the upward progress, and it is only at the great height that Galahad knows himself as really the Wounded Keeper and that thus, in the last resource, the physician heals himself. Now this is the mystery from everlasting, which is called in the high doctrine Schema misericordiæ. It is said: Latet, ceternumque latcbit, until it is revealed in us, but as to this: Te rogamus, audi nos.

SECRET TRADITION IN CHRISTIAN TIMES

August, 1907

I

Echoes of Manichæan Sects

T HOUGHT in the Middle Ages moved, like external science, through a world of mystery, and the Christ-light moved through the mist-light, filling the bounds of sense with the shapes and symbols of vision. It follows, and this naturally, that at a period when all things were dubious in respect of knowledge most things seemed possible, and apart from the power of religion, which tinged life itself with the lesser elements of ecstasy, there was the kind of enchantment which dwells always about the precincts of unknown vistas. Apart from the shapes of imagination, there were the extravagances of minds seeking emancipation from law and authority, more especially in the matters of faith. The Books of the Holy Graal do not belong to the last category, but after their own manner they are like echoes from far away, because the secrets of the Greater Mysteries have not been written, nor do the Holy Assemblies issue proceedings. The value of the Graal legends is like that of other legends—I mean, in the mind of the mystic at this day: it is resident in the suggestions and the fights which it can afford us for the maintenance of that concordat which constitutes the Divine Alliance. Having found that we are dealing with a body of writing which puts forth strange claims and suggests concealed meanings, having found also that it is a literature which was acquired to develop these particular interests, and being desirous of knowing the kind of intervention and the particular motives which were at work, if this indeed be possible, we are naturally disposed to ask whether there were other concealed literatures at the same period, and what fight—if any—they cast upon these questions. The great school of Christian mystic thought within the official Church was concerned wholly with a mystery of sanctity, the term of which was identical with that which I have sought to put forward as the term of the Graal quest, but it had no secret claim and no concealed motive. We cannot, therefore, explain the one by the other. There were, however, independent schools of literature belonging to the same period which do give us certain lights, and it is otherwise reasonable to suppose that so far as there are difficulties in the one path we may receive help from the collateral paths, and thus derive some better understanding of the whole. If a particular spirit or secret mind, school or sodality, took over the old folklore legends, infusing a new motive therein, which motive is akin to the purpose discernible in coincident literatures, that which intervened in the one case was probably in relation with the others. I propose, therefore, to consider these extrinsic schools shortly, and to show that throughout a number of centuries we can trace successively the same implicits, it being understood that they are always put forward in a different way. In this manner we shall come to see that there have been several interventions, but taking place under such circumstances that those who intervened may have been always the same secret school, on the understanding that this school does not correspond to the idea of a corporate institution. It is necessary, however, to deal in the first place with one attempt to account for the Graal literature which has been already put forward, because there are certain directions in which it is idle to look and it is well to know concerning them.

It is now been many years since M. E. Aroux either found in its literal form or beheld in some glass of vision that wonderful romantic book published in 1834 by Gabriele Rossetti and entitled The Anti-Papal Spirit which preceded the Reformation. It was intended as literary and historical criticism, but it is a great flight of imagination. It maintained the existence of a secret allegorical language in which certain books of the Middle Ages, including those of Dante and Petrarch, were written indifferently; it was especially the tongue of the troubadours. Rossetti did not mention the books of the Holy Graal and he scarcely referred to those of chivalry. His thesis was that the language of literature, above all poetical language, was the voice of a secret school, protesting against Rome in the name of doctrine and also of policy and conduct. The secret school expressed aspirations like those of the Albigensian sects. After Rossetti there came M. Aroux, who treated Dante and his compeers as heresiarchs and revolutionaries, concerning himself, especially with the romances of chivalry and hence with the Holy Graal; but in the last respect, his pages give evidence that his acquaintance with the texts was exceedingly slight. I believe that some of the lesser metrical literature of Southern France at least exhibits the use of veiled language, but Aroux and Rossetti are too fantastic to enter within the horizon of serious criticism. The alleged motive is, moreover, distinct from that which I recognize in the Graal literature and is therefore not to our purpose.

Perhaps no Christian sect has been the subject of more foolish misapprehension than the Albigenses, and this on all sides, but more especially on the part of writers who are on the borderland of mystic thought. Against the iniquity of Albigensian persecution in the past, we have later the folly, not unmixed with dishonesty, of the protestant apologists; but worse perhaps than the rest is the folly which has attempted to connect them with the Graal literature. For the purposes of this investigation, I care nothing whether the Albigenses were pure Christians, as pure Christianity is understood according to sectarian canons, or whether they were Manichaeans. The all-important question is the light under which they presented Eucharistic doctrine, from which standpoint it is certain that they could have had no connexion with the development of the Graal cycle. From eclectic Gnosticism, which took over from Christianity what was of kinship with its purpose, to Vaudois and Lollards, there is not one anywhere which sought to develop or exalt the sacramental teaching of the ancient Church. The Manichaeans had a tinkered sacrament, from which nothing could follow in respect of the Graal mystery. As regards the Albigenses, it is certain historically that they denied transubstantiation, though they accepted some qualified sacramental teaching in connexion with the Lord's Supper.

II
Coincident Schools of Symbolism

It will be understood that the sects of Southern France, holding the offices of protestation, testified by act and word that the gates of hell had prevailed against the Latin church, and that the efficacious doctrines, the plenary rights, were in their hands. In other words, they had a great office in religion and, I must add, the fatality of a superior process—all of which tells us precisely why the mystery of the Holy Graal was beyond their horizon. Outside these sects, there were two great concurrent schools of mystic thought which were developing in Europe at the period of the Graal; there was the wonder and the rumor of alchemy and the great, sacred mystery of Kabalistic Jewry. The first was scattered all over the western countries, and its reflection at the period in England was Roger Bacon. The seat of the other was in Spain, but it had important academies coming into being in the South of France. In our consideration of Alchemy and Kabalism the first is the more important, and its interpretation depends upon a construction of symbolism which has not entered previously into the heart of criticism. If the question be whether there is any concurrent school of literature which deals with the correspondences of a sacramental mystery outside the mystery of the Eucharistic Graal, the answer is that of the alchemists, but of a particular section only among the followers of the Hermetic Tradition. As, however, it is not given us to find anywhere the material of demonstration, so I must warn my readers that the art of the alchemists does not offer us during the twelfth and thirteenth centuries the full condition which is necessary to our purpose; their testimony belongs really to a later epoch. At the period of the Holy Graal the books of the Hermetic Adepts were in a state of transition, or alternatively they correspond to the elements of folklore before the great Christian hallow reigned in the Kingdom of Romance. In other words, the material school of alchemy was taken over subsequently and at a time when the Graal literature was only a sacred memory. It is this mystery which was the next witness in the world. The fact that it was taken over is, however, of all importance. We have thus to realize that there were two alchemical schools making use of the same language in a distinct sense, the one branch seeking the transmutation of metals and the art of prolonging life, the other branch investigating the mysteries of the soul. It is to the latter that I refer when I say that there was an intervention in Alchemy by which it was assumed and, while preserving the same veils of language, was transformed in respect of its purpose. I deal, therefore, with the corpora spiritualia of the mystic school; we can leave to the physical alchemists those things of Caesar which belong to them, retaining the things which concern the mysteries of divine symbolism.

Now, as it is certain that the stone of the Graal is not actually and literally a stone, it may follow as a rational inference that, except for symbolical representation, the cup or chalice is not actually or literally a cup, much less a vessel which contains blood, Sang Real or otherwise. In like manner, if there is one thing which appears more clearly than most other things in the books of the Philosophers, it is that the stone of Alchemy is not a stone at all, and that the elixir of Alchemy is not a brew or an essence which can be communicated in ewers or basins. The stone represents more especially the visible sign of the mystery, and it is spoken of as offering two phases, of which one is white and the other red. To bring these ideas into correspondence with the form of Graal symbolism, I will speak of them for the moment by their alternative mysteries, that is, Bread and Wine. The Eucharistic Bread signifies the super-substantial sustenance, and the Wine is arch-natural life. It is for this reason that the Alchemical Stone at the red has a higher tingeing and transmuting power than the Stone at the white. The first matters of the alchemical work, to make use of another language of subterfuge, are Sulfur, Mercury and Salt; but these are the elements of the Philosophers and not those of the ordinary kind. In other words, common Sulfur and Mercury correspond to the Bread and Wine before consecration, and the philosophical elements are those which have been transubstantiated by the power of the secret words. That which is produced is called Panis Vivus et Vitalis and Vinum Mirabile, instead of the daily meat and drink by which we ask to be sustained in the Lord's Prayer. The Salt is that which is called the formula of consecration; it is that which salts and transmutes the natural earth. When Christ said: If the Salt loses its savor, wherewith shall it be salted?—this can be understood of the superexcellent and extra-valid consecration; the removal of the Graal signifies that of a certain arch-natural salting, yet the true salt of grace remains, like that of nature, and in its way also it communicates. Christ further said: You are the salt of the earth—and this is the true priesthood.

That which the textbooks have agreed from time immemorial to term a stone is that also which we find in greater Gospel books, where it is described as a stone not made with hands, and the transmutation performed thereby is the work of inward conversion, resulting in the condition which one of the adepts recommends to his disciples when he exclaims: Transmutemini, transmutemini a lapidibus mortuis in lapides vivos philosophicos. The possession of the stone is, in other words, the possession of the tingeing Christ.

It should be understood, therefore, that the First Matter in transcendence must be taken to signify the elements after conversion has been operated by the secret words of consecration. But the words signify here the Divine Life, and the process which really takes place is represented by the most sacramental of all terms: Et verbun caro factum est; And the Word was made of flesh. In this new light of alchemy, we may continue, if we please, to regard the elements of the Graal as the communication of the Eucharist in exaltation, of which our own Eucharist is only a shadow and substitute; or we can do what is the same thing and is preferable in respect of finality, that is, we can transfer the entire symbolism to man, who is the recipient of the Eucharist, the vessel of reception, the subject of conversion, the container which in the outward order is less than the thing contained, the life which receives the life above all life that is manifest and known. Without man, the conversion and transmutation of elements would be void of all offices, since there would be no terminus ad quem.

Prior to the efficacious consecration, we may assume that the simple elements are those substances, or, if we prefer it, are that one substance variously manifested, which, as the alchemists tell us so expressly, may be found everywhere. It is of no account till the Wise have introduced their mystical ferment therein. Having concealed it under a thousand names, they say in their strange manner that it is known by these; and so also some of them have declared in their derision, as against all the untutored material operations which involve a prodigal outlay, that he who spends upon the Great Work more than thirty thalers has already passed aside from the whole truth of the process. It follows from these elucidations that the higher understanding of the Eucharist and the mystic side of alchemy are concerned with the same subject, that is to say, with man, his conversion and transfiguration: the implicits are therefore the same, and of these things' alchemy was the next witness in the world after the epoch of the Holy Graal.

The schools of Kabalism can scarcely be said to have emerged into public existence when the canon of the Graal literature was already closed; in these schools there were great masters of mystic thought, though, in most cases, more especially on the intellectual side. In its own way, the theosophical scheme of Jewry in exile is a story of loss like the Graal, though it is one which ends in expectation or, I should say, in certainty: it is not, however, in this direction that we can look for more than sidelights and occasional analogies. The reason is that, although the root matters must be identical when the term in finality is one, we are dealing in respect of the Graal with a manifestation in Christendom, but in

Kabalism with a manifestation in Israel. Those who are in search of such analogies will find that the story reflected by Wolfram from Guiot de Provence, concerning the initial discovery of the Graal mystery in the starry heavens by a Jew of Toledo, rests on Zoharic authority, and is exactly the kind of thing which a Kabalistic Jew might have claimed, could we assume, which seems intolerable, that he was concerned in the quest of the Graal, either for its elucidation or invention. In the whole extent of the heavens, according to the Zohar, there are figures and signs—that is to say, there are Hebrew letters—"by means of which we may discover the deepest secrets and mysteries." These figures are formed by constellations of stars, which are for the sage "a subject of contemplation and a source of strange delight." We know further that the High History tells how behind the Graal castle there is the Earthly Paradise, and that this is the castle of souls. Now, we learn from the Zohar that the Garden of Eden is placed in a position which corresponds to that of the Graal itself. By the nature of their office, neither the essence of the Christian Hallow nor the Secret Garden originally belonged to this world; both subsequently were located therein; both in fine were removed, the Graal into the heavenly places and the Garden of Eden into that which is not manifest. The latter was connected closely with the great sanctuary wherein all souls await incarnation in turn, for according to Kabalism their creation was not successive, or dependent on earthly generation, but eternal in the heavens. It will be seen, therefore, that Kabalism has strange things to tell us which connect with the subject in hand, though they are perhaps rather in analogy with the accidents than with the essence of our scheme. There are many other correspondences, could space allow of their enumeration; but, in order to draw the comparison as closely as possible, I must say only that the substitution which according to the Graal legends is left with the Christian Church in place of the living sanctities is paralleled by the legend that the stress and inhibition of Israel is because the divine Word has been withdrawn from the Holy Place, and that instead of the true Tetragram we have only the name Adonai. Amidst such substitutions, therefore, Israel is also waiting by the waters of Babylon, and it has come to pass that we are beside her in those symbolic places, remembering, I think, more dimly, and yet with deeper yearning, the glories that once were in Zion.

III
Analogies of Masonry

In so far as we can regard it as a succeeding witness, the epoch of Kabalism was prolonged, like that of Alchemy, to the seventeenth century by the scholiasts of the Zohar, at which time Symbolical Masonry was beginning to emerge. No one can say at what period the old building mystery was taken over in this high interest, or when the symbolical school first acquired the remnants and traditions of the Templar chivalry. As regards this, when I first began to study the literature, and before I was acquainted with its criticism, I observed what others have observed, that some of its Templar suggestions seem almost transparent, and apart from all verbal and literary criticism I had reason to appreciate how much stronger they are than is known to those who are outside the initiations of Masonry and of those more secret fraternities which lie perdu behind and within it. I still think that herein is a key to the Parsifal of Wolfram, but the German poem is the mystery of the Graal presented on the non-Eucharistic side. Between Templarism and the rest of the texts it is impossible to institute a comparison, for if there is any reliance to be placed under any reserves upon the official process against that chivalry of old, it would appear that the voice of their doctrine on the Eucharist tended to reduce its office or make it of no effect. There is much that remains to be said that must be left at this point; and as regards Masonry there came a time, as it came also in respect of the crude non-Christian elements of the Graal literature, when the mystery, such as it was, of the old Building Guild was assumed by another mystery, as a consequence of which it was re-expressed with a different intention. So, as a shadow of things beyond it, there came into being that association which we understand as the symbolical art. The seeds of the transformation were brought from very far away, and the craft, as we have it, is not an example of growth after the ordinary kind, but of exceedingly curious grafting. That which took over the old mystery knew, though we know not how, the purport of the ancient mysteries, or under all its veils and subterfuges we could never have had its central legend, nor the memorable closing which is attached thereto. Let me say here, to those who can understand, that an amazing inference follows from the craft legend concerning the stultification of the House of Doctrine before its erection was finished. I am the first member of the Masonic fraternity who has ever seen that the mystical temple at Jerusalem was never built according to its proper plans. The secret died with the Master Builder, and it is for this reason that every brother is supposed to be concerned in research which so far has never attained its term. Those who took over the common mystery of the craft degrees had assuredly no interest in the history of an external building. That which is made void by the craft legend is the Jewish House of Doctrine, since the vital secret was taken away.

The step beyond this is to show that there is a parallel in Masonry concerning Christian doctrine, but it is found in a high degree, and in one which is militantly Christian. A certain rite sets before us a picture of all Christendom, personified by the flower of its chivalry, standing guard, amidst the adjuncts of pomp and ceremony, over a vacant sepulcher—the shrine from which a God has departed. Could anything signify more profoundly the apparent stultification of a Christian House of Doctrine? There is, however, another grade which is, comparatively speaking, obscure, though it is still worked in England. In this there is shown the symbolical counterpart by alternative of that intimation with which I have just dealt. It dissolves at a certain stage into yet another degree, and in the successive points of these two rituals, the candidate is brought to a period when all Earthly Houses of Doctrine give place to the High Spiritual House of Eternal Wisdom. As a preliminary to this, the external House, represented by the Holy Sepulcher, is made subject to a triple visitation, with the result that it is found empty, and those who look therein are told in a veiled manner that in such a place it is useless to go in search of lost secrets, because the Divine Warden has risen and gone away. I suppose that the analogy of this symbolism with the history of the Holy Graal would almost speak for itself in the mind of the reader. That history shows how the House of the Hallows was visited by sin or sorrow, and how it was made void, the secret things being transferred therefrom. In no case, however, is the mystery of intention behind these schools of symbolism and legend to be understood as anti-Jewish or anti-Christian. Institutors of Craft degrees or of grades of Christian Chivalry, it follows that those who set forth the widowhood of the House of Doctrine spoke not from without but from within; they all looked indifferently for the return of that which had been taken away for a time. When they tell us of what was lost to Jewry, they were never more assured of the wisdom which once dwelt in Israel; when they mourn over the Holy Sepulcher, they were never more certain that what has been removed is alive. In other words, it is the intimation of the secret schools that somewhere in time and the world there is that which can confer upon the candidate a real as well as a symbolical experience. Above all, this is the message of the Graal literature. It speaks from within the official House of Doctrine concerning that which once inhered therein and is now in the state of withdrawal or profound latency; but it offers all honor and devotion to the substituted sanctuary which remains, as Masonry offers it, in the higher understanding, both to Jew and Christian.

I have made it plain already that in so far as there is mystic purpose or hidden doctrine in the Graal literature, it is at most an echo from afar—a rumor, a legend which had fallen into the hands of romancers. It is as if Sir Walter Montbeliard, the patron of Robert de Borron, being by the hypothesis a Templar, had told a strange story to the poet of things which he also had heard from afar concerning the Sons of the Valley; it is as if Guiot de Provence, having seen a transcript from Toledo, had compared it with some Templar records belonging to the house of Anjou. These are not the directions of research, but they stand for more likely ways, and I put forward as so many materials of assistance, so many traces of the same implicits perpetuated through several centuries, (a) the Sacramental Mystery of Alchemy as corresponding to the Eucharistic Mystery of the Holy Graal; (b) the mystical pageant of Kabalism as analogical to the Graal pageant; (c) certain quests in Masonry as synonymous with the Graal quest. The conclusion is that from the middle of the twelfth century and so forward there has been always a witness in the world that the greatest and the highest among the holy things have been represented by a certain substitution within the official Churches. The Churches have not been made void; they are still "those holy fields"; but they bear the same relation to the sacred mystery behind them that Sinai and Horeb, Tabor and Carmel, Gethsemane and Calvary, bear to the official Churches. Remember that the highest office in no sense makes void the second best among any offices that are inferior.

The Supernatural Graal is without prejudice to the instituted sacrament, even as the transliterations and complexities of Kabalistic interpretation reduce nothing in the literal word. The great rites are celebrated, the high offices continue, the moving liturgical formulae are recited from day to day and year after year; we pass hurriedly through the crowded streets, over the quiet country sides; we pause by solitary seas. The veiled voices signify the Presence, yet the Master is taken away, and we know not where they have laid Him. The great legends tell us that He has been assumed into Heaven because of the evil times, or that

He is in a place of concealment, or that He is not seen so openly. Prohibited, spoliated and extirpated with fire and sword, the memory of the dead sects of Southern France can offer us at their highest only the help of the noble lady Esclairmonde communicating the osculum fraternitatis—a consolamentum of all things saddest—through the flames of the auto-da-fe.

One Masonic chivalry consents to protect us from the insidious attacks of the infidel if we visit the holy fields, but it is confessed that the sepulcher is empty and we know that the worst danger is from the infidel who is within. A later and more obscure chivalry, with a vainer office of observance, keeps ritual guard over the shadow of a sacred legend, we are asking the daughters of Zion whether there is any greater desolation. It pledges us to maintain the Sepulcher when it is agreed that the Master is not there, and we continue to say with our lips: Et unam sanctam catholicam et apostolicam ecclesiam, with a certain relief that the word Credo stands far away in the symbol. Saddest and proudest of all, the great craft legends of Masonry tell us that until that which from time immemorial has been lost in the secret places is at length restored to the mysteries, the true temple can only be built in the heart.

The Kabalistic sages are also waiting for the word, that there may be mercy on every side, and the stress and terror of the centuries is because Adonai has been substituted for Jehovah in the true form thereof. It is only the higher side of Alchemy which, without faltering, has continued to point the path of attainment, speaking of no change, no substitution therein—telling us of the one matter, the one vessel, the one way of perfection, yet also saying that except the Divine Guidance lead us in the path of illumination, no man shall acquire the most hidden of all secrets without a Master, which is another mode of expressing the same thing. I suppose that there is no more unvarying witness continued through the ages, through all which we have felt, as we still feel, that only a small change in the axis of inclination would transform the world of greatest inhibition into that of the greatest grace. It is as if we were in the position of Perceval, according to the High History—as if we had failed only on account of "one little question."

But we do not know what it is, or rather we know it only in its external and substituted forms. We go on, therefore, sadly enough and slowly, yet in a sense we are haunted men, with a voice saying ever and again in our ears: Ask, and ye shall receive; search your heart, for the true question is within and the answer thereof. All this is not to say that the high offices fail, that the great conventions are abrogated, that the glorious sense of chivalry towards our second mother in those sodalities which are external, but yet in that order are some intellectual and some also spiritual—that this sense is not of the highest counsel. But a time comes when the "glory to God in the highest," having been declared sufficiently without, is expressed more perfectly within, and we know in fine that this glory is to be revealed.

The same story of loss is therefore everywhere, but it is never told twice in the same way. Now, it is a despoiled sanctuary; now a withdrawn sacramental mystery; now the abandonment of a great military and religious order; now the age-long frustration of the greatest building plan which was ever conceived; now the Lost Word of Kabalism; now the vacancy of the most holy of all sepulchers. But the sanctuary is sacred, the king is to return, the Order of Chivalry has not really died; at some undeclared time, and under some unknown circumstances, the word which gives the building plan will be restored, and meanwhile the quest after it is continued for ever; the true Word will also be restored to Israel, and so from age to age goes on the great story of divine expectation. Meanwhile, the Christian mystics say: Take no thought for the morrow, because it is here and now; and to this grand antiphon, the response of the Hermetic Mystery is: Even so, in the place of wisdom, there is still the Stone of the Wise.

THE HOLY ASSEMBLY

September, 1907
The Hermeneutics of the Holy Graal

THE Mysterium Fidei is the Eucharist. The Greek Epiclesis clause may pass, with liturgical experts who have also the gift of the mystic, as the nearest approach to a rite above all things valid, that is, manifesting supernaturally. Its history is one of the most interesting in the wild garden of liturgical formulae. But it should be understood that in the earlier days of the Church, there was not a method of consecration which prevailed everywhere; the Latin rite held, with certain variations, to the canonical words of institution, as I have shown in a previous paper; but there are traces of instances in which consecration was performed by the recitation of the Pater Noster over the elements, thus, by the hypothesis, converting the daily bread into heavenly manna. By the hypothesis also, the Epiclesis clause brought down upon the elements the influence and even the presence of the Holy Ghost, and it must be admitted that this contains, ritually speaking, a very high suggestion. At the Council of Florence, the Latins required the Greeks to expunge the Epiclesis, with all forms of invocation, and there can be no doubt that they were doctrinally and technically correct, because it was admitted on all hands that the words of institution produced the valid Eucharist, and the principle of invocation was to give the officiating priest an express and personal part in the mystery of consecrating, which, by the same hypothesis, must be regarded as superfluous. The clause remains to this day in the Greek Church, and for those who lay stress on its efficacy that Church has therefore the words but not seemingly the sign of life which should be resident therein.

On the other hand, at the period of the Graal literature, two unhappy ferments were working in the Western Church: (1) The denial of the chalice; (2) the various doctrinal tendencies which resulted in the definition of transubstantiation.

From this point of view, the wound of the Latin Church is that it misconstrued the Mysterium Fidei. It had, in fact, five wounds corresponding to the five changes of the Graal. Of these changes the last only had perhaps the appearance of a chalice, but at that time it is said elsewhere in this particular romance that there was no chalice, and the mystic reason of this is that the Dominus qui non pars est sed totum is not contained in a cup, though the Lord is Pars hereditatis meæ et calicis mei.

The Latin Church cannot be accused of having failed to discern the Body of the Lord, but it may seem at first sight that its discernment, like that of the Greek orthodoxy, was apart from the life which their own scriptures tell them is resident in the blood—that is to say, it is the symbolical seat thereof. And yet on the basis of transubstantiation it is difficult to reject the Roman plea, that he who receives the Body receives also the Blood, because that which is communicated in the Eucharist is the living Christ made flesh. Perhaps, however, the implicit of the symbolism is really in the contrary sense, and the elements are dual to show that the flesh of itself profits nothing, while the spirit and the truth are in the communication of divine life. By those who regard transubstantiation as the burden of the Church which defined it, there will be a disposition to consider the Latin Eucharist as still a dismembered sacrament; by those who look upon it simply as a memorial, all subtleties notwithstanding, there will be a feeling that the remembrance is broken, and that the isolated sign does not signify fully. On the other hand, that view which belongs more especially to the mystics, namely, that the covenant of Christ to His followers concerns the communication of divine substance, will, I think, be aware that the accidents of such a communication are not of vital consequence; that perhaps the official Church was even more subtle than it knew, because it is certain that transposition or substitution in the external signs cannot occasion even the shadow of vicissitude in the mystery which is imparted.

I think, there is no question that the Mysterium Fidei according to any secret rite of which the Graal romances are the shadow and the rumor may, ex hypothesi, have been contained in a missal, and this missal would then have been Liber Gradalis, for the reason which Paulin Paris gave now long ago. It may have contained only the variations of an Oriental Rite, but it may also have embodied more generic differences, belonging to a mystic sect within the Church.

It should therefore be noted that transubstantiation does not enter the romances except in the last texts, that is to say, the great prose Perceval and the Galahad quest. Now, it is in the latter more especially that the Graal legend seems to have reverted to the official Church, whose purpose was obviously to remove the great Eucharistic Symbol once and for ever. It follows that the Galahad quest and the great prose Perceval belong to the same sacramental school. From the mystic standpoint, the explanation is, of course, different; the Latin Church, like the lesser sects of Christendom, had tinkered the Eucharist, firstly, by the division of the symbols and, secondly, by the materialization thereof, and it was, speculatively speaking, the prevalence of the teachings which I have mentioned which caused the Graal to be described as taken away; that is, it ceased to manifest outwardly. The effect was then that the official Church was cut off from the secret Church, as in the Cosmic Fall of Kabalism the Sephiroth were dismembered like the Eucharist and there was not the facilis ascenus Superno, to divine knowledge in Daath.

Now, seeing that in one case the Keeper of the Graal is supposed to have fallen from righteousness and therefore awaited healing from a source outside his own House of Doctrine, one would be disposed at first sight to conclude that the Graal Church may stand for Latin Christianity. Let us for a moment examine the texts from this point of view, taking the quests for our guidance. That of the Didot Perceval and the Lesser Chronicles leaves the original and the new Keeper either despoiled of the Hallows or they have all passed into final seclusion. The text is so vague that it is difficult to speak certainly—difficult indeed to know that Merlin himself did not take away the Holy Graal. In the first case, though there is no logic in the scheme, the romance was evidently meant as a pronunciation against the Latin Church, which lost the Mystery of Faith. But if this were the intention, the Coming of Perceval would be idle and the healing of no effect. In the second case, neither one nor the other Keeper could represent an official Church, seeing that the latter did not go into seclusion. On the other hand, if Brons or Perceval represent a secret Church, the meaning of the text must be that the Hallows remained with them and they were secluded therewith. To express it in another way, the Son of the Doctrine was received into the House of the Doctrine and had the great secret imparted to him. Faintly and far away, the Didot Perceval shows how the aeonian Keeper has waited in the castle of the soul till the natural man, who is the scion of his house, comes in and asks the question of the union. The natural man understands nothing and does not ask till he is driven, but he is driven at last. As faintly and still further away, the Conte del Graal tells the same symbolical story with many variations; but as it reaches no term till a later period in time, when it is simply a reflection of other texts, and has hence no independent implicits, there is no call to examine it in this connexion. It may be noted, however, that the prologue, which is its latest part, speaks of things which exceed experience—that is to say, evidence—of sins against spiritual life and of return to the House of the Father, as aspiration returns to its source. The German Parsifal tells how the House is always in the world, but that it is only attainable by great sanctity, which is sufficient to show that it does not symbolize the institutes of external religion. It has, however, a strange and undeclared sacramental side, which seems to indicate that the Eucharist in its highest efficacy comes down from Heaven direct. It therefore incorporates not indeed a distinct motive, but the terms of another school. To conclude concerning it, it is obvious from the beginning that the Keepers of the German Graal were a secret order of chivalry, after the manner of the Templars, and its meaning is that the Mystery of Faith was in the custody of a special election, though there is nothing to suggest that it was opposed to the official Church. The great prose Perceval lifts up a different comer of the veil, reciting that one Keeper died unhealed and that the last Warden of the Mysteries was taken away, though the Holy Things remained. We have now only the still greater and more paramount quest left for consideration, which is that of Galahad, and it tells how the Warden of the Mysteries, together with the Holy Things, was removed once and for all, as if the House of Doctrine were itself nothing and the term of research everything. This great quest was written with the perfect sanctity as its actuating motive and we can do no otherwise than accept it as an instance of the literature at its highest. It forms with the great prose Perceval the consummation of the cycle. These quests are mirrors of spiritual chivalry, mirrors of perfection, pageants of the mystic life, and it does not matter what the legend was prior to their appearance. They are the teaching of the Church spiritualized, if I may be pardoned such a term, and it is they which offer in romance form a presentation of the soul's legend.

So far therefore from the Graal sanctuary representing the Latin or any other external Church, we find that the mystery of the sanctuary within is written through all the romances, though it is in the words of the sanctuary without and the savor of the external incense is more noticeable in some quests than in others.

In this light, we shall still find the Didot Perceval a little deficient in consequence and the Conte del Graal too primitive and too composite to reflect any full light of intention. As regards the German cycle, it shows how the great mystery descends and abides in us. The High History empties the House of Doctrine and leaves it as a vacant sign before the face of the world. The Galahad quest says that the world was not worthy. Yet in a sense all this is comparative, and is the several presentations of the various aspects of that which is one at the root, for the secret Church says: Mysterium Fidei, and the official Church says: Corpus Domini; but these two are one.

II
The Catholic Secret of the Legend

In our consideration of certain coincident and successive literatures, we have seen that there was the Graal literature, saying now that the secret words, which were of the essence of the Mystery of Faith, had passed out of all common knowledge; now that the true succession from Christ had been resumed into Heaven; again that the sacred mysteries were reserved in an inaccessible mountain from all but the highest sanctity, or alternatively that the House of Doctrine stood vacant, as if a testimony to the external world. There was also the literature of alchemy, saying that He is truly here, but that the way of His attainment comes only by the revelation which He gives, and for all else, there are only the age-long processes of Nature. There was further the literature of Israel in exile, saying: By the Waters of Babylon—yet also to those who could hear it: Enter into the nuptial joys of Rabbi Simeon! There was, lastly, as there is also, the great witness of Masonry, saying: Not yet, in quiet lie—to every heart of aspiration seeking to build the temple otherwise than in the heart. And so, from age to age, the story of substitution continues, but with a hint everywhere that still there is known somewhere that which the sign signifies. The Wardens are withdrawn, but they are alive. There is a cloud upon the Sanctuary, but the Sanctuary is within the Church, and other rumors distinguishable throughout the centuries speak of a Holy Place which is behind the manifest Altar, of a deeper mystery of love behind the world of grace—a rumor, a legend, a voice, an unknown witness, speaking of a more Holy Assembly, of an Interior and more Secret Church.

It is obvious that the romances of the Graal are either legendary histories of religion, and as such are concerned with the quest of conversion, that is, with Christianity colonizing, or they are spiritual histories with a strong individual element. The first class would include the metrical Joseph and the Grand St. Graal, while the most notable examples of the second are the Parsifal, the High History and the Galahad Quest. The idea of their secret meaning must be held to reside, as regards the first, in the claims which they put forward and, as regards the second, in the special application of the stories. Here, therefore, follows a fuller consideration of the several grades in the mystery designed to constitute the harmony of all quests equally with all histories. The inward man, as I have said, is the wounded Keeper, and he is indeed in the Castle of Souls, which is the Graal Castle, as it is also Eden, Paradise and the Body of Man. That is to say, it is the Earthly Paradise, but behind it there is another Eden. The Keeper has been (a) wounded for immemorial sin; (b) he is infirm by reason of his long exile; (c) he has become maimed for some profanation of the mysteries; or (d) he suffers from the failure to ask one little question. That question is: Who is served of the Graal?—and here are the equivalents of the formula: What part is the Lord? Art thou He that is to come? Who goeth into the Mountain of the Lord? The answer to this last is: The innocent of hands and clean of heart. The Keeper is, in fine, healed and set free by one who comes from without—by Perceval and Galahad, who lay down their arms in a state of purity. Gawain cannot help him, because he is the natural man, unconverted, and the day of Sir Bors is not yet. After the former Keeper's healing, he sometimes remains with the new Keeper, his successor, whom he has incorporated into the mysteries, and this represents one stage of the progress; in other stories, he passes away and is succeeded. The explanation in either case is that the bondage, the desolation, the lapse of the immortal spirit into earthly life is here shadowed forth, in which state the spirit can only be helped from without, that is to say, by the mortal half, the external nature; and its great deliverance is by such a transfiguration that the one is succeeded by the other and the two are one henceforth. Hereof is assuredly the tradition of some secret sanctuary and its application may be found by those who will work out the details, seeing that it prevails through all the quests. There will be no need to say, even to the unversed student, that in the wilderness of this mortal life that which maintains the spirit is that which is involved by the higher understanding of the Holy Graal. But at the same time, it is also a Feeding Dish, a Dish of Plenty, because the life of the body comes from the same source. When the natural man undertakes the great quest, all the high kingdoms of this world, which cannot as such have any part therein, look for the ends of everything. It is the quest of that which is real, wherein enchantments dissolve and the times of adventure are also set over. The enchantments are in the natural world, and so again are the adventures, but the un-spelling quest is in the world of soul. The witness of this doctrine has been always in the world, and therein it has been always secret. The knowledge of it is the Shekinah restored to the sanctuary; when it is over-shadowed, there is a cloud on the sanctuary. It is the story of the individual man passing into the concealment of the interior and secret life, but carrying with him his warrants and his high insignia. In a word, it is that doctrine the realization of which in the consciousness I have called, under all reserves, and for want of a better term, the Secret Church, even the Holy Assembly—I should say rather, the cohort of just men made perfect.

III
The Good Husbandman

The external Church is that body in which the work of regeneration takes place; it is the life everlasting projected on the perishable plane. It is in this sense the condign and legitimate governor of all the external places. The Church is the good husbandman, who prepares the ground and tills the earth of humanity. It fertilizes that earth after various manners, as, for example, by the laws of moral conduct, by the great doctrines and the great literatures, by the high consecration of the seven sacraments, by the water, the oils and the wine. In all these ways, it sows with a generous hand the seeds of secret life. But the earth is hard, and the earth is also unresponsive. The seed will germinate in many directions and the earth will therefore be irradiated by a certain undeclared presence of the secret life; but it issues above the ground only in a few cases, and then the individual enters into the manifested life of sanctity. It is a question thereafter of the particular quality of the earth and the environment of the life. Generally, the growth is stunted and too weak to put forth its powers. It is only on rare occasions that they spring up into the high light and the clear air, lifting the radiant glory of a perfect head amidst their peers.

The hidden life of the soul is well known to the doctors of the soul, and the Church has also its hidden life, wherein it communicates with all things nearest to the Divine in the higher consciousness. Official doctrine is, however, in the same position as normal consciousness; it covers a part of the field only. There is therefore, on both sides, a certain sense of the incommensurate, and perhaps it is for this reason that the Churches are desolate; this desolation is, however, on account of that which is in hiding, not of that which is withdrawn. The offices are not abrogated and the sacraments are still administered, being valid and efficacious up to a certain point. Perhaps also the desolation is more especially in ourselves, and it is we who, individually and collectively, have helped to make void the House of Doctrine. The fact that the external Church is from this point of view in widowhood makes its desertion a graver offence against the high unwritten code of chivalry, just as a dereliction of masonic good conduct is implied in forsaking one's mother lodge. At the same time, the good work can sometimes be done from without as well as from within, but in this case that work is an approximation towards the Church which is within.

IV
The Mystery Which is Within

On the historical side, the Secret Church is the shadow of a hypothesis at best; on the spiritual side of the intellect, it is an implicit, but it is that irresistibly; mystically, it is a truth which is not less than obvious, but it should be understood that it is apart from all forms, conventions and instituted existence. When in our highest moments we conceive with the least unworthiness of the Church on the ideal plane, we approximate, but still under the reserves of our own insufficiency, to the Holy

Assembly. It is the unity of arch-natural minds. It is that in which, by the mediation of the creeds, we confess our belief daily—the communion of saints. If we like to express it in such words—and they are excellent apart from their unhappy associations—it is the choir invisible. It is even like the priesthood of the Graal sanctuary, as we judge by the romances concerning it; it does not ordain or teach; it fulfills its office sufficiently because, speaking symbolically, it is "in the foremost files of time." It is like Saint Martin—its feet are on earth and its head is in Heaven.

The Secret Church has said: Introibo ad altare Dei, and it has entered and gone in. When it comes out, in the person of one of its members, it carries bread and wine, like Melchisedech. The conditions of its membership correspond to the condition's requisite for the finding of the Holy Graal, as described in the German Parsifal. If it were possible to regard the Graal priesthood as an order, it might be said that its device is: Behold, I am with you always, even unto the consummation of the world. It is the place in which Mary conceived in her heart before she conceived in her body. As already indicated, it has not issued manifestoes, but things have transpired concerning it, and thus we have the Characteristics of the Interior Church by Loupoukine, the Cloud upon the Sanctuary by Eckhartshuasen, Werner's Sons of the Valley, the Eucharistic side of Alchemy and the rumor of the Holy Quest. It gives to those who can receive it a full answer to the question: Art thou He that is to come, or do we look for another?

The presence of this Secret Church is like that of angels unawares. In the outer courts are those who are prepared for regeneration and in the adyta are those who have attained it: these are the Holy Assembly. It is the place of those who, after the birth of flesh, which is the birth of the will of man, have come to be born of God. It is in the persons of those who are regenerated that the gates of hell cannot prevail against the Church. The place of the Holy Assembly is the place of Eden and Paradise; it is that whence man came and whither he returns. It is also that place from which the Spirit and the Bride say: Come; or it is the place of the Waters of Life, with the power to take freely. It is like the still, small voice; it is heard only in the midst of the heart's silence, and there is now no written voice to show us how its rite is celebrated. There is no sodality, no institution, no order which throughout the Christian centuries has worked in such silence. It is for this reason that it remains an implicit in mystic literature rather than a formal revelation; it is not a revelation but an inference; when it is not an inference, it is an attainment.

The mystery in chief of the Secret Church is that of Divine communication, of which it has the sanctifying sacraments, but so far as these are typified symbolically it can have no more efficient and unspotted outward signs than the bread and wine for oblation. It is in this sense that it connects more especially with the Eucharist. The Churches with open doors are the thresholds of the Church which is not entered by doors because it has not been built with hands. The Secret Church is the manifest Church glorified and installed in the spiritual kingdom, as it was first set over the kingdom of this world. It is, therefore, the soul of the outward Holy Assembly, and it would be unreasonable for those who acknowledge the body to deny that which informs it. But to speak of a soul which thus informs a body is to say that, although the lesser is contained by the greater, the latter is until now not without the former nor apart therefrom, and its mode of manifestation, in so far as it can be said to manifest, is not otherwise than within. There is no separate incorporation. If I have spoken of it as leading the official Church, there is here an imperfection of expression, because it is speaking after a formal manner concerning modes which are apart from all whatsoever that we understand by convention. Without in any sense representing and much less exhausting the process, I should prefer to repeat that it draws rather than leads, and if I may attempt one further definition, I would describe the Secret Church as the integration of believers in the higher consciousness.

V
Conclusion

We know that in its higher grades, the spirit of imagination moves through a world not manifest, and this is the world of mystery; it is that also in which many are initiated who are called but not chosen; yet it is that in which the epopt is at last enthroned—that the world in which the Graal Castle, Corbenic or Mont Salvatch, the most holy temple and secret sanctuary, are attainable at any point, all points being out of time and place. It is the world of quest, which is also the world of attainment. There, in fine, at the striking of a certain mystic hour, that translation takes place in which the soul is removed, with the Graal thereto belonging, and it is idle for anyone to say that it is shown henceforth so openly. It is then that the offices of all the high degrees meet in the term of their unity, and the great systems also, at which height we understand vitally what now we realize intellectually—that the great translation of Alchemy, the passage from kingdom to crown in Kabalism, the journey through Hades to Elysium in the Greek Mysteries, or in Dante as their last spokesman, and lastly the great quest of Galahad, are the various aspects and symbolical presentations of one subject. We may never know how the luminous shadow of these mysteries was cast upon the hearts of the romancers, but as they appeal, all of them, to some great antecedent record, and although we cannot suppose that this was itself otherwise than a bright reflection in a mirror, it is not unreasonable to accept what they say tentatively. The news of the great quest overshadowed them somehow, and I for one am acquainted with other places wherein are corresponding reflections, wherein also we see, however vaguely and dimly, the trail of their garments to whom these great things are not a matter of dreaming.

At this stage of the interpretation, I shall not need to point out that, in the final adjustments, even the highest symbols are merely pretexts; they are tokens, "lest we forget"; and this is for the same reason that neither chalice nor paten really impart anything. They are the great conventions to which the soul confesses on the upward path of its progress, and within their proper offices, they are not to be set aside. The explanation is not that they impart from their own virtue, but through them the high graces communicate in proportion to the powers of reception. The soul which has opened up the heights of the undeclared consciousness within partakes as a great vessel of election, while another soul may receive nothing.

And now to make an end of these pleadings: I have chosen to give some account of the Holy Graal as it was and as it is, that I could lead up to what it might be, that is to say, how it could be realized in high literature, because in other respects the things which might be in the ideal order are those also which are—and God redeems the future as well as the past. As regards therefore the true theory of this mystery, with others of the mystic school, we may hope in the Lord continually, even as one who believes that he will not be confounded in eternity. Reason has many palaces, but the sovereign peace rules in a single place. Dilated in the mystery of cloud and moisture and moonlight, the Graal appears even now, and that suddenly. The spirit of the holy quest may be as much with us in the study of the literature of the quest as if we were ourselves venturing forth in search of the Graal Castle. Herein is the consecrating motive which moves through the whole inquiry. I have allocated a great experiment in literature to a great consanguineous experiment in spiritual life. I have not so much demonstrated the value of a pure hypothesis as elucidated after what manner those who are concerned with the one subject do from all points return triumphantly thereto. As a seeker after the high mysteries, at this last I testify that whosoever shall in any subject offer me daily bread, I will say to him: But what of the Panis vivus et vitalis? What of the supersubstantial bread? And if there be anyone who deals therein, under what rules soever of any houses of exchange, I will have him know that if he sells in the open market even, I am a buyer. So therefore, the writer of these papers gives thanks that he has written concerning the romance pageants and sanctity as of the eternal secrets of religion.

MADAME GUYON

June, 1908

FENELON and Madame Guyon are both beacons on the mystic path, but I think that their light is thrown upon those directions wherein there is no final harborage. Between them there stands the circumspect figure of Bossuet, as an undesired moderator between them, carrying all the official warrants, to all of them loyal, signal as the author of the Variations of the Protestant Sects, negligible as a teaching authority on the great subjects—perhaps, it may be said, more especially as he appears in the once celebrated and now forgotten Instructions on the States of Prayer. It was a remarkable, a momentous conjunction and opposition of planets which do not group usually after this manner. It is not easy to characterize or to compare them. It is not quite easy to adjust them to their environment or to their brilliant, faithless, dissolute period of Louis Quatorze. It would be ultra vires at any time to set Bossuet in judgment on Fénelon or Madame de Maintenon on Madame Guyon, giving the best intentions to all parties; yet Bossuet was the spokesman of the Church, and Madame de Maintenon was in a certain fluidic sense one mouthpiece at least of the political party. There is a great deal to be said for the position of Bossuet, who was in the face of a grave difficulty; but he had the incompleteness of the logical understanding when it deals with those highest subjects which exceed its canons. There is a great deal to be said for the position of Madame Guyon, against whom he was instrumental in moving the vast machinery of the

Church; but she had some errors of the mystic consciousness married to a logical understanding which was equipped at the best imperfectly. This notwithstanding, she was a shrewd woman after her own manner, and manifested on one occasion an extraordinary aptitude for business of a complicated kind.

MADAME GUYON.

As regards the deep things of experience which are involved in the whole subject, I set down in the first place the principles hereinafter following: (1) Hereof is the purpose and term of the inward life—that a man should know in fine Him in Whom he has believed at first, which itself is the justification of that faith whereby it is said that in the beginning we are ourselves justified; and this was the condition which Madame Guyon claims to have attained in the repose of her own soul. (2) It is this state which the men and women in the world do not know, and there are few who can tell them effectually, so that even a preliminary certitude can enter their hearts; it is also that state of which people under the external obedience and ministry of the official churches for the most part dream only—even if they dream indeed—and it is at a long distance. (3) The root of our consciousness may grow into a great tree by which we shall ascend into heaven, and so did Madame Guyon ascend in her spirit, according to her unwavering testimony. (4) The ground of this is that we are of the true legitimacy, Sons and Daughters of the House, and it is our fault if we do not enter into our own; but in respect of Madame Guyon, she had come to know of her inheritance, that this was indefectible, and though she did not read perfectly the language of the Divine Law, she had begun, as she best could, the investigation of her title deeds. (5) She did not understand fully that it is not on account of our imputed "vileness," our miserable plight and the compassion which this state may be supposed to Kindle, but because of our genealogy, and because of our implied possibilities, that God has given to His elect that which we know to have been given. (6) The secret which begins in conformity is the great secret which ends in the Divine Union, and—within and without—Madame Guyon knew many depths and some of the heights which are implied in the uttermost subjection of the will to God. (7) She knew also that the way of subjection, of conformity and of advancement by one step at a time, is the way of love.

FRANÇOIS DE FÉNELON.

Now, if I were speaking as a mystic to none but those who were mystics, who had accepted—at least intellectually—all the dedications of the inward life, I should conceive that this recital was adequate by way of a memorial as to the personality of Madame Guyon; but I am addressing a mixed audience, and I must say that which is necessary concerning her in the external state, and its relations, before it will seem warrantable to proceed, however shortly, to the real matter of this thesis. It must be understood, for those who can hear it, that what follows in the barest summary is rather alien than otherwise to my proper purpose.

Madame Guyon, née Jeanne Marie Bouvières de la Mothe, was born on April 13, 1648, and she was still in her childhood when Queen Henrietta Maria, the widow of Charles I, King of England, visited her father at Montargis in the province of Orleanois. This is sufficient to indicate the social condition of her family, and I have said already that in France it was the period of Louis XIV. She was a child of conventual life, almost from the beginning—a neophyte in Ursuline, Benedictine and Dominican schools of teaching—and—under whatever limitations—she not only learned early, but realized something of the ways of God with man, in virtue of which the chosen souls are drawn "from tents of Kedron to Jerusalem." She was married in her sixteenth year to Jacques Guyon, who was approaching forty, and by the intervention of his mother she was brought too soon, and, indeed, immediately, into familiar acquaintance with the sorrows of a persecuted life. It was not otherwise a happy, though apart from her it might well have been an endurable marriage. She became the mother of five children, and she lost her husband when she was still under the age of thirty years. There are grounds for believing that her disposition towards the spiritual life had helped to alienate his affections, but his death brought about her liberation from the yoke which his mother had imposed. I suppose, I should mention further that among the lesser inflictions, her considerable personal attractions were ravaged by smallpox. She had lost also two of her children, to all of whom, in the midst of her religious dedications, she was attached deeply. Those dedications passed through the usual stages which characterize the life of the soul—seasons of joy, seasons of illumination, seasons of sanctifying grace, and in fine a long period of privation, drought and inhibiting darkness. But perhaps her signal of misfortune was to mistake the absence of joy and consolation for a sign that Divine Grace had been withdrawn as well—by which I understand the Plenary and not what theology calls the Sufficing Grace. Such privations seem almost invariably to carry with them an implied guarantee, seeing that in the annals of sanctity there is no instance of their endurance beyond a specific period. In the case of Madame Guyon, they lasted, I think, longer than usual; but they ended, as this experience ends always, more suddenly than they began, and this was in response, as she tells us, to the concurrent prayers of herself and her spiritual director, Father Lacombe. The change came in July, 1680; there was no permanent recurrence of the experience, and she felt in possession henceforth not only of the God who is power, but also of the consoling God.

I believe, it may be said that at this period she had taken already a certain place as a teacher of the inward life; but it was assumed and reserved always within the restricted circle of her private acquaintance, of those who sought her, and of the poor and distressed, to whom her material wealth enabled her to minister materially. She was at no time in public evidence as a teacher, reformer, or prophetess; and it is to be noted especially in her favor that although she was the recipient of many sensible favors in vision, she never presumed upon these, as if they constituted warrants of themselves, but relied upon that which had been given her in the palmary degree—the realization of Divine Life communicated in supernatural faith.

As regards her external condition at this time, she was drawn so much towards retirement that she thought seriously of the conventual life. She renounced it on account of her children, as later—but for other reasons—she renounced an episcopal offer which would have given her a high conventual place, nominally at least. On the other hand, she was approached in three instances with a view to a second marriage, and it seems certain that in one direction she was conscious of natural predisposition, but she had resolved already to belong only to God. She continued, therefore, for the moment her own way of dedicated activity in retirement, with an audience which increased insensibly, speaking, as I think, not of herself, but of that which had been given to her in trust, and exercising such influence that even in the case of her director she led rather than was directed. In conjunction with him and with D 'Aranthon, Bishop of Geneva, she was for a period at Gex on the Swiss borders, where she devoted herself to works of charity and religious instruction. But that which had come to be termed the new doctrine— that which was briefly and simply sanctification by faith—had gone abroad as a rumor in this part of the world, from the center-in-chief at Paris, and it was here that her trials began. Father Lacombe preached on the experience of holiness, and incurred the displeasure of the bishop, largely through the intervention of his advisers, and he who had welcomed at first both him and Madame Guyon, allocating the spirit of the teaching to her whose teaching it was, resolved to terminate her work within the limits of his diocese, unless he could adapt it expressly to his particular ends. Originally, in his own mind, he had designed that work solely as a ministry of charity, not of religious instruction, with which object he now proposed that she should become the prioress of one of his conventual houses. Recognizing that in this manner a period would be put to her mission, she left Gex—as an alternative—and repaired to Thonon, where, however, the feeling of ecclesiastical authority towards the inward life was illustrated by the burning in public of books which treated thereof.

It was after her practical expulsion from the diocese of Bishop D'Aranthon that some part of her experience and illumination began to pass into writing. A thesis entitled Spiritual Torrents was written at Thonon, and at Grenoble, her next place of sojourn, she began her mystical commentary on the Old and the New Testament. She appears also to have held private assemblies for prayer and conversation. She published, in fine, that Short Method of Prayer by which she remains to this day more especially known and valued as a writer on the contemplative life. The cloud, which perhaps was no bigger than a hand at Gex, extended over this book and began to break in tempest. Under friendly episcopal advice, she left Grenoble for Marseilles, but it was stirred up against her speedily. She found refuge for a period in Italy and thence returned to Paris in the summer of 1686, being still under forty years of age. Here there was a lull of some months, and Madame Guyon gathered into her circle several who were distinguished by their rank, and some by their sanctity. But scarcely had a year elapsed when the first bolt fell from the sky of Rome, working through the Court of France, by the imprisonment of Father Lacombe, who, for the remaining seven-and-twenty years of his earthly existence, was consigned from dungeon to dungeon, with the Bastille as a beginning and the Castle of Oleron as a term. It is pitiful to record that the instigator of this transaction was a certain Father La Mothe, the half-brother of Madame Guyon, and there is no question that through her spiritual director he was attacking her. This policy continued, and after a period of slanderous accusations, involving her personal character, she was herself imprisoned in a convent. There, amidst privations and indignities, she had at least the opportunity of writing, of which her own extensive memoirs were, I believe, the chief result. Through the good offices of Madame Miramion, who is known otherwise to history as a woman of spiritual life, the influence of Madame de Maintenon—previously hostile—was brought to bear upon the throne, and Madame Guyon's release was secured after a confinement of eight months. This act on the part of the King's morganatic wife brought the two women into acquaintance, and the one who had misconstrued the other now learned to admire her.

It should be observed that it was subsequent only to Madame Guyon's first imprisonment that the star of Fénelon rose over the horizon of her life. It was not, therefore, as many may have supposed, an early or a very long acquaintance, and as no one was in a better position to be informed concerning her than the Archbishop of Cambrai, he must have acted from the beginning with his eyes open. There is little doubt that into the spiritual side of her heart he was taken at once by her; there is no doubt that she appealed to him as a new director, at least on the doctrinal side of her literary work; and there is, finally, no doubt that she did bend him towards her mystic purpose in the world. Between them there was long and frequent correspondence, and between them there were various meetings. He, on his part, became an apostle, in a manner, of the inward life; but though he could counsel at need, and correct perhaps at need, in matters of technical doctrine, he could so little in extremity save her that he was almost lost himself. His patronage, therefore, availed less than little, except that it must have increased her vogue; in 1689 her book upon Prayer was burned by hundreds in public, and about the same time those who, on a previous occasion, had sought, it is said, to ruin her by means of a forged document are believed to have tried poison by means of a bribed servant.

The next event in her history was the intervention of Bossuet, who, in a book which I have already mentioned, pronounced, somewhat late in the day, against her opinions, but without involving her name. He sat also in judgment upon her, with other commissioners, but there was no specific condemnation, and it seems certain that his overt actions were rather through the pressure of her enemies than his own direct inclination. The result in either case was her second imprisonment, this time in the castle of Vincennes. Subsequently, he was removed to Vaugirard and thence to the Bastille, where she remained for four years, and was then at length released. She lived thereafter as an enforced exile at Blois, where she died in the year 1717, having—all her vicissitudes notwithstanding, and all her persecutions—attained the age of nearly seventy years.

We have now to consider a much more important matter than one of external history and of the suffering thereto belonging: it is the attitude of the ecclesiastical power towards that which it termed Quietism, or alternatively to that condition of repose in the inward life by the identification of the will with God. The official Church, even in her most intolerant form, is not of necessity an enemy of the inward life because she is the custodian and teacher of the outward doctrine, with the practices and ceremonies attaching thereto. There are many for whom this statement will have almost the idleness of a commonplace, but there are others for whom there is no proper correspondence between that which is without of the Church and that which is looked for within, and we have further to deal with the question of strenuous fact that she did proscribe the doctrines of inward life as expressed by Madame Guyon and Fénelon. A t the same time, the mystery of that life, the counsels of perfection which belong to it, and the sanctity which has been its witness are written over all her literature. I am also assured personally that, as the vital organism of a corporate body, the Latin Church is conscious—and conscious keenly—that all which belongs to her without depends from her as she is within. She may say—and otherwise she would be scarcely an external Church—that her teachings are to be accepted in their literal sense; that her practices are the rule of faith; that her ceremonial is authorized and holy; but she has never said that the mysteries of divine truth do not exceed all measurements of experience and all dogmatic expression, while no institution has maintained more continuously that the Kingdom of Heaven is within. But this being so, why did the Church persecute and imprison either Molinos or Madame Guyon? Why did Rome close the mouth of Archbishop Fénelon by a quasi-condemnation of his Maxims of the Saints? I believe that there is a very clear and a cogent answer.

We must take in the first place the case of Molinos, who was actually the antecedent of Madame Guyon. He said in Spain that which in its basis was the same as Madame Guyon said a very little later in France. He was still in the prison of the Holy Office at Rome when she was in danger of the judgment at Vincennes. Though so nearly allied in time, there is no reason to suppose that she knew of him then otherwise than at a distance; but at some later period of her life The Spiritual Guide may have come into her hands, while, in spite of certain forged letters—or letters so accounted—it is unlikely that her name and repute ever entered within his horizon, seeing that his outward life was confined to the four walls of his dungeon. The sum of those principles and that practice which received in the case of Molinos the name of Quietism—by the way, it was a term of contempt—corresponded sufficiently to the principles and practice of Madame Guyon for her system to be designated by its enemies after the same manner. Molinos taught the doctrine of present and effective sanctification by the way of faith. Madame Guyon taught the mystery of entrance into God through Christ, also by the way of faith, the necessity in all things of complete dedication to God, and the ministry of inward holiness as the consecration of outward life. The end on earth was the attainment of that state which she terms Pure or Unselfish Love, the nearest approach to the Divine Union of which it was given her to speak. I see nothing in this naked expression of principles to which Rome need have taken exception; I see nothing which it did not at need approval. As it so happens, however, the expression does not exhaust the content of that which was implied in the principles, and there is hence a certain intellectual warrant, for the sake of the truth of things, to exercise justice towards that Church which has arrogated to herself a license to exterminate by all means whatever she regards as heresy. We know that this title does not inhere in churches or other institutions, however consecrated, and we may reserve all rights as to how we characterize the claim; but at the moment this exceeds the issue, and the fact remains that the Church, from her own standpoint, was face to face with a movement which, quite unconsciously to itself, tended to make void her office. After common Protestant heresies had divided the world from Rome, there seemed on the point of springing up within its own bosom, and claiming to be a part of itself, a school of secret thought, as the prince of some other world wherein the Church had not anything.

Quietism was a product of its period, and at the root it does not differ from the universal principles of the mystic life; it was the inclination of the axis of the period which caused the Quietist to say that mystic love at its height forgets solicitude even for the lover's salvation: that was its answer of the secret soul of man to the doctrine of rewards and punishments—with its concomitants, the commercial transactions in forgiveness and indulgences, its trade in prayers and masses. It was also an answer to the imposed rule of the ascetic life, though those who put it forward were not aware of this fact, and themselves, in the person of Madame Guyon, adopted on occasion revolting forms of penance. But, in the last resource, Quietism signifies the repose of the soul in God as the resting-point of all that ardor of activity which takes the soul to the center. It is obvious, therefore, that the relation between this view and the doctrines of the Union, as expressed by the great company of all the saintly doctors, is one of identity rather than of analogy; and it has been pointed out that Margaret Mary Alacoque was beatified—under popular pressure, perhaps, but beatified she was—for saying the same things after nearly the same manner as Molinos did before her—both being Spanish contemplatives—and things far exceeding Fénelon, who in addition to the mystic consciousness had the logical understanding in the reasonableness of sweet marriage therewith.

When Fénelon, by the necessity of things, was driven to try conclusions with Bossuet, and with the power which was behind Bossuet, it is said—and credibly enough—that he regarded the doctrine of the Interior Life as being itself upon trial, and as, for him, that Life signified Christianity in its essence, therefore Christianity also would stand or fall with him. The bone of contention was the little work entitled Maxims of the Saints, and the complicated issues which were involved, owing to the position of the writer, caused the condemnation which overtook it to be worded with such caution that it fell upon the constructions which were or might be put on it without accusing the mind of Fénelon of being at variance from the mind of the Church. This wonderful policy notwithstanding, the book offers fullest evidence that the root and the trunk of that tree which had begun to grow in France, as once it had attempted in Spain, put forth some strange branches and strange blossoms. The most express clauses which can be cited as part of that evidence exhibit the following claims: (1) That a holy soul may deduce important views from the Word of God, which would remain otherwise unknown; (2) that the decisions of the soul in a state of continuous faith are the voice of the Holy Ghost in the soul; (3) that souls which have experienced the higher sanctification have not so much need of times and places for worship as others. The fact that these statements are moderated and even minimized as the spirit of the prelate intervenes could make them a little less unsavory in the mouth of the Church, and there is no doubt that what is negative and implied in Fénelon becomes positive and explicated in Madame Guyon, who, by her doctrine of justification through faith, apart from works, had passed, without intending it, over to the camp of the Protestants. On all the higher planes, the issues for her are between the soul and God, whence I find no room in her system for the intervention of the Church and its sacraments. I do not wonder, therefore, that Madame Guyon and Fénelon were signal dangers to the great, jealous, exclusive institution which claims to be the sole depository of the faith delivered to the saints and the sole interpreter of its purport. And seeing further that in their light and their particular quality of sanctity, I do not find the mystic light of all; that in Madame Guyon, the mode of expression is too often one of sentiment passing towards hysteria; while in parts too many the Maxims of the Saints are scarcely saved from the commonplace; I recur to the point whence I started and record in fine that their theosophical system offers no abiding harborage.

It follows from all the considerations which have been enumerated here that Madame Guyon had the consciousness of the mystic term and I am sure that she had some of its experiences. Perhaps in his own more reposeful, more reasoned and reserved way, Fénelon saw a few things more clearly; but they too were in the initial stages only. And I am not condoning the ways and methods of the Church to which they owed their first inspirations and drew their first teaching, if I say that they, and she more especially, would have done well to recognize more fully that the gate of ceremonial, strict observance and external offices is a true enough gate in its way and can admit the soul to the path. With a little more wisdom, Madame Guyon would not have been chastised and might have been even beatified.

That which has served as a pretext for the present paper is the recent re-issue of T.C. Upham's well-known Life of Madame Guyon. Had space served me, I should like to have said something of this biography—so sympathetic and appreciative that to those who know the subject it cannot fail to be charming in a certain sense. But it is not a critical work, and in this, as in other respects, its limitations are strongly defined.

One only word in conclusion: To-day the mystic life is again on its trial, but in a different sense than it was at the time of Fénelon; it is not before the court of Rome or the court of King Louis, but before the face of the intellectual world, as the one claim which remains to be tested after all other modes have been found wanting, and those even who had the highest stakes in them have confessed to their failure.

MORE DEALINGS WITH THE DEAD

July, 1908

DURING the ages of Latin Christianity, the desire of the living or the dead was only of peace for the soul; no one tolerated the idea of seeing them, no one sought to communicate with them. It was known that they were Messed, assuming that they died in the Lord; it was believed that "Masses on the earth" would aid them "at the throne of the Most Highest." The Paradiso of Dante represents the highest water-mark of some far-off idea of re-union, but it was so sublimated that it gave no reflection to the sympathies and sorrows that must have reigned in the lower world of thought and life. That this is all changed, and indeed centuries ago, is assuredly an indication that something which has always been implied in human consciousness has become manifest, and marks a stage in the development of the soul. Mystically, it has been always recognized, so far as Christianity is concerned—as our creeds show; but the communion to which our faith is pledged thereby was not of that kind which either sought or would have tolerated the idea of individual communication. To speak plainly, and under due correction in respect of sporadic differences, this has been, both as regards the assumed facts and the expressed aspiration, a growth of the last century or two, and if it is not, in its later development, the work of modem spiritualism, it has at least grown largely out of the phenomena which are familiar under that name, regarded as evidences testifying to the desires of the human heart, which at their period had become far more strenuous. Unfortunately, the history of communication with "the world of spirits" under this auspice has not produced absolute certitude that its experimental research has ever dealt really with departed intelligence, though it has created certain strong presumptions. Unfortunately, also, it has given us, on any assumption, no real knowledge of man's estate in the universe after his passage through physical life. The revelations continue, but even as before, they minister to each circle of investigation according to the belief of that circle. The pathological facts are very curious, as strong witnesses of our undeveloped potencies, but overall the records there is written in other respects a great note of interrogation.

If we take as our example for the moment the literature of automatic writing, this is becoming large at the present day, like that of trance-speaking in the past. Its evidential value is another matter and the unprejudiced mind has a full opportunity in the records which occasion this notice to appreciate its value under circumstances which may be regarded as, on the whole, somewhat favorable. They are the records of a private circle whose members are personal friends of Lady Paget, and our guarantee concerning them is the guarantee which has satisfied her, namely, that she has entire faith in their sense of honor. As a fact, the members are two only, of whom one has acted as the medium and the other as the interrogator in chief. The triad is completed by the disincarnate spirit from whom the communications originate. The recorder has been simply an editor who does not appear to have been actually present at the sittings. The occurrences stand, therefore, at their recorded value, and in dealing with them, it seems perfectly safe to assume the good faith of everyone concerned, at least on this side of life. Of the communications, as such we shall probably know beforehand how unlikely they would be to contain either new truth or old truth re-expressed in a higher or better way. Of all those who have gone up into the mountain of the Lord, there is no voice that has come down; but in the place of these, within the sphere of modem spiritualism, there is a cloud of witnesses, and there has been through all its years an inchoate clamor. It is Babel saying that it has taken form and that it possesses a real program. Perhaps these Colloquies stand outside the usual class of automatic communications by their remarkable historical portions. From this point of view, it would be difficult to say that so interesting a book of its kind has been published for some years, and among the persons to whom it appeals, it is sure to find a willing and perhaps a large audience. On the other hand, interesting as these stories are, it is for much the same reason that the pleasant tales of Patronio are, as they term themselves, pleasant tales; they are not convincing, nor do they indeed carry with them any tincture of likelihood. The great events of Europe at the end of the eighteenth century could not have happened in the way that is suggested, and it would be idle to reason critically on what it is so difficult to take seriously. Within the range of our own subjects, so far as I can follow their trend, they are almost peculiarly ill-informed. The Rosicrucian references, in the course of one of the narratives seem the work of a person who, to speak frankly, does not know what he is talking about; and even in lesser matters, we are sometimes brought up shortly by a textual contradiction which is not less than surprising. There are very few references to what may be termed doctrinal matters, but there is one remark on the subject of the Eucharist which shows quite plainly that the communicating spirit was without even the elementary knowledge of a child. So also, the Tarot cards are mentioned in connexion with folklore, to which they have never properly belonged. There is teaching on reincarnation, but it is simply by way of reflection, and all that is said of Atlantis is also by way of reflection, adding nothing to our existing range of highly empirical knowledge. If this is the position in respect of things which can be checked, or at least sightly, it is useless to estimate what must stand by its own appeal, as we have no means of knowing. Somehow the communicating intelligence belongs to an active school of the catholic charity founded by St. Francis; somehow St. Francis was a reincarnation of Christ; somehow the school at one period was answerable indirectly for the horrors of the French Revolution. All this is childish and a little pitiable, but it stands at its own value, and that is transparent.

Some who are mystics may know, on other warrants than those of modern spiritualism, and outside all the range of its phenomena, that when it was said of old: Bear ye one another's burdens, the message was to pray for the dead; but that which was understood by the prayer comes scarcely within the range of official conventions. These Colloquies are another instance of the best that we can expect, apparently under the best circumstances, from within the sphere of spiritualism. After the sixty years already mentioned, we have still heard nothing that could satisfy and very little that it has been possible to accept, even tentatively. With spiritualists themselves, the standard is apparently different, and perhaps even the experienced in this school are apt to regard everything from the standpoint of its highest market value. It would seem, apart from them, that the only term of aspiration, the only term of thought, was expressed long ago by St. Monica, as rendered by Matthew Arnold: "Life in God and union there."

THE LATIN CHURCH AND FREEMASONRY

WHEN Father Benson decided that the coming of the Destroyer was a fit and proper subject for treatment in sensational romance, he looked about him for certain materials which might respond for the antecedents of the evil time and the all-malefic persona. He would find many naturally and among the plethora he chose a few. That, however, which was most to his purpose, which obscurely enough was most after his own heart, proved to be the Masonic Order; and he may have even laid down on paper, to be re-embodied subsequently, a kind of ground plan or schedule of future Masonic development, which hypothetical schedule it remains easy to extract from his tale of wonder. I will present it in so far as it is necessary to explain the purpose and causation of the brief criticism which is designed in the present paper. It may be termed a scheme prophetic of the Masonic Constitution 100 years hence, and it includes: (1) great access of Jews to the fraternity; (2) abolition of the idea of God therein; (3) special disclosures with regard to the Mark Masons; (4) responsibility of Masonry in its higher grades for a movement against religion over the whole world;

(5) admission of women as a master stroke; (6) affiliation of Antichrist with Masonry, and this as the only known antecedent concerning him; (7) the surrender of all schemes for future progress and for the brotherhood of nations into the hands of the Order, to counterbalance the false notions of unity and spiritual fraternity as conceived by the Church; (8) The establishment of a non-theistic form of religious observance—a religion infante—based on Masonic ritual; (9) The Church as before and now goes on denouncing. These are the implied prolegomena to the coming of the Man of Sin and the concomitants thereof.

It will strike the reader who is perhaps versed in romances rather than in matters historical as a curious piece of invention, with an actuating grain of spite, signifying little and producing nothing probably, except some further doubt on the part of a few young ladies or still inexperienced wives as to what in the world's name takes either father or husband to the Lodges of the Masonic Society. The Mason, on his own part, if he reads such romances, will say that Father Benson is a priest of the Latin Church, which has always persecuted Freemasonry; that he is, moreover, a convert of recent years comparatively; and that such kind of people lean a little naturally to the extreme side. If the position were in this manner exhausted, nothing would be offered to criticism which would be worth the pains of a column in a common newspaper. There is more, however, in the signs of the times than appears on their surface always, and it is because in the present connection I have particular reasons for realizing this fact that I have thought it worthwhile first of all—and perhaps more than all—to read The Lord of the World, or any other story about the world's end and the Prince thereof; and, secondly, to reproduce a schedule containing accusations which do not much matter against certain concealed mysteries which on one side of them do. In case this paper, by the office of some star of literature, should come under the eyes of Father Benson, I will ask him to observe, and alternatively any members of the community to which he belongs, that I do not expostulate with him personally, or with any other man who is living. I am a mystic, carrying as such in my heart an eirenicon for all the faiths, and I can recite with his own sincerity every line and phrase of the Pange lingua, down even to those last words which he hears in his mind rising clear and high over the dissolution of the cosmic order— Procedenti ab utroque

Compar sit laudatio.

I know also that the time comes when this world passes, and the glory of it—though it is not in the sense that he pictures—and that the sacraments of the mystic Church—suffering, militant, or triumphant—are of those things which emerge into the new order when the Mystery of God is declared to each soul of us, as that order comes down out of heaven. If the story of Father Benson can be said as its root-matter to have one thesis, I suppose it is the old prophetic forecast that when the scheme of God's providence draws to its close, the last struggle, symbolized by the idea of Armageddon, will be that of the Roman Church, as the one surviving witness of Christ, with all the powers of Apollyon, as the sum of the spirit of this world. Seeing that there will never be any such struggle—for, on the contrary, the spirit of God by the slow process of the centuries will change the substance of the spirit both in the Church and the world—there is no call to consider the merits of the suggested alternative. Out of its presentation, however, one issue arises which is exceedingly clear, and this is that the Latin Church, for reasons, of which some are obscure and some moderately transparent, has agreed to regard Freemasonry, and the secret societies which are by imputation therewith connected, as the culminating type, representative and summary of those forces which are at work in the world against the work of the Church in the world. The thesis, which would be adduced and is indeed adduced continually in support of this thesis, is (a) that the French Revolution was the work of the secret societies, and of Masonry chiefly; (b) that the concurrence of those forces out of which came United Italy, with the subversion of the temporal power, had Masonry as their point of convergence; (c) that the unhappy position of the Church in France has been created by Masonry; and (d) that in so far as the other Latin races are disaffected towards Rome, and are tending towards naturalism in place of religion, this is also a Masonic tendency. Now supposing that this view had to support it the historical evidence—abundant, sufficient, or even presumptive tolerably—which we who are Masons have been looking for our enemies to produce, we should be left simply in the position of the Latin Church when that is confronted by competitive exponents of the truth of God. As this truth, from the standpoint of that Church, is unaffected by the pretensions of rival orthodoxies, pure apostolic Christianities and sects generally, so the Mason, who knows well enough what is the true purpose and term, what are the explicits and implicits of the mystery which initiation has reposed in his heart, will know also that Masonry would emerge unaffected, supposing that Grand Lodges, Grand Orients and Supreme Councils passed into corporate apostasy. If in certain countries and at certain distracted periods we find that the apparatus of the Lodges has been made to serve the purpose of plot and faction, Masonry as an institution is not more responsible for the abuse than is the Catholic Church as a whole for the poisoned eucharists of a Borgia pontiff.

It has been said very often that English Masonry is not to be judged by Masonry of the continental species; that communion with the Grand Orient of France has been severed by the Grand Lodge of England; and that Craft Masonry in the Latin countries generally has ceased almost to be Masonic at heart. But this is only a branch of the whole truth; what is true of Great Britain is true in one form or another of the United States, Canada, Australia and, among continental kingdoms, of Sweden, Norway, Denmark, Germany and Holland. The Latin countries remain over—with a few others about which we know little masonically, seeing that they are in the South of Europe—and Russia also remains. Of these last nothing can be said with certainty, but in the Latin countries the position of Masonry is the work of the Church which condemns it.

There is no charge too banal, no soi-disant confession too preposterous in matter or manner, to be successful with the Catholic Church when its purport is to expose Freemasonry. The evidence for this is to be found, among things that are recent—or this at least comparatively—In the Masonic impostures of the late Leo Taxil and his gang of confederates, to whom more than one section of the Church lent a willing ear, whom also it abandoned only when their final unmasking had become a foregone conclusion. It will be here sufficient to say that Leo X granted an audience to Leo Taxil and that the Cardinal-Vicar Parocchi felicitated him for exposing the turpitude of the imaginary androgyne lodges. Of two other squalid impostors, Adolphe Ricoux stood for an unimpeachable witness with Monsignor Meurin, Archbishop of Port Louis, while Margiotta had the papal benediction and a sheaf of episcopal plaudits. I do not doubt that even at this day, within the fold of the Latin Church, many persons are and will remain convinced—priests and prelates included—that Masonry is dedicated to the practices of Black Magic and to the celebration of sacrilegious masses. From the Humanum genus encyclical to the findings of the Trent Congress, a long confusion of issues and identification of a part with the whole has characterized all the pronouncements. Craft Freemasonry in its intellectual centers represents and mirrors of necessity the flux of modern opinion upon all speculative subjects, outside belief in a personal God and the other life of humanity, which are the fundamental parts of its doctrine. Beyond this sphere, it has no accredited opinions in matters of religion, while so far as the high grades are concerned, those are few and unimportant which do not exact from their candidates a profession of the Christian faith. We are therefore in a position to adjudicate upon the qualifications of the Trent Congress, which decided that the religious teachings of Freemasonry were those of Nature worship, and that the public beliefs of Freemasons were those of Monism, Idealistic Pantheism, Materialism and Positivism, the connecting link between all being the identification of the universe with God. Doubtless craft Freemasonry, even in England, includes in its ranks the shades of philosophical thought which correspond to these findings, but indubitably the same might be said of any large assembly, public or private, in any part of the world; and hereof is the folly of the judgment. Freemasonry also numbers spiritualists, theosophists and representatives innumerable of the higher schools of mysticism. If it does not include convinced Catholics—and as regards intellectual certitude, apart from formal practice, it does include them assuredly—it is because the obedience of the one through the intolerance of the other makes the dual obedience impossible, though in itself it is natural and reasonable within its own lines.

So much on the general subject, which has been familiar to me in its chief ramifications for nearly fifteen years, and as regards the forecast of Father Benson, I do not deal in prophecy, and I will leave its value to be inferred by past experience gathered from similar quarters and already summarized briefly.

The element of joy in the whole curious collection is that, by an intervention of the special providence which decides that indiscriminate hostility shall make itself ridiculous in the end, Father Benson has selected for a point in the center of his schedule that order of Mark Masonry which, among all grades external to the craft itself, is the least known on the continent, which of all and above all has the least connection with any event in history, which is the most simply symbolical, and in fine carries no double meaning whatever. Masonry could, I think, ask nothing more of its enemies than to choose Mark Masonry as their object of attack on the score of any disaffection, political or religious.

It follows, as one inference from these statements, that certain high-grade orders do carry a second sense in their symbolism, and so do the great craft grades, but it is neither of Natural Religion, Idealistic Pantheism, Monism or much less of Materialism or Positivism. It is of that great experiment which is at the heart of all the religion, being the way of the soul's reintegration in God. I believe personally that the sacramentalism of the Christian scheme holds up the most perfect glass of reflection to the mystery of salvation, and in this sense that the Church contains the catholic scheme of the Mysteries, but I know, after another manner, which is also the same manner, that there are mysteries which are not of this fold, and that it is given unto man to find the hidden jewel of redemption in more than one Holy Place. I say, therefore, with the Welsh bards, that I despise no precious concealed mysteries, wherever they subsist, and above all I have no part in those Wardens of the Gates who deny in their particular enthusiasm that things which are equal to the same are equal to one another, since these Wardens are blind.

THE HERMETIC AND ROSICRUCIAN MYSTERY

W E are only beginning, and that by very slow stages, to enter into our inheritance from the past; and still perhaps in respect of its larger part we are seeking far and wide for the treasures of the mystic Basra. But these treasures are of more than one species and more than a single order; for that measure to which we are approximating and for that part which we hold, we shall be well advised to realize that there are some things which belong to the essences while some are of the accidents only. I do not think that among all the wise of the ages, in whatsoever regions of the world, there has been ever any difference of opinion about the true object of research; the modes and form of the quest have varied, and that widely, but to one point have all the roads converged. Therein is no change or shadow of vicissitude. We may hear of shorter roads, and one would say at first sight that such a suggestion may be true indubitably, but in one sense it is rather a convention of language and in another it is a commonplace which tends to confuse the issues. It is a convention of language because the great quests are not pursued in time or place, and it would be just as true to say that in a journey from the circumference to the center all roads are the same length, supposing that they are straight roads. It is a commonplace because if anyone should enter the byways or return on his path and restart; it is obvious that he must look to be delayed. Furthermore, it may be true that all paths lead ultimately to the center, and that if we descend into hell, there may be still a way back to the light, as if one ascended to heaven; but in any house of the right reason, the issues are too clear to consider such extrinsic possibilities. Before I utilize these random and, I think, too obvious considerations to present the root-thesis of this paper, I must recur for one moment to the question of the essence and the accident, because on the assumption from which the considerations originate—namely, that there is a secret tradition in Christian times, the place of which is in the West—or rather that there are several traditions—it seems desirable to realize what part matters vitally among them. I will take my illustration from alchemy, and it should be known that on the surface it claims to put forward the mystery of a material operation, behind which we discern—though not, it should be understood, invariably—another subject and another intention. Now, supposing that we were incorrect in our discernment, the secret tradition would remain, this notwithstanding, and it would remain also if the material operation were a dream not realized. But I think that a tradition of the physical kind would have no part in us, who are concerned with another conversion than that of metals, and who know that there is a mystic stone which is unseen by mortal eyes? The evidences of the secret tradition are very strong in alchemy, but it must be accepted that, either therein or otherwise, I am not offering the proofs that the tradition exists. There are several schools of occult literature from which it follows that something was perpetuated belonging to their own order, as, for example, the schools of magic; concerning these latter I must say what to some persons may seem a rule of excessive severity—that they embody nothing, which is essential to our purpose. It is time that we should set apart in our minds the domain of phenomenal occultism as something which, almost automatically, has been transferred to the proper care of science. In so doing it is our simple hope that it may continue to extend a particular class of researches into the nature of man and his environment which the unaccredited investigations of the past have demonstrated already as productive to those who can be called open to conviction. The grounds of this conviction were manifested generations or centuries ago, and along both lines the research exhibits to us from time to time that we—or some of us—who know after another manner, have been justified very surely when, as if from a more remote region, we have returned to testify that the great mysteries are within.

I have no need to affirm that the secret tradition, either in the East or the West, has been always an open secret in respect of the root-principles concerning the Way, the Truth and the life. It is easy, therefore, to show what it is not, and to make the distinction which I have attempted between the classes of the concealed knowledge. It is not so easy to define the most precious treasures of the King—in respect of that knowledge—according to the estimate concerning them which I have assumed tacitly to be common between persons confessing to mystic predispositions at this day. The issues are confused throughout, all our high predilections notwithstanding, by the traditional or historical notion concerning the adept, which is that of a man whose power is raised to the transcendent degree by the communication or attainment, alter some manner, of a particular and even terrible knowledge of the hidden forces of nature. I have heard technical and imputed adepts of occult associations state that those who possess, in the actual and plenary sense, the gifts which are ascribed to themselves by the simplicity of an artificial title, are able so to disintegrate the constituted man that they can separate not only the body from its psychic part but the spirit also from the soul, when they have a sufficient cause in their illumination against a particular victim. If things of this kind were possible, they would belong to the science of the abyss—when the abyss has been exalted above all that is termed God; but there is no need to attribute an over-great seriousness to chatter and traffic of this kind, which has been all too prevalent in a few current schools of inexactitude. The tendency contributes, as I have said, to confuse the issues and, though it may seem a perilous suggestion, one is tempted to say that, in all its higher aspects, the name itself of adept might be abandoned definitely in favor of that of the mystic—though on account of the great loose thinking it is only too likely—and there are signs sufficient already—that it would share a similar fate of misconstruction.

There was a time perhaps when we could have listened, and did even, to descriptions of this kind, because we had only just begun to hear of adepts and sages, so that things were magnified in the half-light. The scales have fallen now, and though the light into which we have entered is very far from the high light of all, it is serviceable sufficiently to dispel many shadows and to dissipate many distractions. The difficulty which is here specified is increased by the fact that there are certainly powers of the height, and that the spirit of man does not in its upward path take all the heavens of aspiration without, after some manner, being set over the kingdoms which are below it. For ourselves, at least, we can lay down one irrevocable law—that he who has resolved, setting all things else aside, to enter the path of adeptship must look for his progress in proportion as he pursues holiness for its own sake and not for the miracles of sanctity. It will be seen that I am disposed to call things by their old names, which have many consecrations, and I hope to command sympathy—but something more even—when I say further that he who dreams of adeptship and does not say sanctity in his heart till his lips are cleansed and then does not say it with his lips, is not so much far from the goal as without having conceived regarding it. One of the lesser masters, who has now scarcely a pupil amongst us, said once, quoting from somewhere: Vel sanctum invenit, vel sanctum facit; but I know that it must be a long resident in our desires before it can be declared in our lives.

I have searched the whole West and only in two directions have I found anything which will compare with pure monastic mysticism; one of these is the mystic side of alchemy, while the other is that body of tradition which answers most fully to the name of Rosicrucianism. There are other places in which we find the same thing, or the substance of the same thing, and I believe that I have given faithful testimony already on this point; even in the lesser schools I am sure that it was always at the roots, but except in so far as a personal sympathy may direct us, or the accidents of an historical study, I do not know that there is a direct gain—or that there is not rather a hindrance—by going any distance afield for what is so close to our hands, and into side issues for what is in the straight road—whether this be broad or narrow. There is no doubt that from one point of view Christian mysticism has been on the external side, bewrayed rather seriously by its environment, because of the inhibitions of the official churches; in saying this, I hope that the time has come to all of us when the cheap conventions of hostility towards these churches, and especially towards the Latin Rite, have ceased to obtain in our minds and that we can appreciate, in however detached a manner, the high annals of their sanctity. If so, we shall be able to appreciate also, at the proper value, an external and historical side on which the Latin Church approached too often that picture in the story of the Holy Graal of a certain King of Castle Mortal, who sold God for money. The difficulty which the Rite has created and the inhibitions into which it has passed arise more especially not alone on the external side but from the fact that it has taken the great things of symbolism too generally for material facts. In this way, with all the sincerity which can be attached to its formal documents, produced for the most part by the process of growth, the Church Catholic of Latin Christianity has told the wrong story, though the elements which were placed in its hands are the right and true elements. I believe that the growth of sanctity within the Latin Church has been—under its deepest consideration—substantially hindered by the over-encrustation of the spirit with the literal aspect, though this at the same time is indispensable to expression. I believe that in the minds of the mystics, this hindrance has operated; of all men on earth, they have recognized assuredly the working of the spirit; but they sought to attain it through the veils of doctrine, and they did not utterly and wholly part the curtains thereof. The result was that these trailed after them and were an impediment as they entered the sanctuary. The process itself was, in one sense, the wrong process, though on account of their environment, it was almost impossible that they should adopt another. We have agreed long ago that to work up from Nature to Grace is not really the method of the wise, because that which is below is the branches and that which is above is the roots, and the tree of life is really in this sense, and because of our distance from the center, as it were, upside down. So also, the true way of experience in the mystic fife is to work outward from within.

It is natural, of course, and this is of necessity also, that we should receive our first intimations through the letter, but when it has exhibited to us some reflections of the fight which is behind, we must not suffer our course to be hindered by the office of the letter, but should set it aside rather, to abide in the root-meaning which is behind the symbols. There is a later stage in which we shall revert to the external and to the meaning that is without, bringing back with us the inward light to interpenetrate and transform it. Perhaps an illustration will explain better the order of procedure than a formal statement merely, though I do not think that there is even a surface difficulty concerning it. We have been taught in the infancy of the mind the great story which is the root and heart of external Christianity. That is not the letter which kills but the cortex of a vessel behind which are the eternal fountains of life. I need not say that many of us do not get beyond this cortex and, fortunately; it is not a dead husk, but a living body through which Grace flows to us after the measure of our capacity. But it may come to pass that the inward sensorium is opened—by the mediation, as it may well be, of the great books of the Church, or in what manner soever—and we then see that the great story, the old story, the story which is of all things true, is that of our own soul. I mean this not in the sense of the soul's geniture, but in the sense of its progress, as it is here and now environed. We are then looking towards the real road of our redemption, and it is at this stage that the letter should be set aside for a period because everything has to be enacted anew. The virgin must conceive and bear her son; in the grand rough outline of Saint Martin, the son must be born in the Bethlehem of our human life; he must be presented in the temple which stands in the Jerusalem within; he must confound the doctors of the intellect; he must lead the hidden life of Nazareth; he must be manifested and must teach us within, in which way we shall return to the world of doctrine and shall find that all things are made new. It is not that there are new doctrines, but there is another quality of life; thereby the old symbolism has been so interpenetrated that the things which are without have become the things which are within, till each seems either in the power of the pace and in the torrent of the life. It is then that we cease to go out through the door by which we went in, because other doors are open, and the call of many voices, bidding us no longer depart hence, says rather: Let us enter the sanctuary, even the inmost shrine.

I desire, therefore, to make it plain that the Secret Church Mystic which exists and has always existed within the Church Militant of Christendom does not differ in anything from the essential teaching of doctrine—I mean Quod semper, quod ubique, quod ab omnibus; that it can say with its heart what it says also with its lips; that again there is no change or shadow of vicissitude; but in some very high sense the pound of the essentials has been removed. The symbolum remains; it has not taken on another meaning; but it has unfolded itself like the flower from within. Christian Theosophy in the West can recite its Credo in unum Deum by clause and by clause, including in unam sanctam catholican et apostolicam ecclesiam, and if there is an arriere pensee it is not of heresy or Jesuitry. Above all, and I say this the more expressly because there are still among us—that is to say, in those circles generally—certain grave misconceptions, and it is necessary to affirm that the path of the mystic does not pass through the heresies.

And now with respect to the secret schools which have handed down to us at this day some part or aspects of the secret tradition belonging to Christian times, I must leave out of consideration, because there are limits to papers of this kind, the great witness of Kabalism which although it is a product of the Christian period is scarcely of it, and although therein the quest and its term do not assuredly differ from that of the truth which is in Christ, there are perhaps other reasons than those of brevity for setting it apart here. Alchemy may not have originated much further East than Alexandria, or, alternatively, it may have traveled from

China when the port of Byzantium was opened to the commerce of the world. In either case, its first development, in the forms with which we are acquainted, is connected with the name of Byzantium, and the earliest alchemists of whom we have any remains in literature constitute a class by themselves under the name of Byzantine alchemists. The records of their processes went into Syria and Arabia, where they assumed a new mode, which bore, however, all necessary evidence of its origin. In this form, it does not appear to have had a specific influence upon the corpus doctrinale. The records were also taken West, like many other mysteries of varying importance, and when they began to assume a place in western history, this was chiefly in France, Germany and England. In other words, there arose the cycle of Latin alchemy, passing at a later date, by the way of translation, into the vernaculars of the respective countries, until finally, but much later, we have original documents in English, French and German. It follows, but has not so far been noticed, that the entire literature is a product of Christian times and has Christianity as its motive, whether subconsciously or otherwise. This statement applies to the Latin Geber and the tracts which are ascribed to Morien and Rhasis. The exception which proves the rule is the Kabalistic Aesh Mezareph, which we know only by fragments included in the great collection of Rosenroth. I suppose that there is no labyrinth which it is quite so difficult to thread as that of the Theatrum Chemicum. It is beset on every side with pitfalls, and its dues, though not destroyed actually, have been buried beneath the ground. Expositors of the subject have gone astray over the general purpose of the art, because some have believed it to be: (a) the transmutation of metals, and that only, while others have interpreted it as (b) a veiled method of delineating the secrets of the soul on its way through the world within, and besides this nothing. Many text-books of physical alchemy would seem to have been re-edited in this exotic interest. The true philosophers of each school are believed to have taught the same thing, with due allowance for the generic difference of their term, and seeing that they use the same language it would seem that, given a criterion of distinction in respect of the term, this should make the body of cryptogram comparatively easy to disentangle. But as one of the chief difficulties is said also to reside in the fact that many of them do not begin at the same point of the process, the advantage of uniformity is canceled largely.

There are affirmed to be experimental schools still existing in Europe, which have carried the physical work much further than it is ever likely to be taken by any isolated student; but this must be accepted under several reserves, or I can say, at least, that, having better occasions than most people of knowing the schools and their development, I have so far found no evidence. But there are testified otherwise to be—and I speak here with the certainty of first-hand knowledge—other schools, also experimental, also existing in Europe, which claim to possess the master-key of the mystical work. How far they have been successful at present in using that key I am not in a position to say, nor can I indicate its nature for reasons that, I think, must be obvious. It so happens, however, that the mystery of the processes is one thing and that which lies on the surface, or more immediately beneath the externals of the concealed language, is, fortunately, another thing. And, as often happens also, the enlightening correspondences are offering their marks and seals—if not at our very doors—at least in the official churches. Among all those places that are holy there is no holy place in which they do not abide a mane usque ad vespertinum, and the name of the correspondence-in-chief is the Holy Eucharist.

I propose now to tabulate certain palmary points of terminology which are common to all the adepts, including both schools indifferently, though we are dealing here—and this is understood—with the process of one school only. By the significance of these points or terms, we shall see to what extent the symbolism of the higher alchemy is in conformity with mystic symbolism and with the repose of the life of the Church in God. It should be realized, however, that there is nothing so hard and so thankless as to elucidate one symbolism by the terms of another—and this notwithstanding an occasional identity which may manifest in the terms of each.

It must be understood further and accepted that all alchemists, outside the distinctions of their schools, were actuated by an express determination to veil their mystery and that they had recourse for this purpose to every kind of subterfuge. At the same time, they tell us that the whole art is contained, manifested and set forth by means of a single vessel, which, amidst a manner of minor variations, is described with essential uniformity throughout the great multitude of texts. This statement constitutes a certain lesser key to the art; but as on the one hand the alchemists veil their hallow-in-chief by reference, in spite of their assurance, as above noted, to many pretended vessels, so has the key itself a certain aspect of subterfuge, since the alleged unity is in respect only of the term final of the process in the unity of the recipient. This unity is the last reduction of a triad, because, according to these aspects of Hermetic philosophy, man in the course of his attainment is at first three—that is, when he sets out upon the great quest; he is two at a certain stage; but he is, in fine, one, which is the end of his evolution. The Mack state of the matter on which the process of the art is engaged is the body of this death, from which the adepts have asked to be detached. It is more especially our natural life. The white state of the stone, the confection of which is desired, is the vesture of immortality with which the epopts are clothed upon. The salt of the philosophers is that savor of life, without which the material earth can neither be salted nor cleansed. The sulfur of the philosophers is the inward substance by which some souls are saved, yet so as by fire. The mercury of the sages is that which must be fixed and volatilized—naturally it is fluidic and wandering—but except under this name, or by some analogous substitute, it must not be described literally outside the particular circles of secret knowledge. It is nearer than hands and feet.

Now the perfect correspondence of these things in the symbolism of official Christianity, and the great mystery of perfect sanctification, is set forth in the great churches under the sacramentalism of the Holy Eucharist. This is my point, and I desire to make it clear: the same exalted mystery which lies behind the symbols of bread and wine, behind the undeclared priesthood which is according to the order of Melchizedek, was expressed by the alchemists under the guise of transmutation; but I refer here to the secret school of adeptship, which had taken over in another and transcendent interest the terminology and processes of occult metallurgy.

The vessel is therefore one, but the matter thereto adapted is not designated especially, or at least after an uniform manner; it is said to be clay by those who speak at times more openly in order that they may be understood the less, as if they also were singing in their strange chorus:

Let us be open as the day,

That we may deeper hide ourselves.

It is most commonly described as metallic, because on the surface of the literature there is the declared mystery of all metals, and the concealed purpose is to show that in the roots and essence of these things there is a certain similarity or analogy. The reason is that the epopt, who has been translated, again finds his body after many days, but under a great transmutation, as if in another sense the panis quotidianis had been changed into the panis vivus et vitalis, but without mutation of the accidents. The reason is also that in normal states the body is here and now not without the soul, nor can we separate readily, by any intellectual process, the soul from the spirit which broods thereover, to fertilize it in a due season. It is, however, one vessel, and this makes for simplicity; but it is not by such simplicity that the art is testified to be a lusus puerorum. The contradistinction hereto is that it is hard to be a Christian, which is the comment of the man born blind upon the light that he cannot see. There is also the triumphant affirmation of the mystical counter-position, that to sin is hard indeed for the man who knows truly. The formula of this is that man is born for the heights rather than the deeps, and its verbal paradox is facilis ascensus superno. The process of the art is without haste or violence by the mediation of a graduated fire, and the seat of this fire is in the soul. It is a mystery of the soul's love, and for this reason she is called "undaunted daughter of desire." The sense of the gradation is that love is set free from the impetuosity and violence of passion and has become a constant and incorruptible flame. The formula of this is that the place of unity is a center wherein there is no exaggeration. That which the fire consumes is certain materials or elements, which are called recrementa, the grosser parts, the superfluities; and it should be observed that there are two purgations, of which the first is the gross and the second the subtle. The first is the common process of conversion, by which there is such a separation of seemingly external components that what remains is as a new creature, and may be said to be reborn. The second is the exalted conversion, by which that which has been purified is so raised that it enters into a new region, or a certain heaven comes down and abides therein. It is not my design in the present place to exhaust all the sources of interpretation, because such a scheme would be impossible in a single paper, and I can allude, therefore, but scantily to the many forms of the parables which are concerned with the process up to this point. The ostensible object, which was materialized in the alternative school, is the confection of a certain stone or powder, which is that of projection, and the symbolical theorem is that this powder, when added to a base metal, performs the wonder of transmutation into pure silver or gold, better than those of the mines. Otherwise, it prolongs life and renews youth in the adept-philosopher and lover of learning. In the second case, it Is spoken of usually as an elixir, but the transmuting powder and the renewing draught are really one thing with the spiritual alchemists. It must be also affirmed that, in virtue of a very high mysticism, there is a unity in the trinity of the powder, the metal and the vase. The vase is also the alchemist on his outer side, for none of the instruments, the materials, the fires, the producer, and the thing produced an axe external to the one subject. At the same time, the inward man is distinguished from the outward man; we may say that the one is the alchemist and the other the vessel. It is in tins sense that the art is both physical and Spiritual. But the symbolism is many times enfolded, and the gross metal which is placed within the vessel is the untransmuted life of reason, motive, concupiscence, self-interest and all that which constitutes the intelligent creature on the normal plane of manifestation. Hereof is the natural man enclosed in an animal body, as the metal is placed in the vessel, and from this point of view the alchemist is he who is sometimes termed arrogantly the super-man. But because there is only one vessel, it must be understood that herein the stone is confected and the base metal is converted. The alchemist is himself finally the stone, and because many zealous aspirants to the art have not understood this, they have failed in the great work on the spiritual side. The schedule which now follows may elucidate this hard subject somewhat more fully and plainly.

There are (a) the natural, external man, whose equivalent is the one vessel; (b) the body of desire, which answers to the gross matter; (c) the aspiration, the consciousness, the will of the supernatural life; (d) the process of the will working on the body of desire within the outward vessel; (e) the psychic and transcendental conversion thus effected; (f) the reaction of the purified body of desire on the essential will, so that the one supports the other, while the latter is borne upward, and from such raising, there follows this further change, that the spirit of a man puts on itself a new quality of life, becoming an instrument which is at once feeding and is itself fed; (g) herein is the symbol of the stone and the great elixir; (h) the spirit is nourished from above by the analogies of Eucharistic ministry; (i) the spirit nourishes the soul, as by bread and wine; (j) the soul effects the higher conversion in the body of desire; (k) it thus comes about that the essence which dissolves everything and changes everything is still contained in a vessel, or—alternatively—that God abides in man. This process, thus exhaustively delineated in the parables of alchemy, is put with almost naked simplicity by Eucharistic doctrine, which says that material lips receive the supersubstantial bread and wine, that the soul is nourished and that Christ enters the soul. It seems, therefore, within all reason and all truth to testify that the panis vivus et vitalis is even as the transmuting stone and that the chalice of the new and eternal testa¬ment is as the renewing elixir; but I say this under certain reasonable reserves because, in accordance with my formal indication, the closer the analogies between distinct systems of symbolism the more urgent is that prudence which counsels as not to confuse them by an interchangeable me.

All Christian mysticism came forth out of the Mass Book, and it returns therein. But the Mass Book in the first instance came out of the heart mystic which had unfolded in Christendom. The nucleus of truth in the missal is Dominus prope est. The Mass shows that the great work is in the first sense a work of the hands of man, because it is he officiating as a priest in his own temple who offers the sacrifice which he has purified. But the elements of that sacrifice are taken over by an intervention from another order, and that which follows is transfusion.

Re-expressing all this now in a closer summary, the apparatus of mystical alchemy is indeed, comparatively speaking, simple.

The first matter is myrionimous and is yet one, corresponding to the unity of the natural will and the unlimited complexity of its motives, dispositions, desires, passions and distractions, on all of which the work of wisdom must operate. The vessel is also one, for this is the normal man, complete in his own degree. The process has the seal of Nature's directness; it is the graduation and increasing maintenance of a particular fire. The initial work is a change in the substance of will, aspiration and desire, which is the first conversion or transmutation in the elementary sense. But it is identical even to the end with the term proposed by the Eucharist, which is the modification of the noumenal man by the communication of Divine Substance. Here is the lapis qui non lapis, lapis tingens, lapis angularis, lapis qui multiplicetur, lapis per quem justus aedificabit domun Domini, et jam valde aedificatur et terram possidebit, per omnia, etc. When it is said that the stone is multiplied, even to a thousandfold, we know that this is true of all seeds which is sown upon good soil.

So, therefore, the stone transmutes, and the Eucharist transmutes also; the philosophical elements on the physical side go to the making of the stone, which is also physical; and the sacramental elements to the generation of a new life in the soul. He who says Lapis Philosophorum, says also: My beloved to me and I to him: Christ is therefore the stone, and the stone in adept humanity is the union realized, while the great secret is that Christ must be manifested within.

Now it seems to me that it has not served less than an useful purpose to establish after a new manner the intimate resemblance between the higher understanding of one part of the secret tradition and the better interpretation of one sacrament of the church. It must be observed that we are not dealing in either case with the question of attainment. The analogy would remain if spiritual alchemy and Christian sacramentalism abode in the intellectual order as theorems only, or as part of the psychic dream which had never been carried into experience. It would be more easy (if there were here any opportunity) to offer the results of the experience as recorded in the Ives of the saints than to discuss the traditional attainments which are held to have passed into actuality among the secret schools; but the veiled literatures must be left to speak for themselves, which—for those who can read—they do, like the annals of sanctity; as to these—those who will take the pains may seek verification for themselves. My task in respect of spiritual alchemy ends by exhibiting that this also was a mystery of sanctity concerned ex hypothesi with the communication of Divine Substance, and that this is the term of the Eucharist. It is this which the doctrine of sanctity offered, to those who entered the pathway of sanctity, as the foretaste in this life of the union which is consummated in eternity, or of that end beyond which there is nothing whatever which is conceivable. We know from the old books that it has not entered into the heart of man, but the heart which has put away the things of sense conceives it by representations and types. This is the great tradition of that which the early alchemists term truth in the art; the end is representation after its own kind rather than felicity, but the representation is of that order, which begins in ecstasy and ends in absorption. Let no man say, therefore, that he loses himself in experience of this order, for, perchance, it is then only that he finds himself, even in that way which suggests that after many paths of activity he is at length coming into his own.

It might seem that I have reached here a desirable point for my conclusion, but I am pledged, alike by my title and one antecedent reference, to say something concerning Rosicrucianism, which is another witness in the world on the part of the secret tradition. There is one respect in which it is simpler in its apparatus than the literature of the purely Hermetic tradition, for it lies within a smaller compass and has assumed a different mode. It is complicated by the fact that very few of the texts which are available among the things of the outside world have a title to rank in its tradition. This, I suppose, is equivalent to an intimation that the witness is still in the world after another and more active manner, which is true in more than a single way. I am not the ambassador, and much less the plenipotentiary, of the secret societies in the West, and independently of this statement I fed sure that I shall not be accused of endeavoring to assume the role or to create the impression. I know only that the societies exist, and that they are at the present time one means of perpetuating that tradition. I do not suggest that there are no other means, because I have indicated even from the beginning that the door looking towards heaven and the sanctuary, which is its ante-chamber, was opened long centuries ago by the official churches. But the tradition itself has been rather behind the churches and some part of the things for which we are all seeking is to be found therein—all which is without detriment to the light of the East, because this is also the light of the West under another veil. Even in the esoteric assemblies which are now and here among us, the tradition is, in a sense, veiled, and, of course, in speaking publicly one has always to cloud the sanctuaries rather than to say: Lift up your eyes, for it is in this or that comer of London, Paris or Prague.

If there is one thing more regrettable than the confusion in forms of symbolism, it is the identification of separate entities under a general term which has only a particular meaning so far as history is concerned. The name Rosicrucian, has suffered from abuse of this kind, bang used almost interchangeably with that of Alchemist by popular writers. I must ask to be disassociated from this error when I say that the external history of the Rosy Cross, in so far as it can be said to exist, has only one point of correspondence with Rosicrucian traditions perpetuated by secret societies in a few centers of Europe. The point of correspondence is the legend-in-chief of the Order, detached from the pseudo-historical aspect which it bore in the early documents, and associated with a highly advanced form of symbolism. It is in this form only that it enters into the sequence of the mysteries, and exhibits how the priest-king does issue from Salem, carrying bread and wine. We have, therefore, the Eucharistic side in the higher Rosicrucian tradition, but if I may describe that which is greater in the terms of that which is lesser—because of the essential difficulty with which I am confronted—it has undergone a great change, not by a diminution of the sacraments but because they are found everywhere. The alchemical maxim which might be inscribed over the gate of any Rosicrucian temple is—Est in Mercurio quicquid quarunt sapientes.

The Eucharistic maxim, which might be written over the laboratory of the alchemist, in addition to Laborare est orare, would be;

—Et antiquum documentum

Novo cedat ritui;

praestet fides supplementum

sensuum defectui.

The maxim which might be written over the temples of the official churches is Corporis Mysterium, that the mystery of the body might lead them more fully into the higher mystery of the soul. And, in fine, that maxim which might, and will be, inscribed over the one temple of the truly catholic religion when the faiths of this western world have come into their own—that which is simplest of all, and of all most pregnant, would be mysterium fidei, the mystery which endures forever and forever passes into experience.

In conclusion, as to this part, Rosicrucianism is the mystery of that which dies in manifestation that the life of the manifest may be ensured. I have found nothing in symbolism, which accounts like Rose-Cross symbolism for that formula, which on one side is the summary expression of mysticism: "And I look for the resurrection of the dead and the life of the world to come."

And now in conclusion generally:

I have spoken of three things only, and of one of them with great brevity, because the published literatures have to be set aside, and of that which remains it does not appear in the open face of day. The initiations are many and so are the schools of thought, but those which are true schools and those which are high orders issue from one root. Est una sola res, and those whose heart of contemplation is fixed upon this one thing may differ widely but can never be far apart. Personally, I do not believe—and this has the ring of a commonplace—that if they came to understand one another, they would be found to differ widely. I know not what systems of the eons may intervene between that which is imperishable within us and the union wherein the universe will, in fine, repose at the center. But I know that the great systems ay, even the great processes—of the times that are gone, as of those which now encompass us—do not pass away, because that which was from the beginning, is now and ever shall be—is one motive, one aspiration, one term of thought remaining, as if in the stillness of an everlasting present. We really understand one another, and our collective aspirations are united, the world without end.

THE PICTORIAL SYMBOLS OF ALCHEMY

November, 1908

THE Hermetic Mystery—upon the higher interpretation of which I have spoken at considerable length in the previous paper and have created an analogy between its hidden meaning and that which I should term the center of the Religious Mystery in Christendom—is the only branch of mystic and occult literature which lent itself to the decorative sense. I suppose that there are few people comparatively who at this day have any notion of the extent to which that sense was developed in the books of the adepts. It will be understood that in speaking now upon this subject I am leaving my proper path, but though the fact does not seem to have been registered, it is so utterly curious to note lo w a literature which is most dark and inscrutable of all has at the same time its lighter side—a side, indeed, of pleasant inventions, of apologue, of parable, of explicit enigma, above all of poetry. The fact is that alchemy presented itself as an art; its books were the work of artists; and for the sympathetic reader, even when he may understand them least, they will read sometimes like enchanting fables or legends. When in this manner some of the writers had exhausted their resources in language, they had recourse to illustrations, and I wonder almost that no one has thought to collect the amazing copperplates which literally did adorn the Latin and other tracts of the seventeenth century.

As I propose to print some selected specimens of the pictorial art in alchemy because they are exceedingly curious, and not for a deeper reason, the reader will not expect, and for once in a way will perhaps be rather relieved, that I am not going in quest especially of their inner meanings. So far as may be possible, the pictures shall speak for themselves, seeing that I write for the moment rather as a lover of books—a bibliophile—than a lover of learning. I will begin, however, with a definition. The alchemists whom I have in my mind may be classified as artists on the decorative side and in their illustrations—but I know not whether they were their own draughtsman—they approached the Rabelaisian method. The school on both sides is rather of Germanic origin; and it is such entirely, so far as the pictures are concerned. The French alchemists had recourse occasionally to designs, but they are negligible for the present purpose. This is a clearance of the ground, but it must be added that the great and authoritative text-books have not been illustrated—as, for example, The Open Entrance to the Closed Palace of the King, which is the work of Eirenæus Philalethias, and the New Light of Alchemy, which is believed to be that of Alexander Seton. If I may attempt such a comparison, Philalethias—in the work mentioned—reads rather like a Pauline epistle and Seton like an Epistle to the Hebrews; but the analogy in both cases is intended to be allusive only, and strict in no sense. So also, they read here and there as if they were almost inspired, but they could not be termed decorative. The really practical works—as, for example, the Latin treatises ascribed to Geber—are never illustrated, except by crude sketches of material vessels used in the material art for the aid of the neophyte on his way to the transmutation of metals. I do not think that they really helped him, and they are of no account for our purpose. The pictures of the adepts were the allegorical properties of the adepts, and though the criticism has a side of harshness, they were almost obviously provided for the further confusion of the inquirer, under the pretense of his enlightenment. At the same time, authors or artists were sages after their own manner, their allegories had a set purpose and represent throughout a prevailing school of symbolism. It is quite easy to work out the elementary part of the symbolism; it is not difficult to speculate reasonably about some of the more obscure materials. But the true canons of alchemical criticism yet remain to be expounded; and I believe that I have intimated otherwise the difficulty and urgency attaching to this work, so that there may be one unerring criterion to distinguish between the texts representing the spiritual and those of the physical work. On the latter phase of the subject, it would be useless—and more than useless—to discourse in any periodical, even if I could claim to care for anything and to know sufficiently thereof. I know neither enough to hold my tongue nor enough to speak, so that I differ in this respect—but for once only—from my excellent precursor Elias Ashmole. Like him and like Thomas Vaughan, I do know the narrowness of the name Chemia, with the antiquity and infinity of the proper object of research; thereon we have all borne true witness in our several days and generations.

It is a matter of common report that the old Hermetic adepts were the chemists of their time and that, as such, they made numerous and valuable discoveries. This is true in a general sense, but under what is also a general and an exceedingly grave reserve. There is little need to say in the first place, that the spiritual alchemists made no researches and could have had no findings in the world of metals and minerals. Secondly, there was a great concourse of witnesses in secret literature, who were adepts of neither branch; but they expressed their dreams and speculations in terms of spurious certitude, and were often sincere in the sense that they deceived themselves. They produced sophistications in the physical work and believed that their tinctures and colorations were the work of philosophy; these discovered nothing, and misled nearly every one. They also—in the alternative school—pursued erroneous ways or translated their aspirations at a distance into the root-matter of spiritual Hermetic tradition; they reached the term of their folly and drew others who were foolish after them, who had also no law of differentiation between things of Caesar and God. Finally—but of these I say nothing—there were arrant impostors, representing the colportage of their time, who trafficked in the interest of the curious, assuming alchemy for their province, as others of the secret sciences were exploited by others of their kindred. Now, between all these, the official historians of chemistry in the near past had no ground of distinction, and there is little certainty that they were right over many or most of their judgments. Once more, the canon was wanting; as I have shown that in another region it is either wanting for ourselves, or—to be correct—is in course only of development. This work, therefore, was largely one of divination, with a peculiar uncertainty in the results.

I have now finished with this introductory part, and I offer in the first place a simple illustration of the alchemist's laboratory, as it was conceived by Michael Maier at the beginning of the seventeenth century. He had a hand in the Rosicrucianism of his period and published some laws of the brotherhood, or alternatively those of an incorporated sodality based on similar lines. He was a man of great and exceptional learning, but withal of a fantastic spirit; he is proportionately difficult to judge, but his palmary concern was the material side of the magnum opus. He may have veered, and did probably, into other directions. The illustration is chosen from The Golden Tripod, being three ancient tracts attributed respectively to Basil Valentine, Thomas Norton, and John Cremer—a so-called abbot of Westminster. It is these personages who are apparently represented in the picture, together with the zelator, servant or pupil, attached to the master of the place, whose traditional duty was the maintenance with untiring zeal of the graduated fire of the art.

Basil Valentine, in the course of his tract, makes it clear that he is concerned therein only with the physical work, and in the decorative manner which I have mentioned he affirms that if the three alchemical principles—namely, philosophical Mercury, Sulphur and Salt—can be rectified till "the metallic spirit and body are joined together inseparably by means of the metallic soul," the chain of love will be riveted firmly thereby and the palace prepared for the coronation. But the substances in question are not those which are known under these names, and it is for this reason, or for reasons similar thereto, that no process of metallic alchemy can be followed practically by the isolated student, because everything essential is left out. The tradition is that the true key was imparted orally from the adept to his son in the art. This notwithstanding, Basil Valentine calls the particular work to which I am here referring, The Twelve Keys, and it is said that they open the twelve doors leading to the Stone of the Philosophers and to the true Medicine. The same terminology would be used by the spiritual alchemists in another and higher sense; but this school possesses a master-key which opens all the doors. Basil Valentine's second key is that of Mercury, as it is pictured here below.

This, it will be seen, is the crowned or philosophical Mercury, bearing in either hand the caduceus, which is his characteristic emblem, and having wings upon his shoulders, signifying the volatilized state. But there are also wings beneath his feet, meaning that he has overcome this state, and has been fixed by the art of the sages, which is part of the Great Work, requiring the concurrence of the Sun and Moon, whose symbols appear behind him. The figures at either side carry on their wands or swords, respectively the Bird of Hermes and a crowned serpent.

The latter corresponds to that serpent which, by the command of Moses, was uplifted in the wilderness for the healing of the children of Israel. As in this figure, Mercury has become a constant fire, one of the figures is shielding his face from the brilliance. He is on the side of the increasing moon, but on the side of the sun is he who has attained the Medicine, and he looks therefore with a steadfast face upon the unveiled countenance of the vision. According to Basil Valentine, Mercury is the principle of life. He says also that Saturn is the chief key of the art, though it is least useful in the mastery. The reference is to philosophical lead, and he gives a very curious picture representing this key, as it is shown on the next page.

The King in Basil Valentine's terminology is the stone in its glorious rubefaction, or state of redness, when it is surrounded by the whole court of the metals. The Spouse of the King is Venus; Saturn is the Prefect of the royal household; Jupiter is the Grand Marshal; Mars is at the head of military affairs; Mercury has the office of Chancellor; the Sun is Vice-Regent; the office of the Moon is not named, but she seems to be a Queen in widowhood. Before them there is borne, the banner attributed to each: that of the King is crimson, emblazoned with the figure of Charity in green garments; that of Saturn—which is carried by Astronomy—is black, emblazoned with the figure of Faith in garments of yellow and red; that of Jupiter—which is carried by Rhetoric—is gray, emblazoned with Hope in parti-colored garments; that of Mars is crimson, with Courage in a crimson cloak, and it is borne by Geometry; that of Mercury is carried by Arithmetic, and is a rainbow standard with the figure of Temperance, also in a many-colored vestment; that of the Sun is a yellow banner, held by Grammar and exhibiting the figure of Justice in a golden robe; that of the Moon is resplendent silver, with the figure of Prudence, clothed in sky-blue, and it is borne by Dialectic. Venus has no banner apart from that of the King, but her apparel is of gorgeous magnificence.

I pass now to another order of symbolism which delineates the spiritual work by means of very curious pictures, accompanied by evasive letterpress. These are also from a Germanic source, and the writer—if not the designer—was Nicholas Bamaud, who went among many others in the quest of Rosicrucian's, but it does not appear what he found. I will give in the first place a symbol which represents Putrefaction, being the disintegration of the rough matter in physical alchemy and on the spiritual side, the mystery of mystical death.

FIG. 3.

FIG. 4

According to The Book of Lambspring, which is the name of the little treatise, the sages keep close guard over the secret of this operation, because the world is unworthy; and the children of philosophy, who receive its communication in part and carry it to the proper term by their personal efforts, enjoy it also in silence, since God wills that it should be hidden. This is the conquest of the dragon of material and manifest life; but it is like the old folklore fables, in which an act of violence is necessary to determine an enchantment for the redemption of those who are enchanted. The work is to destroy the body, that the body may not only be revived, but may live henceforth in a more perfect and as if incorruptible form. The thesis is that Nature is returned unto herself with a higher gift and more sacred warrant; and the analogy among things familiar is the sanctification of intercourse by the sacrament of marriage. The dragon in this picture is destroyed by a knight, but we shall understand that he is clothed in the armor of God, and that St. Paul has described the harness. The next illustration concerns the natural union between body (UNICORN) soul and spirit; it is represented pictorially

Fig. 5.

in the tract after more than one manner, as when two fishes are shown swimming in the sea, and it is said that the sea is the body. Here it is a stag and a unicorn, while the body is that forest which they range. The unicorn represents the spirit, and he who can couple them together and lead them out of the forest deserves to be called a Master, as the letter-press testifies. The reason is that on their return to the body, the flesh itself will be changed and will have been rendered golden. In respect of the alternative illustration, the mystery of this reunion is likened to a work of coaction, by which the three are so joined together that they are not afterwards sundered; and this signifies the Medicine. In yet another picture, the spirit and soul are represented by a lion and lioness, between which an union must be effected before the work upon the body can be accomplished. It is an operation of great wisdom and even cunning, and he who performs it has figure 6 merited the meed of praise before all others.

FIG. 6.

I suppose that rough allegory could hardly express more plainly the marriage in the sanctified life between the human soul and the Divine Part. Neither text nor illustration continue so clear in the sequel, more especially as different symbols are used to represent the same things. In the next picture the war between the soul and the spirit is shown by that waged between a wolf and a dog, till one of them kills the other, and a poison is thus generated which restores them in some obscure manner, and they become the great and precious Medicine which in its

Fig. 7.

turn restores the sages. The tract then proceeds to the consideration of Mercury, and to all appearance has changed its subject, though this is not really the case, as might be demonstrated by an elaborate interpretation; but I omit this and the pictures thereto belonging, not only from considerations of space but because the task would be difficult, since it is not possible to say what the spiritual alchemists figure 7 intended by Mercury, this being the secret of a particular school. When the sequence is again taken up, the human trinity is presented under another veil, being that of the Father, the Son and the Guide. The symbolism is strangely confused, but some apologists would affirm that this was for a special purpose. In any case, the soul now appears as a boy; the Guide is the Spirit, and the illustration shows them at the moment of parting, when the soul is called to ascend, so that it may understand all wisdom figure 8 the splendors of the celestial canopy exhibited above them.

Fig. 1.

It is said to be a mountain in India, which in books of the Western adepts seems always to have been regarded as the symbolical soul's
home and the land of epopts. The text states, notwithstanding, that the
mountain lies in the vessel, and those who remember what was set forth
in my previous paper will know exactly what this means—an intimation
on the part of the alchemist that he is dealing only with events of experience belonging to the world within. That which is expressed, however,
as a result oi the vision is that the soul remembers the body—spoken
of here as the father—and longs to return thereto, to which the Spirit
Guide consents, and they descend from that high eminence. Two things
are illustrated hereby—(1) that the soul in its progress during incarnate
life has the body to save and to change, so that all things may be holy;
but (2) that it is possible—as is nearly always the case in parables of this
kind—to offer a dual interpretation figure 9 and the alternative to that
which I have given would be an allegory of return to the House of the
Father in an entirely different sense. But it is obvious that I cannot speak

Fig. 9.

of it—at least, in the present place. The next picture—and assuredly the most grotesque of all—represents the reunion of body and soul by the extraordinary process of the one devouring the other (Fig. 10), during which operation it should be noted that the spirit stands far apart. The text now approaches its close and delineates the construction of a re-born and glorified body, as the result of which it is said:

FIG. 10.

"The son ever remains in the father, and the father in the son. . . . By the grace of God, they abide forever, the father and the son triumphing gloriously in the splendor of their new Kingdom." They sit upon one throne and between them is the spirit, the Ancient Master, who is arrayed in a crimson robe. So is the triadic union accomplished, and herein figure 10 is the spiritual understanding of that mystery which is called the Medicine in terms of alchemical philosophy. The finality of the whole subject can be expressed in a few words, and although it may be a dark saying for some of my readers, it may prove a light to others, and for this reason I give it as follows: The experiment of spiritual alchemy was the Yoga process of the West. The root-reason of the statement must be already, as I think, obvious—probably from the present paper and assuredly from that which preceded it.

The physical experiment of the magnum opus may have been carried in the past to a successful issue. I do not know, and of my concern it is no p a rt; but those who took over the terminology of the transmutation of metals and carried it to another degree had figure 11 opened gates within them which lead into the attainment of all desire in the order which is called absolute, because after its attainment all that we understand by the soul's dream has passed into the soul's reality. It is the dream of Divine Union, and eternity cannot exhaust the stages of its fulfillment.

Fig. 11.

SOME MEMORIALS OF A MYSTIC

February, 1909

THE records of the saints who are included by the calendars of the Church are glorious testimonies concerning that great people who have been gathered into the Kingdom of Heaven during the centuries of Christendom. But how many would deserve a place therein, disciples of the most hidden life of sanctity, could we only know concerning them, and had those who beatify and canonize the power of reading in the heart! Besides these there is also that great multitude whom no man can number, out of every tongue and tribe and people and nation, on whose places of earthly rest it might be written of one and all that "of such is the Kingdom of Heaven." Not the least, though among the latest, in this choir invisible is the profound, enlightened and lovable spirit whose literary remains have just now been published under the careful and affectionate editorship of one who is a kindred spirit, Professor W. F. Barrett. The title of the slender volume which lies before me describes it as enshrining the Thoughts of a Modern Mystic and alternatively as A Selection from the Writings of the late C. C. Massey (London: Kegan Paul, Ltd., 1909). Professor Barrett, in one excellent chapter which memorializes a long-continued friendship, tells us not perhaps all that we could desire but all that is necessary for us to learn concerning the personal history of his subject—one with whom so many of us were acquainted in the past, with whom few perhaps were so familiar as he was, but one whom all respected and, of those who knew him better, all, I am sure, loved. Outside this chapter, the volume includes, firstly, an important selection of private letters written to various friends and, secondly, certain papers, nearly all of which appeared in a magazine called The Unknown World, of which I was editor in 1894 and 1895, or during all its short lease of existence.

It will be new to my readers—or so almost certainly—and it will explain my own position, if I offer a brief extract from this periodical. In those days, less experienced than these, I also was acquainted with C. C. Massey, and he commanded then, as he would again command now, my particular admiration and sympathy. He was a regular and extensive contributor to The Unknown World, and having asked him at its inception to define Mysticism from his own standpoint, I said as follows, when introducing the remarks which he furnished:—"There are some who are born mystics, and to this richly gifted class belongs Mr. C. C.

Massey. . . . Perhaps a time will come when these writings"—his contributions on mystic subjects to periodical literature—"will be recovered and collected into another of the great books of man's spirit." Professor Barrett gives the extract at greater length than I have ventured, and of the magazine itself he speaks with the kindly insight which characterizes his literary work. C. C. Massey died on March 29, 1905, and this memorial volume fulfills the hope which I expressed those long years ago, without of course arising therefrom.

The chief question which occurs for our consideration is the view taken of Mysticism by this "modem mystic," whether in 1894 or subsequently and generally. Professor Barrett, expressing his own standpoint and reflecting that of his friend, says that it is "the merging, or sublation, as Mr. Massey puts it, of our alien and separative self-consciousness into the Divine and Universal Life." Certainly, in the one and doubtless in the other case, this merging is not to be regarded as submerging, or the annihilation of human consciousness; and on this understanding, it is a true and high definition. In 1894, Massey said that Mysticism is "a peculiar vital apprehension of spiritual principles and energies, and of their functional operations in or through man and nature." But this is what Mr. Massey might have called otherwise a "stage in the cognition" of the world within; the transcript of Professor Barrett deals rather with the terra; but both definitions are valuable and may be said to complete one another.

There are some and there are perhaps many in the younger generation to whom Massey will be only a name; there are a few to whom he may not even be that. I had better, therefore, mention that he was unknown in literature by the publication of any original works in book form, of which there is no record, but he had earned a distinct reputation by two excellent translations from the German—in particular by his rendering of Carl du Prel's Philosophy of Mysticism. Outside these he contributed only to the periodical press of the time along the lines of his particular concerns, but most largely to the spiritualistic journal Light and as it is desirable to say, it should, I think, be said that this paper had then, as it still has, several titles to consideration outside the special interest in which it exists officially. The contributions to its columns over the recurring signature of "C. C. M." were those which first attracted me to the work of Massey and the present memorial volume has drawn something from this source, but more fully from another, the existence of which could have been always predicated reasonably—namely, the occasional correspondence to which I have referred already. We were brought for a short season into closer touch when the Leo Taxil conspiracy against Continental Masonry was approaching its breaking point; many letters, if I remember, were exchanged between "C. C. M." and myself in the columns of Light, and when my story of the conspiracy appeared under the title of Devil Worship in France, it was reviewed by him at extraordinary length in that organ. This literary accident brought him into touch with a priest of the Latin Church, towards which he had leanings, both then and subsequently. I heard some account of letters that passed between them; but he found no satisfaction—in part perhaps for the reason that I gave him, namely, that the ecclesiastic in question, whom I had once known, was an amiable rather than an intelligent man. Massey may not have been meant for active membership of any official church, but having passed through the curriculum of research with which we have all made acquaintance in one or other of its modes, he returned—as some of us return, and, I think, an increasing proportion—with a profound acquired sense of the deep things of God which repose within Christianity. It is that sense through which we who have been so schooled are entitled to call ourselves—as he also did—Christian mystics. In the intellectual order—or that chiefly—I sometimes feel that we use it with a fuller apprehension than it could have been used of old, because of our schooling and the grinding mills thereof—that we apply it to ourselves in a wider intellectual sense than might have been possible with those greater men who spoke from more direct experience, who knew indeed the heights but not the arduous and complex paths of thought peculiar to these later days.

There are many precious things in what must, I suppose, be regarded as the by-ways of intellectual thought, the product of men and women who, through no want of capacity, have not entered—or indeed sought to enter—the front ranks; and the task of rescuing some at least of their remains is a pious, as it is also an important work. Once again, therefore, Professor Barrett deserves our grateful recognition, and as he tells us that he has ample materials for another volume, may the present one have that reasonable encouragement which will prompt him to continue his labor of love!

DEALINGS IN LEGITIMACY

April, 1909

THERE are many paths of suffering which do not lead into glory, many crosses which scarcely find their term in erection on Calvary, many crowns which are thorny enough, though not actually the crown of thorns; in fine, there are many casual and putative illuminations which do not attain the apotheosis of crucifixion. I think that some of these might be symbolized, at certain epochs, in the crown of France. There stood once, and there may still stand, a tombstone in the old cemetery of Delft, in Holland, which bore this memorable inscription: "Here lies Louis XVII, Charles Louis, Duke of Normandy, King of France and of Navarre, born at Versailles on March 27, 1785, died at Delft on August 10, 1845." This stone either covers the remains of Charles Edward Naundorff, whose life of imposture was perhaps tempered by hallucination towards its close, or it is the place of rest which, so far as his body is concerned, was at length reached by the last lawful King of France. This appears at first sight to be rather a simple issue, which ought to be determinable by the choice of one of its alternatives. But, as it happens, there is a French cemetery, which is that of Gleize, and there also is a monument, which bears on one side a dubious inscription, as follows: "1785. None will say over his tomb, Poor Louis, how much wert thou to be pitied I Pray God for him." This is questionable enough, and might pass for a simple eccentricity; but on the other side of the stone, for long, and still perhaps, set against the wall of the chapel, there is yet another inscription, and this reads: "Here lies Louis Charles of France, son of Louis XVI and of Marie Antoinette, born at Versailles on March 27, 1785, died at Gleize on August 10, 1853." Now, this stone either covers the remains of the ex-Baron de Richemont, whose life of imposture was at no time tempered by hallucination, or it is the place of rest which, so far as his body is concerned, was reached by the last lawful King of France. The issue is therefore to this extent complicated, but it does not rest here; we shall see very shortly after what manner it is yet more deeply so; at the moment I will add only that in the far-off western world there is again another cemetery, and another tomb again, which either covers the remains of Eleazar Williams, of dubious or unknown parentage, whose life of piety and self-devotion was contaminated by no pretensions but those that were thrust upon him, whose hallucination is not suggested, and—under the circumstances—is not likely, or, once more, it is the place of rest which, so far as his body is concerned, was at length reached by the last lawful King of France.

It is obvious that in these cases—as indeed in others innumerable—there is a very important implicit in the words: "Here lies Louis XVII"—or in their variants, actual and possible. The implicit is that the second son of Louis XVI, who became Dauphin of France on the death of his sickly brother, did not himself perish from natural causes, through ill-treatment, or by poison, as the result of his imprisonment in the Temple dining the French Revolution. The fortunes of this question are rather like the fortunes of kings themselves and their substitutes, for they have been exceedingly checkered. Prior to the year 1812, the state of Royalist feeling is probably represented by the Journal du Temple, which was published by M. Clery, who was the King's valet de chambre. That the Dauphin ever escaped the toils of his prison did not here occur to one who seems to have been mournfully familiar with the brutal precautions taken to render it impossible, and it is therefore left doubtful whether he died by poison or from disease and the effects of ill-treatment, the disposition being against the first hypothesis. At this period, the only pretenders who had appeared were unquestionable impostors, one or both of whom had based their claim upon a novel of the day, now apparently forgotten, in which the Dauphin's escape was depicted. The second stage is marked by the appearance of certain historical memoirs by M. de Beauchesne, which, if not produced under the authority of Louis Philippe, had certainly the royal approval, and once at least were quoted by his son, the Prince de Joinville. The claimants and their evidence had become at this time something approaching a thorn in the flesh of the powers that were, and in 1852 M. de Beauchesne, with every appearance of detachment, brought his knowledge of the past—and this also was intimate, though not in the very close sense of M. Clery—to allay the grave doubts and disperse the conflicting rumors. He said that the positive fact of the Dauphin's death was for him authentically demonstrated, that he really died in the Temple, and that he—de Beauchesne—knew personally the two last jailers in whose arms the boy passed away.

THE LITTLE DAUPHIN.

From the Engraving by Cousins after the portrait by Greuze.

On the one hand, therefore, the hope or possibility had never entered into the heart of the King's valet in 1812, and on the other—for what it is worth—it is denied with all earnestness—and almost with imprecations on himself if he bears false witness—by one who affirms that he has no pretension of pleading a cause. But how does it stand now? Well, I think that M. de Bonnefon does not unreasonably express the opinion by the opening words of his recent work as follows:—"That the Dauphin, son of Louis XVI, was deported from the prison of the Temple—this, among all the mysterious events of that tormented life, is the least open to discussion and is also the least discussed. And Miss Welch, who in her monograph—also recent—rejects all the claimants without being manifestly unfair to any of them, rejects also what she terms "the conventional story of the Dauphin's death." With considerable moderation and restraint, she says: "That there are in connection with the official ending of Louis XVII's career a dozen suspicious details, not one of which is of prime importance, but all of which considered together, cannot but raise a serious doubt that the King died in the Temple, particularly in view of the weighty reasons why his escape might have been desired not only by Royalists, but by some of the Republicans as well."

Louis XVI.

The opinion of a partisan on a particular side is here well balanced by the coinciding opinion of one who is no partisan, though otherwise she has her limitations and a few prejudgments. In my own detached mind, the reasonable inference that the Dauphin did not perish in the Temple depends (1) in part from testimony put forward by those who were in a position to know, and more especially from the confession—seemingly authentic—of Simon his jailer's wife that she herself was instrumental in his escape; (2) in part from the dubious medical attestations to the fact of his death, by which I mean the uncertain note struck by the death-certificate; (3) in part by the incertitude as to what body—if indeed any—was interred; (4) in part from the strange way in which the proposal to hold some kind of funeral service in commemoration of the young King was thwarted, possibly by the intervention of the Latin Church; and, in fine (5), when the time came for the erection of monuments to the memory of other members of the royal family, from the nonerection of that which was intended to commemorate Louis XVII. I set aside all that has been inferred from the life-long conduct of Madame Royale—i.e., the Duchesse d'Angoulême; from the belief of old intimates of the family like Madame de Rambaud, and from the alleged knowledge of the beloved Madame de Beauhamais, afterwards the Empress Josephine; because these things rest either on dubious assumptions, are confused by speculative elements, or are awaiting complete demonstration.

MARIE ANTOINETTE.

THE TEMPLE.

(From the Engraving in the Carnalet Museum. By kind permission of Messrs. Methuen.)

The accounts of the Dauphin's removal, on the assumption that he left the Temple, are suspicious enough as to many matters of detail, more especially in so far as these have been furnished or extended by those who in later times claimed identity with him. If the evidence of the jailer's wife is of fact and not of invention, it has the further merit of simplicity, for it is said that she carried him outside the walls of the town as part of a laundry bale. He was in ill-health at the time, and is affirmed to have been replaced by an incapable and dying boy, or otherwise by a deaf-mute. But it is further suggested that there was more than one substitution, and as the claimants were not always at peace with themselves, much less with one another, it will be seen how the difficulties multiply. Naundorff, for example, once stated that what was originally introduced was a lay figure.

As regards the claimants I estimate that a mere collation of the available documents, so as to determine how far the most important pretenders made use in their several interests of public facts in common, and in some cases borrowed each other's inventions, would occupy three years on a moderate computation, and would require to be done in France. The word impossible is therefore written across the whole question so far as a short article is concerned. Miss Welch, who sometimes strikes a note that sounds a little disconcerting, and in spite of several disclaimers is, on the whole, rather in a condition of suspended judgment, shows that there were forty Dauphins in all, but three only with any tangible evidence which seems to construct in their favor. These are Eleazar Williams, Richemont and Naundorff. On the other hand, since there is no canon of control for enumerations of this kind, Mrs. Weldon reports that, coincidently and in succession, within that period when it was, humanly speaking, possible for a son of Louis XVI to be alive, some two hundred false claimants appeared. She reduces the amazing list by a justified process of exhaustion to four persons—Naundorff, Augustus Meves, Richemont and Eleazar Williams. This quartette she shortens, in fine, to one by assuming that, of the other three, two were persuaded into their belief by the subtlety of statecraft as an offset to the dangerous pretensions of the real claimant. These were Meves and Williams. As for Richemont, he was "a paid agent of the police," produced for the same reasons. I do not see that the evidence for this view quite appears in Mrs. Weldon's monograph, but she testifies to the sincerity of the two, whose lives, as it happened, lent themselves to the precarious possibility and who accepted that which was told them. Curiously enough, Meves was a broker of French parentage, in business on the London Stock Exchange, and his identity with the Dauphin was revealed to him by his reputed mother under a covenant to reserve his speech while she at least was in life. He came to believe that she had been in the service of Marie Antoinette, but he took no public steps, leaving the question as a legacy to his son, who was concerned in the publication of a few books, after which he dropped out of notice. There is no reason for suggesting—though this has been done—that he was either hallucinated or an impostor, but the first impeachment might obtain in the case of the lady. Other explanations are possible, but it is not worthwhile to consider them. As Meves died in 1859, he was one of the most long-lived pretenders, but within certain limits, his is evidently a story of dream. The earliest claimants in point of time—whom I have mentioned briefly already—were Jean Marie Hervagault, the insolent and beautiful son of a small tailor, and Mathurin Bruneau, the son of an agricultural laborer. The one is said to have died in 1812, or still earlier, and the other about 1825, in prison. Both attained notoriety in respect of their claims, for which no particle of evidence was ever forthcoming, and of their impostures there is no question. I mention them only because of the next case, which is that of Baron de Richemont, in whose interest M. de Bonnefon, or his precursor de Beauchamp, has revived one of Hervagault's inventions.

THE DAUPHIN.

To confuse the disconcerting facts which bore witness to his own parentage, Hervagault said that one of the boys substituted for the Dauphin in the Temple was the child of a tailor bearing the name that was unjustly imputed to him. We shall see how this has been utilized, and also the case against Bruneau. The dossier of the Baron de Richemont, which is long, curious and persuasive, may be summarized briefly as follows. The Dauphin was received from the Temple by a certain Ojardias at the instigation of the Prince de Condé. Ojardias was assassinated.

THE DAUPHIN.

[From a painting by Kucharsky. By kind permission of Messrs. Mathews]

He was placed in the care of the Comte de Frotté, who was shot. He came also under the momentary protection of Mme. de Beauharnais, of whose fate we know. He was taken, disguised as a girl, to the camp of Général de Charette at La Vendée, thence to La Rochelle, and in 1796, he joined the Prince de Condé in Holland. Reasons of policy having led this prince, his knowledge notwithstanding, to coincide in the nominal proclamation of the Comte de Provence as Louis XVIII, the Dauphin was transferred to Rome, again in feminine disguise. There he was received by his father's aunts, who remitted him to their almoner at Milan, whence he proceeded to the Dowager Duchess of Orleans at Barcelona. He was next confided to the Regent of Portugal, and on returning to France, with no stated chaperon, he was wrecked on the coast of Normandy. There he was arrested as a vagabond, and being acquainted—though it is curious to say—with the fact that the tailor's boy, Hervagault had been substituted for himself at the Temple by the fiction of the alternative Dauphin, he veiled his identity under that humble name. This caused his restoration to the reputed father, which must have led to complications, but we learn only that he wandered from the unwelcome asylum, was again arrested, and then confessed to his identity with the son of Louis XVI. His subsequent life is the history of successive imprisonments, occasioned for the most part by reiterated claims for recognition, though he was disposed to deny any ambition to wear the crown of France. He went to Brazil in 1810, where he was protected by John VI. But when the fall of Napoleon brought Louis XVIII actually to the throne, he again returned to France, again put his claim forward, and seeing that Hervagault, real or imaginary, had been attested dead in 1810, the Dauphin was now—in 1815—incarcerated as that other pretender Mathurin Bruneau, who, according to the defense of Richemont, did not perish as a prisoner in 1825, but at his father's house in 1812. There is no call to recount the further judgments, the innumerable escapes, the endless wanderings, followed by fresh imprisonments, which befell Richemont. I will say only that his imputed sister, Madame Royale, never acknowledged this—or indeed another—pretender, though she had been brought with him once into personal contact. One of his last acts was to cite her before the Civil Tribunal of the Seine, but she died in 1851 before the summons was returnable, and he himself passed away on August 10, 1853. As he was never married, his claim lapsed with him, and was asleep for many years, indeed till M. de Bonnefon awakened it by the publication of his Dossier du Roi. I confess that, after making allowance for the documents which he does produce, and his allusions to others, it remains difficult to check many important points of his narrative.

The next claim which comes for our consideration does not exactly arise in the order of time, but it is placed here between that of Richemont and that of Naundorff as something which is apart from either, entirely sui generis, and in several respects remarkable. It is that of Eleazar Williams, the news of which reached England from America in the early part of 1853 and was known concurrently in France, if at no earlier period. I can give the story only in the barest possible outline. Williams is said to have been a sickly and imbecile boy, one of a family of French refugees who reached New York in 1795. The boy was left in the care of a half-breed Iroquois Indian, and money was provided from France, as it is alleged, for his education.

LE BARON DE RICHEMONT,
(Soi-disant Louis XVII.)

An accident practically—or to all intents and purposes—restored his faculties, but he knew nothing of his past life. He had some experience subsequently in the war of 1812; thereafter, he became a lay missionary to the Oneida Indians, and was ordained by a bishop of the Protestant Episcopal Church in 1826. In 1841, the story says that he was sought by the Prince de Joinville, who revealed to him, under a seal of secrecy, that he was the son of Louis XVI. The alleged purpose of the recital was to obtain from Eleazar Williams a deed of abdication in favor of Louis Philippe, the reigning King of France, the consideration for which was to be "a princely establishment, either in France or in America, together with the restoration of the private property of the royal family, confiscated during the Revolution, or fallen afterwards into other hands." This overture was refused, but Williams regarded himself as bound by the pledge of secrecy, until later revelations intervened. So far, however, from advancing any claim, the unexpected suggestion of royal status was a position from which he desired only to be delivered, saying that he sought a heavenly but not an earthly crown. He died in 1858. He is the most interesting of all the pretenders, and he really pretended to nothing. He refused the advances made to him on the warning of his conscience, and in the words which the Comte de Provence is said to have used when replying at Warsaw to the ambassador of Napoleon: "Though I am in poverty and exile, I will not sacrifice my honor." He was never mentally strong, but there are grounds on which it seems difficult to suppose that he was hallucinated about the visit of the Prince de Joinville; and the historical grounds are indubitable.

ELEAZAR WILLIAMS.
(Facsimile of a pencil sketch from a Portrait of 1804.)

If this be so, he was either the Dauphin of France, or, alternatively, the son of Louis Philippe, as Mrs. Weldon would probably say, had entered into an iniquitous conspiracy to obtain a pretended abdication as a counterpoise to the troublesome claims of Naundorff. But how the prince de Joinville came, in this case, to hear of Williams as a person with lost antecedents who might serve his purpose, I should not pretend to say. The fact that they did meet transpired through the publication of an article in Putnams Magazine, copies of which were sent to the Prince, who replied through his secretary, admitting that the conversation took place, broadly under the circumstances mentioned, but affirming that it was confined to the French history of North America during the previous century. Here the matter remains, so far as the two principals are concerned, and there is no one at this day who can judge between them. It is said that in 1904 a grandson of Williams was still living, and regarded himself as the last of the Bourbons; it is not said that he advanced any claim, but, whatever his sentiments, they will reach their term with himself, for he is without issue to continue his strange particular phase of the true legitimacy.

The living interest of the whole subject centers, however, in an alternative French pretender, one of whose descendants is still termed by his supporters the King of France, and there are two monthly periodicals devoted to his cause. So far also as there is any expression of opinion outside the sphere of partisanship, there is a disposition in recent times to regard the Naundorff claim as the least intolerable of all. I think, for example, that a few additional lights would make Miss Welch one of its converts, awaiting which event it may be said that even abstruse Kabalistic calculations—for what these are worth—have been pressed into the service of the theme,

It is beyond the scope of this brief paper to enter into a discussion of the Naundorff pretensions, about which Mrs. Weldon has given us rather an account of her convictions than a consecutive narrative of the evidence, such as it may be held to be. She has herself passed through many ordeals, to some of which she alludes in her preface; but if I speak of them here, in such late days as these, it is only to say that they have not destroyed her enthusiasms. They have rather kindled her sympathies with some who bear witness of themselves, but do not obtain recognition. In the comparatively narrow limits to which her work is restricted, she has had no opportunity to tell the whole story, or to produce more than a simple synopsis of the evidence, giving details only where she has been impressed especially herself. It should be understood, therefore, that much remains to be said, both for and against the claim, so that those whose interest may be enlisted here and now by this obscure side-issue of history must go further if they desire to learn more fully. They will find a good deal to their purpose in La Survivance du Roi Martyr, par un Ami de la Vérité, Toulouse, 1880, and in L'Enfant du Temple, Paris, 1891, by Baron de Gaugler. These writers are on the side of the defense; on another side there is that Story of Louis XVII of France, by Mrs. Elizabeth Evans, about which I have already spoken, and there is the diatribe, which exhausts language, in the work of M. de Bonnefon. They are all indifferently the work of pronounced partisans; Mrs. Evans is the kinswoman of the rival claimant, Eleazar Williams, while Mrs. Weldon has early memories of other ties than those of blood which connect her with the Naundorff claim.

THE REV. ELEAZAR WILLIAMS.
[From a Painting by the Chevalier Fagnani.]

The predispositions of the one have no doubt caused her to present Naundorff in the worst possible light, and those of the more recent writer have led her to depend too largely on depositions which rest more particularly on the personal authority of the claimant, to the depreciation of critical value. For myself, it should be needless to say that I represent no side, and if I hold any opinion, it is that neither by Naundorff himself, nor by Mrs. Weldon, nor by any other person from any point of view, has the tale of the Dauphin's survival in any one pretender been adjudicated upon in unquestionable accordance with the historical sense. Such a task must involve much which would scarcely occur except to an expert in research and from which the expert might shrink, because, in respect of the issues or anything that would follow therefrom, there is little left to repay the pains. The cause of all the direct claimants has long since been committed to the hands of God, and I question whether it is likely to be pronounced upon by a truly competent authority in this world.

In respect of Naundorff, he was first heard of at Paris in 1833, as one who had entered that city from Prussia. He assuredly convinced many in respect of his claims, but I do not think that Mrs. Weldon has dealt adequately with the fact that French at the time was evidently to him a foreign language. His own imputed reminiscences of his early life suggest that if he had forgotten much during the torment of his life in the Temple, he might at least have remembered his native tongue. Mrs. Weldon rather derides criticism of this kind and Miss Welch, for some reason, ignores it. The hinted excuse is that out of the twenty-four first years of his life, he spent, according to his story, some seventeen in dungeons.

KARL LOUIS NAUNDORFF.
(Soi-disant Louis XVII.)

I will not speak of these imprisonments, of his life as a watchmaker in Berlin, or of the successes and failures which befell him when he began to prosecute his claim. These things are within the easy reach of everyone. The point to observe is this—that when he could and did in fine come forward, the policy of the government in respect of the other pretenders was reversed. As Miss Welch points out, it seemed to fear the public advertisement of his pretensions; it did not imprison or try him, but drove him out of the country. "It is difficult," she adds, "to avoid the conclusion that the government that so plainly avoided coming to an issue with this man did so from fear." He found a refuge in England, and, as we have seen, he attained his earthly term at Delft in Holland. The method by which he reached it is sometimes affirmed to have been poison, administered by an unknown hand, and there is evidence that this was his own belief. He died maintaining his claim and asking at a higher tribunal for that imperishable crown, the pallid reflection of which was denied him on earth. Though his various partisans were utterly disconcerted, and though there is something to be said for the children whom he left, those who believe in him now—and in France this is said to be still a burning question—may be counselled to console themselves by one of two considerations: if they please, he was spared further tribulation in a cause that was hopeless; but if they can rise to the opportunity, he escaped the crown of France.

In order to dispose of the claims of Naundorff it is advanced (a) that he was one of the substituted boys set up to cover the escape of the real Dauphin, or (b) that he came into connexion with the latter soon after his escape, and personated him when he died—which, by the hypothesis, was before long. The logical inference from these competitive assumptions is that his pretensions are not easy to dispose of otherwise. In order to destroy the case of Richemont it is supposed—as we have seen—that the power which sought to counterbalance the dangerous aggression of the true claimant, Naundorff, put up fantastic impostors from time to time, thus distracting inquiry and confusing all the issues. This is a Favorite hypothesis, but having regard to the multiplicity of pretenders, I think that it proves too much. In order to scatter the case of Eleazar Williams, it is speculated that the prince de Joinville, son of Louis Philippe, played an imbecile practical joke on a devout missionary, using for that purpose the most explosive of all instruments; and I think that this is absurd.

A curious side issue of the whole subject is the material and financial maintenance of some of the claimants. If Richemont were other than the Dauphin, we know not whence he came or from what stock. He followed no profession—not even that of a chevalier d'Industrie—and had no visible resources, yet he never seemed wanting for means, though he showed no signs of affluence. He was a wanderer over the face of the earth and the ordered narrative of his adventures, which has more than one touch of kinship with the books of knight-errantry, has this also—an entire lapse of memory as regards essential matters of detail, for example, whether he carried a purse and a change of clothes and linen. Cervantes rails at such omissions in the Spanish books of chivalry, and they offer a note of unreality in the special pleading of M. de Bonnefon.

The appeal of Naundorff was obviously much stronger; it became a financial undertaking and is still a going concern, a vested interest. In the course of the years, he must have proved a heavy tax on the wealthier contingent of his believers.

As against the renunciation of Eleazar Williams, we have the disconcerting, but yet comprehensible fact that Naundorff lived on his claim, and at one period of his residence in England, he maintained a large establishment. I think that he has been judged too harshly in many quarters; I think that he was received too lightly in many others. There is something to be said for his claim, if we can put that of Williams' aside. It was believed in by Victorien Sardou. It was supported at much cost to himself by Jules Favre. On the alternative side there is a bare possibility that he also was deceived, and the last word may not have been said (a) upon the visions and revelations of the French peasant Martin concerning La vraie Légitimité, and their not unlikely effect on a mind which may have been prone to strange impressions, or (b) upon the imputed visions of Naundorff himself, who is styled by Mrs. Weldon "the founder of modern spiritualism," and whose so-called "occult works," including La Doctrine Celeste, are very curious memorials, perhaps with a serious pathological side. In truth, the whole controversy, now long since passed into desuetude in respect of its most obvious interests, if it contributes to nothing else, does assuredly yield a substantial increment ad majorem fantasiæ gloriam. Apart from this, amidst so many conflicting interests, who among the wise shall choose? Choose nothing rather between the cohort of false prophets—for they also were many—and the dubious princes! What we can say in our detachment is that the piteous story of the Dauphin boy, whether he escaped or not, is scored in memory as one of those undesigned lessons taught by the mystery of iniquity which works in great revolutions, but the roots of that iniquity are not in the revolutions themselves; they are in the thrones and the powers about them.

THE SACRED TRIAD

June, 1909

AS the consideration of this paper arises out of a book published recently, but does not connect therewith except as the indepen-dent treatment of an identical subject, I shall do well to set aside some unexpressed canons of criticism, to which I should defer generally, by saying a few words concerning the work itself at the very beginning. The Doctrine of the Trinity, by the Rev. J. R. Illingworth, D.D. (Macmillan & Co.), is characterized in its title as apologetic in the proper sense of that term, and to the history of the dogma—which it presents in a sketch at once slight and informing—it adds all that which is actually of the author's special concern. This concern is with the practical value of the doctrine at the present day, its intellectual value, also at the present day and distinguished—as if for the purpose of a schedule—from the practical bearings, which except for the author's defined object is, in the better sense, not a true distinction, since these two are one. In fine, as an argumentum ad hominem, we have a clenching and bringing home of the thesis in the statement, developed fully, that the doctrine is worth the presumption of its truth. As this seems an appeal, and obviously, to the mind of the typical and official churchman, the book may be de-scribed almost as popular in its design, which notwithstanding it is a very simple and useful introduction to the position of the dogma in the life of Christendom, and from this point of view—if from no other—those to whom I speak will do well to make acquaintance therewith.

By the indication that it is worthwhile, I take it to be meant that the doctrine offers to those who receive it truly some experience in the consciousness which makes for an extension of that knowledge which comes out of the life of sanctity, and this is the proper, as it is indeed the only, test of truth in doctrine. Thus, and in every way, from outward to inward, the appeal always moves. Heaven, so far as we can approach it now, is an idea of location transcendentalized to the ineffable degree; but such a location is within, though before we reach our term in that order, we may see many strange places. The vital quality of Trinitarian doctrine—if any—is (a) the declared or undeclared essence by which it can be so translated into our consciousness that (b) we may enter by experience into a fuller union with God. So also, the Persons of the Divine Trinity are the mode in which our consciousness as Christians confesses to the experience of God, and this because our faith in Him testifies ex hypothesi to the fact that He does not deceive His children, and more than all that He does not confuse them by false experiences. This is the assumption, and out of this the question of fact arises, in the terms hereunto following: Seeing that I speak as a mystic and that I address those only who confess to this description, at least by a disposition of the mind, in what respect does it signify to us as mystics whether the unity of God subsists in a Trinity of Persons? If we are Christian mystics in any real sense of the term, it must signify a great deal, because it was not until Christ manifested in flesh, for our redemption after some manner, that the Doctrine of the Trinity was explicated, and according to the Catholic teaching of all the Churches that which manifested then was the Second Person of the Divine Triad. Here it will be, of course, understood that what signifies is not the simple intellectual conception but the inward realization. I have put forward a canon of criticism by which all doctrines must be judged, and that is their capacity for ministration to the need of the soul, so that the soul can advance in the experience of the life of sanctity and shall thus walk not alone by faith but by sight also. Out of this criterion, there arises the further and keener question of whether Trinitarian doctrine responds for us to such a test. We shall arrive at some conclusion on this subject by a consideration of the doctrine itself from the standpoint which I have indicated; but in the first place, it is necessary rather than desirable to say a few words regarding its antecedents in religious and philosophical systems which are other than Christian. Now, the religions that are called pagan had indubitably the analogies of Trinitarian doctrine, but ingenuity has increased artificially the closeness of the likeness, and once, at least, tended to present it in false terms of identity. The development of the critical faculty on the side of its sanity has tended to reduce these exaggerations, and by many it will be admitted now that such analogies are useful chiefly to bring the distinctions into clearer light. In my own view, the non-Christian Triads are so much the mere shadows of the Divine Trinity that in order to avoid confusion, it is a wise plan to set them aside altogether. The only really important collateral fact is the way in which the doctrine developed in theosophical Jewry, during the period of the greater exile, concurrently with and yet independently of its development in Christendom. It is an amazing growth—by its complications, its involutions and the grotesqueness in its mode of expression—but I regard the result as, intellectually speaking, a great light of constructed mystical doctrine and, at whatever distance, the only formulation of the scheme of things with which Christian theology can suffer a moment's comparison. Its major defect is that which is inherent in its conception, and this is that it is devoid of any correspondence with the manifested Christ; yet it was held so sincerely in the past to admit of and even to involve such a correspondence that for generations the Christian students of Kabalism regarded the development of its sole and own implicits as the only form of propaganda which was possible with success in Israel.

The implicits of Trinitarian doctrine are in the New Testament and all that which may be held to lie behind it; those of Jewry are in the Secret Doctrine, of which the Kabalah—vast as it is—seems to be only an expression in part. Whether there was a common source from which both drew must exceed the limitations of a few words on a great subject; but the intellectual life of Christendom during the growth of dogma moved in strange paths and issued from strange clouds of darkness. Whether the Secret Doctrine was indigenous in Jewry, and that from the Mosaic period, or whether it was a derivation from many things antecedent, remains an open question after centuries of discussion. I hold an opinion on this subject which is reflected from the schools wherein I have been nourished theosophically, but in the present place I must set this also aside—not that it is extrinsic to the issues, but because, like the antecedents of Christianity, it opens gates into the infinite, while this is a brief excursus and not a treatise at large. It remains that both systems ended by producing something sui generis. As regards the analogies between them, it must be understood that the Christian apologists who have undertaken to show that the Kabalah contains specific Christian doctrine in the specific Christian sense have carried their enthusiasm beyond the horizon confessed by that literature; they have done exactly what might be expected under the circumstances; they have given the particular meaning to the general and fluidic sense. The doctrine, for example, of the threefold Divine Nature is assuredly in Kabalism, but in the Christian mode it is not there at all; it is there in the Kabalistic mode, and so only. How great the distance which intervenes will be appreciated by anyone who has an acquaintance with the Sephirotic system, as it is found first of all in the ancient Book of Formation and as it is developed into complexity in the Zoharic books. The original

Sephirotic system was the doctrine of the emanation of the universe, or—if this be putting it too strongly—of the manifestation of universal things externally. It contains no suggestion of the Trinity, the explanation of everything is by ten Numerations—of which the first is the Spirit of God explicated as the Divine Name in the forming of things. At a later period, the Numerations, or Sephiroth, were divided into four worlds: the world of Deity, the angelic world, the world of formation, and that of manifested and material things. In some distributions of the Sephiroth among these worlds, the Divine Triad is exhibited in the world of Deity. In others, we have the Great Countenance, wherefrom issues the Father and the Mother, and these together correspond to the first three Numerations, being the Triad in another aspect. The notion of the Divine Son—or Microprosofus—corresponds to the six lower Sephiroth, or the Lesser Countenance. The tenth Sephira, or Numeration, is the Spouse of Microprosopus; it is the kingdom of this world understood in its assumption by the other, and it is thus the Church of Israel, or, according to the precarious speculation of Christian apologists, it is the Holy Spirit, in which sense they carry the Kabalistic system a still greater distance from the Christian idea of the Trinity. A certain general analogy, inheres, deeply imbedded, and this will appear as we proceed. At the moment it remains only to add that as all things are in the mind, but at first by way of root or vestige, so I do not doubt that those who looked for Messias and spoke of the Spirit of God had, from all time, the implicit of the Trinity among them. This is only another way of saying that the experience of sanctity had brought the Church of Israel into a certain exalted degree of consciousness in God.

Recurring to Christian Trinitarian doctrine, the true key to our position as mystics will be found in those words of St. Augustine which are quoted by Dr. Illingworth: "We say Three Persons, not as being satisfied with this expression, but because we must use some expression." In other language, all doctrines are part of the path towards that term which Augustine recognized—the soul's rest in God—but the path is not the term, and it does not yet appear what awaits us in fine. Being Christian mystics, we recognize that Christ was manifested as the Son of God, to communicate to us who are His followers the filial connection with the Divine. If we are the sons of God, there is a beyond question the principle of fatherhood in God, concerning which Christ came to tell us, and hence He is called in orthodox terminology our elder Brother. As Christian mystics, we do not claim to know what fuller and deeper and more exalted mystery of being lies behind the relationship of Christ to the Divine, but we hold it as certain that the Divine had entered into the human consciousness of Jesus as It had never entered previously into man, so far as history has recorded. Whether the entrance was through the extension of human consciousness or through another manner of union, there is nothing in our experience to determine, but beyond those deeps which we can fathom, there are all the unplumbed abysses. Behind the doctrine of God's Fatherhood there rests an implicit of motherhood, and because of its realization at this day among persons disposed towards mysticism, there has been a certain tacit change in the appreciation of the relations one to another of the Divine Persons. As the doctrine concerning the Son of God has created an analogy between the Sacred Triad and the human family, the logic of this analogy seems at first sight to set aside the Filioquce clause of the Nicene Creed, though it does not in any sense bring about a rapprochement to Greek orthodoxy on the subject; it creates rather a procession of the Son from the Father and the Holy Spirit, understood as a feminine Persona. Now, on this difficult question, symbolist as I am, it must be said, through the sense of sincerity, that analogies carried to the absolute degree tend to land us in confusion. In the present instance, we get at the truer view by killing the analogy after it has served our purpose. To do this, we must realize that within God, conceived as the Father, there is that which precedes ex hypothesi the relation of fatherhood—I mean to say that there is Love. But in the Divine Nature, regarded in Itself and Its essence, there is no passage from subject to object, so that the Motherhood of God can be conceived only in the Fatherhood, and conversely. God, the Father is therefore God the Mother, and the procession is God the Son, but as constituting the Duad only. The Sacred Triad is completed by the Holy Spirit, which is the bond of ineffable love between the Father and the Son, but still not passing from subject to object, for of the Three that give testimony in heaven it is said that "these Three are One." The place of the Holy Spirit seems therefore indicated rightly by the clause of the Nicene Creed: Qui ex Paire Filioque procedit. But the Son is the Word of the Father, by which the universe is made—that is to say, the order of things wherein the Fatherhood is manifested through the Sonship, which order the Spirit or Bond of Love also embraces as the Comforter, and is perhaps to be declared more fully at the end of these times, that is to say, when God—through the Comforter—shall be all in all on the manifest plane, awaiting the other more remote, timeless condition, after the balancing of things, when the Son shall deliver up the kingdom to the Father. The words of man cannot describe that union. The analogy hereto in Kabalism, somewhat deeply involved, is: (a) the inaccessible God above the Sephiroth; (6) Macroprosopus, implied in the first Sephira, but still unsearchable; (c) Abba and Aima, the qualities of fatherhood and motherhood conceived in God, allocated to the second and third Sephiroth—in all, one triad, hormis l'Ineffable. We have then Adam Kadmon, Microprosopus, or Messias, and the Spouse—that is to say, Israel, whereon is Shekinah, the cohabiting glory, corresponding to the Spirit. If the first Triad is conceivable as implied in the Divine Fatherhood, we do reach a kind of substituted Trinity, but the Messias is not born on earth, and the analogy remains phantasmal.

In the Christian doctrine of the Trinity, the root-matter is the Fatherhood of God manifested through the Sonship of Christ, by which we are affiliated and enter into the realization of our legitimacy, and this operates through consanguinity with Christ, by enlightenment of the Holy Spirit. I believe that such a doctrine does respond to the test which I laid down at the beginning, that it is the material of experiences by which holy life may enter into holy knowledge, and that it contains a legal abstract of our titles. The root of the Christ-mystery was on the external plane; all symbolism requires this fulcrum from which the great things can move the universe of thought; but they become vital by elevation into the sanctuary of our consciousness, whereby they are made part of our personal history. The historical Christ goes before us eternally, rising from degree to degree in that consciousness, drawing all things after Him, as it is said: Christus autem assistens pontifex futurorum bonorum ... introivit semel in sancta, ætema redemptione inventa. The gist is that He entered and went in; He opened the sanctuary, and we follow, a part of the great procession which has followed previously and which constitutes the true Church.

SHADOWS ABOUT THE THRONE

August, 1909

THERE is perhaps no serious question that when the Comte de Provence became Louis XVIII, he reigned rather as a king in substitution than a king in fact, and destiny exonerated itself in respect of the whole transaction by seeing that he was never crowned and never ceremonially enthroned. The Church also escaped from anointing a dubious successor of St. Louis and a none too worthy namesake. When the Comte d'Artois, that still younger brother of Louis XVI, was actually installed as Charles IX there was no return of an old Saturnian reign, and I do not remember that anyone "spoke or heard" any particular good of the egregious effigy who in his time was Louis Philippe. But this is not to say that if Louis XVII, once Dauphin of France, had, in fine, come into his own, we should have been spectators from near or afar of an ideal rule. His nimbus of suffering looks now like an aureole of sanctity, and we have accounted it to him as including the martyr's palm and pallium. But if the event had given us an opportunity of experience, we might have known another story. The legitimacies come and go, but in their rising or their setting, the Kingdom of Heaven is not for these nearer, or its justice declared in power. It may seem strange, therefore, that in my article on "Dealings in Legitimacy" I should not only have distinguished at some length between the competitive champions of an uncertain claim, and should have regretted that many dossiers fortement documentés have left us despairing of any canon of criticism, but that I should now recur to the subject. What signifies it to me or to most of my readers, who know that the true legitimacies are of another order? It can be only on the assumption of some arrière-Pensée, and, to describe it in familiar terms, this responds to the occult interest. It responds also to something that is more within the lines of my own purpose, for it is a story of occult failure, of vain endeavor and voided presage. As there were three claimants in chief to the honors of the true legitimacy, so were there three prophets—one of whom testified concerning Naundorff, one more especially concerning the principle at stake, though he is also of the Naundorff tradition, and the third concerning a new and regenerated Christianity, the triumph of which would mean the Legitimist triumph, for the King would attain in the newly understood Savior, and the Savior's reign in the heart would be insured by the great restoration; but this prophet was Naundorff himself.

The transcendental witnesses who thus arose out of the legitimist dream were speaking likenesses of the fraud and folly, which are the unvarying concomitants of astral practices. All reflected the religious preoccupations of their place and their period; two of them tampered with, travestied and diluted theological doctrine, proclaiming their orthodox implicits and their high place in the unseen hierarchy; all reflected from the French Revolution and the Reign of Terror, the fond hope of a new external order. The astral machinery was put to work that it might secure its advent; the astral intelligence, under the name of angels and holy spirits, foretold the triumph of the cause; and it ended, as these things end always—in a word, as it was in the beginning, is now and ever shall be—in folly, failure and disgrace for all participants therein.

Now it so happens that the history of a certain defection in the ranks of Naundorff's supporters is also that of his revelations, a fact which even historically kindles interest concerning them, while those who accepted his construction of the world unseen were drawn within the infectious current of enthusiasm set in motion by another prophet of legitimacy, and this raises the whole question as to the thaumaturgic side of the subject. Here is the apparently extraneous issue that I propose to consider in the present paper. That which seemed to be extraneous was, however, deeply implied in all the disordered movement. When the star of royalty was extinguished in the blood and terror of the Revolution, the sentiment of royalty passed in some minds through a phase of nervous exaltation and stood ready on a slight pretext to assume the aspect of religious devotion. Such a pretext was supplied by the old dream of a great king to come, who would inaugurate a new epoch and reign almost over the world from the throne of France as a center. The time-honored prophecy of Orval was the basis of this dream, and one of its occult mouthpieces was the visionary William Postel in the sixteenth century. The martyrdom, actual or imputed, of a Bourbon king centered the hope in that dynasty by the operation of poetical justice, and the possibility of the Dauphin's survival was like fire to the fanatical extravagance, raising it to the pitch of fever. Outside all likelihood, however, it began to take a specific thaumaturgic shape at a point where we can presuppose neither knowledge, interest, nor enthusiasm. In or about the year 1816 a peasant named Thomas Ignatius Martin, located at Gallardon in Beauce, an old division of France between the Seine and the Loire, became a recipient of visions having a political object and involving the pretended intervention of the angel Raphael. I have given some account of these visitations elsewhere, and here it is only necessary to say that, though he does not seem to have been exactly a willing instrument, he spread abroad those prophecies of which he was made the recipient, and these concerned the troubles and turmoil's of France, with the ultimate restoration of peace and happiness by the coming of the expected king, who would be the true son of Louis XVI. He foretold the revolution of 1830; on April 2, 1818, he informed Louis XVIII that he was not the rightful occupant of the French throne; after the Revolution just mentioned, he is said to have announced that the Dauphin was in Germany; and in September, 1833, he saw and recognized Naundorff as the promised savior of the nation. The regnant authorities had tolerated him for so many years that they might have been expected to do so till he reached his natural term, but on April 16, —or alternatively May 8—1834, it is affirmed that he was first poisoned and then strangled. The subsequent exhumation of his body seems to have determined the question in an affirmative sense. It is to be noted for the rest that the mission of the peasant Martin, while, as I have said, political in its object, was also religious to the point of devotion, and in its devotion it was ultra-Catholic, working amidst a cloud of novenas, acts of thanksgiving, masses and offices of prayer; in fine, it offered no novelties in doctrine, and though all the available evidence, together with its criticism, suffers from the partisan spirit, I am disposed to regard the peasant as a real and not a pretended visionary. His prophecies were largely disproved by events, his recognition of Naundorff may have been hallucination in extremis, but his experiences ran the usual course of such pathological occurrences; and he was not, for example, cheated by a sect of political illuminés, using him as a tool for their own ends.

But on August 6, 1839, there arose Eugène Vintras of Cato in Normandy, he also an unlettered peasant, he also a man of vision, he also— but in the first instance more especially—utilized by dubious unseen powers, or imposed upon by some political faction, to further the cause of legitimacy, as represented by the claim of Naundorff. The details are long and complex, but the prime object in view seems to have been an arch-natural anxiety that the putative prince should be rooted in the Catholic faith—which he was not at that time, nor, as we shall see, subsequently. The intervening power was that of the Archangel Michael, for a new prophet had involved a new output on the part of the Blessed Hierarchy. It will be understood, therefore, that Vintras began in the religion of his childhood, and with the kind of supramundane assistance that might have been predicated in the circumstances; he had also particular devotion to the Most Holy Virgin, which probably anteceded his visions. As regards the legitimacy and its claim, it is clear that the survivance du roi martyr had become a tacit assumption which did not call for argument, and that the claimant's after-history was also so far well known that for Vintras there was no other pretender than Naundorff. For the rest, the role of the Orphan of the Temple was held to enter into that Divine plan which the prophet characterized as the Work of Mercy. Whereas, however, Martin remained an unpretentious peasant, fervent in the faith of his fathers, to his day's own end, the seer of Cato had the spirit and ambition of a hierophant; he forgot the imputed necessity of orthodox doctrine for a claimant of the French throne; he forgot the throne and the claimant; it was not enough that he should be visited and advised by St. Michael; the spirit of the prophet Elias had also descended upon him, and in him had retaken flesh. As such, it was inevitable that if Vintras did not come to destroy doctrine; he came at least to fulfill it and to develop it further. This development took the shape of a particular apotheosis of the Virgin. She was the Daughter of Heaven and was actually created Wisdom, which is a private, though not inexact, deduction from many lections in the Roman Breviary. But her spirit was an emanation of the Holy Trinity: it was composed of the power of the Father, the love of the Son, and the wisdom of the Holy Spirit— which is the side whereon the teaching leans to the extravagance of un-authorized theology. Her conception was by the word of her father, St. Joachim, who announced to St. Anne, her mother—she being afflicted by her long sterility—that she would bear the Daughter of Heaven. The implied orthodox basis was the doctrine of the immaculate conception, from which the pre-existence of Mary was inferred. The reign of the Holy Spirit was the proposed term, and Elias, in the person of Vintras, was the precursor thereof.

Louis XVIII.

As a part of his mission, he established the Work of Mercy, but the propaganda suffered proscription at the hands of the Bishop of Bayeux. The writer to whom I am indebted for this statement says that the interest at that time was not a formal association, that it was not hostile to the Church, nor a dispensation of new doctrine; what it promised was more light on existing doctrine. It is evident, however, that there was already novelty enough, and already there were Eucharistic and other miracles, for priests of the Church had by this espoused the cause of Vintras, who also exercised in his own person the sacerdotal function. Altogether, it was more than the Church could stand; the prophet was somehow imprisoned, and over one hundred miraculous hosts—the history of which exceeds this notice—bearing hieroglyphic figures, are said to have been enclosed secretly in the tabernacle of an altar in the cathedral of Bayeux, as sacred goods that had been confiscated. When they were examined four years later, they had undergone no change, but one of them was missing. The curé, La Paraz, one of the Vintras converts, said that it was not yet time to reveal where this memorial had been taken, but it had moved by its own power.

EUGÈNE VINTRAS IN HIS PONTIFICAL VESTMENTS.

In the meantime, Vintras and the headquarters of the proscribed sect were located in London, where, at 31, Marylebone Road, the miracles continued and the claims developed. Out of the Work of Mercy came the Marisiaque de Carmel, having a pro-victimal sacrifice of Mary, celebrated by a woman clothed in a sacerdotal vestment. At a later period Vintras himself assumed the dignity of a sovereign pontiff, and had special insignia revealed to him. They consisted, it is said, of a golden crown having the Indian lingam in front, a purple robe—apparently with an inverted cross—and a magic scepter terminated by a hand, uplifting the thumb and index finger only. The text of the sacrificial ceremony was the praise of wisdom under the form of womanhood, considered as a living tabernacle. It was Eucharistic in character; but there was also at a later stage a sacrifice of Melchizedek. It is obvious that, ex hypothesi, Vintras had received ordination of the arch-natural kind, and he celebrated strange masses, in the course of which, according to Jules Bois, he was raised from the ground; the host which he had consecrated remained suspended over the chalice; and a personal witness deposes that the wine, which seemed of no earthly vintage, was distilled by drops from the atmosphere. On these and other evidences, the unpretending house in London was styled l' Université Ê liaque, and the prophet himself adopted the names of Elie Pierre Michel in addition to his baptismal name of Eugène. His sect being considered, I suppose, the more baleful because of the illicit priesthood involved thereby, it was condemned formally on November 8, 1848, by a brief of Pope Gregory XVI, which act was confirmed at a later period by Pius IX. Vintras died at Lyons on December 8, 1875, being the Feast of the Immaculate Conception; in the cemetery of la Guillotihre his place of earthly rest is marked by a monument erected by his son; but the latter, and so also the wife of Vintras, is said to have discredited his pretensions. The memorials connected with the prophet are (a) Le Livre d'Or, 1849, embodying revelations of the Archangel Michael, delivered between August 6, 1839, and June 10, 1840. This is the thesis at length of the Work of Mercy, including the necessity of a new revelation, and its history. (b) Le Christ devant Rome et la Chrétienté, being a letter addressed to a priest in 1860. It is a belated diatribe on the action of the Bishop of Bayeux. (c) L'Evangile Éternelle, printed at London in 1857 and exceeding 700 pages, but undiscoverable at this day. (d) Le Voix de la Septaine, a journal of the work extending to four volumes, which appeared between 1842 and 1844; for this I have searched vainly in the records of periodical literature. (e) Finally, there are works in manuscript, apparently from the pen of Vintras, which, if printed, would fill a great number of volumes.

The succession of the heresy is traced back in Le Livre d'Or to the year 1772 and to a society of St. John the Baptist. This was founded by a visionary named Loiseaut, to whom the Precursor appeared (1) as a worshipper at his side in a church; (2) as a speaking head swimming in blood on a golden dish; (3) as a mendicant in the streets; and (4) at all times and seasons sub-sequently. The unfailing testimony of this occult personality concerned chastisements which were to overtake France, and disasters which should befall the Church.

LEVITATION OF VINTRAS.

Loiseaut confided these facts to certain persons, who formed themselves into a society which met in great secrecy; the members held hands in a circle, and St. John appeared in their midst; they beheld the scenes of the Revolution to come, but also the great Restoration which would follow thereafter. The circle had a spiritual director named Dom Gerles, who became their leader after the death of Loiseaut in 1788. When he fell under the influence of revolutionary ideas, the circle co-opted a somnambulist named Soeur Françoise André, whose visions sustained them. Dom Gerles became an illuminé on his own account, and had as another somnambulist, Catherine Théot, who healed and prophesied. The original circle found a recorder in the Sieur Ducy, and it dreamed of the rescue of the Dauphin and the wonders of his future reign. Sœur André died and was succeeded by a certain Legros, who was at the Charenton asylum when the peasant Martin was once placed there provisionally for a short period. This is the first succession; the second was that of Thomas Martin, and the third was the well-known Madame Bouche of Avignon, otherwise Sœur Salomé. She is said to have been taken seriously by Pius VII, who regarded her work of regeneration as a holy work. She spent eighteen months in close personal communication with Alexander I of Russia, and ousted from his confidence with the still more famous Madame de Krudener. She foresaw the coming of a great king. The fourth in succession was Vintras, as the witness preceding the Second Coming of Christ.

STIGMATIC HOST OF VINTRAS.

It will be seen that the connection throughout was one of consanguinity in spirit and purpose, but not of formal transmission.

Between the death of Martin and the rise of Vintras, came the experiences of the claimant Naundorff. The chronology of his history is rather curious at this point. He made his first appearance at Paris in 1833; his memorable meeting with Martin took place in that year; by his own evidence, he recognized the peasant, who had often appeared to him in vision. Martin died in 1834, and between this period and 1839 Naundorff was receiving the revelations or excogitating the principles which he embodied at the beginning of the latter year in La Doctrine Celeste, by which he appeared as the founder—so far as intention was concerned—of yet another religious sect. It will be seen that this was almost concurrent with the first experiences of Vintras.

PORTRAIT OF ABBÉ BOULLAN.

When he and Naundorff were both residents in London, it is credible to believe that they met, but in any case, the brief of Gregory VII which condemned the prophet coupled his errors with those of "that lost man who falsely proclaims himself Duke of Normandy"—illius perditi hominis qui falso se Normanniæ ducem jactat. No two heresies could have less in common, except their pretended origination from the angelic world. Vintras produced strange exotics of doctrine, pontifical aspects of rite, above all palpable miracles—a modern and blasphemous repetition of a super valid Mass of the Graal. Had he ever heard of that legend, there is little doubt that it would have been taken into his service. The plebeian mind of Naundorff conceived no decorations, and what he or his inspiring spirits presented for the relief of the age has not been incorrectly regarded as a precursor of the doctrinal part of modern spiritualism—at least, of one of its phases. There is no pseudo-revelation which has touched such uttermost deeps of the mental pit. The so-called celestial doctrine is a kind of recitation de novo in terms of verbiage of Christ's life according to the Gospels and there is some New Testament history subsequently, it being understood that the writings of evangelists and apostles were all falsified as a result of the Council of Nice. Christ is not God, but the first angel created in heaven; Mary, by consequence, is not the Mother of God; the imputed conception by the Holy Spirit is blasphemy against that Spirit. The body of Christ did not rise from the dead, nor therefore ascend into heaven, any more than the Word was made flesh. What appeared after the Crucifixion was a spiritual body. It naturally follows that the mass and all Roman practices are parts of papal reprobation. It took three Angels of the Lord to produce this dossier, and it was confirmed by a putative Christ Himself, as that teaching which He gave during His terrestrial sojourn. It is small wonder that Naundorff's political believers were scandalized, or that others who wanted revelations preferred those of Vintras.

Such are the religious and pseudo-transcendental aspects of la vraie légitimité, and it remains for me to say what became of the Messianic mission when Vintras died thirty years after the pretender whose cause he espoused for a moment. M. Jules Bois once affirmed that the pontiff delegated his powers to an Abbé Boullan, celebrated in the dubious annals of French occultism and veiled by J. K. Huysmans under the name of Doctor Johannes. He inherited the MSS. of the prophet, and Madame Thibault, the clairvoyant and priestess of the Provictimal Sacrifice, was also transferred to his charge. Boullan was once the almoner of a conventual house, but is said to have been unfrocked, for what reason I do not know, except that his brain was turned by theological studies along mystical fines. He went to Rome to plead his cause at the Vatican, which would not receive or hear him. It does not appear under what circumstances, but he came under the Vintras influence and felt himself delegated by heaven to preach the Coming of Christ and of the Divine Paraclete. He combined this with a mission to destroy the secret priesthood of Black Magic, for it was his misfortune to descry their baleful work everywhere, as others see that of Jesuits. He also set free the possessed by his Mass of Melchizedek. Huysmans terms him a singularly erudite mystic, and one of the most amiable of thaumaturgists. His headquarters were termed Carmel, and he believed that the soul of St. John the Divine had incarnated for a second time in his person—pace the late Mr. Edward Maitland. What he celebrated was called a Red Mass, and his consecrated hosts bore strange stigmata; but they were signs of victory and not of suffering, like those of Vintras. Boullan believed that the Ordre Kabbalistique de la Rose Croix, the litterateur Sar Péladan and the occultist Stanislas de Guaita were among the apostles of Black Magic and his sworn enemies. When he died on January 4, 1895, Jules Bois accused de Guaita of his occult murder; this was in the sceptical columns of Gil Blas. Huysmans was rather disposed to the same view and to put it on record in the same way; a little dispute followed which ended in two duels—but these ridiculously, as usual. And as Boullan had no successor, so ended the dealings in legitimacy on the occult side of religion; and so, passed the glory of the world of wonders.

The legitimacy itself remained and is represented at the present day by that descendant of Naundorff who is called Jean III. within the strange circle of his attraction. The cause is comparable to that which inspires the League of the White Rose, if this pleasing and decorative fantasy has not yet been entombed among us. After his father's revelations, it is, of course, unlikely that he hears masses, whether of Melchizedek or pro victimal; he may be a tete fort of the period, in which case I have done. But if there is a trace anywhere of a rite that is now heard of nowhere, if his wonderful court conceals an occult church in crypts, I pray those who know to come forward and tell me, when this memorial shall not be held to have ended but will continue hereafter.

JOHN DEE: IN TRADITION AND HISTORY

October, 1909

AS an illustration of a certain quality of vanity which sometimes characterizes the ardent pursuit of science, the case of Dr. John Dee, in the days of Mary and Elizabeth, offers one noticeable point, and it instances also the persistence of tradition in such a manner that salient facts of an entire life may become obscured and almost effaced. Those who are keen can, of course, go to biographical dictionaries of the larger kind, or to important encyclopedias, and receive a due proportion of correction; but as a counsel of prudence, this is not especially practiced—or in spite of it, the tradition continues. So, it comes about that John Dee, the philosopher of Mortlake and Manchester, is known everywhere as magician and wizard, the skryer and astrologer of Queen Elizabeth, but not at all for his notable contributions to the extension of mathematical science or as the peer and often as a friend of the chief men of learning in Europe at his epoch. His early history recalls indeed that of Picus de Mirandula, for at the age of twenty-four, the rumor of his attainments had gone far and wide in the world. But Picus was steeped in true, theosophical Kabalism, while Dee knew seemingly only its debased and so-called practical side, the art of invoking spirits. Picus was no astrologer and no magician, actual or reputed, Dee, on the other hand, did not die in his youth, worn out by the excesses of study, though he also had risked this danger. He lived to an age which was great in years, though unhappily clouded in honor; it remains for posterity to do what it can to clear him, even if this is rather a confused task. Let me say, on my own part, that I regard him, in a secondary sense, as one of the sufferers for occult science; on the most strenuous side of his so-called magical practices, his own records carry a strong conviction of his sincere and blameless intention, though in one respect—which I shall refrain from specifying—he was led utterly astray. Even then, it was with the utmost reluctance and under pressure which, for him, in his fatal dedication to commerce with lying spirits, can only be regarded as strong.

I have said enough—and many readers will know already—to indicate that the tradition concerning Dee is not less precise in its way, or less well founded, than the mathematical science which he loved. In the mistaken parlance of the period, he was magician, wizard, sorcerer, and so downward to the nethermost gulf of all the evil arts. But in reality, as against these nightmares, he was occupied only with certain ceremonial methods of inducing vision in the crystal, and—as high exotics—with the great work of metallic transmutation and with the great elixir. In these last he was a seeker only, though on one or two occasions it seems very nearly on his conscience that he claimed more. Those who may read the curious, crabbed, but informing life which has given this notice its opportunity will find that he strenuously denied all these practices when he was in danger of the judgment on the part of Queen or King or Council, and when the popular cry of magic had gone out against him; while, for what the apology is worth, he remembered not only an escape from the stake, to which he once looked near, in the days of Mary and Bishop Bonner, but that other time of his absence when the pestilent villagers of Mortlake broke his instruments and burned his priceless library—fortunately, during his absence, or he might have paid the penalty in his body.

JOHN DEE.
(*From an old Steel Engraving.*)

The horror of the wizard and all his ways, to which further impetus and a kind of imprimatur were given in the succeeding reign by the lucubrations of James I, was sufficiently in evidence during that of Elizabeth; and—almost as if it were a derivation from the better traditions of occult science itself—there was, firstly, especial detestation of necromancy as the most decried—though hypothetical—part of witchcraft; and, secondly, there was the ignorant confusion of common magical pneumatology with the abominated ceremonial evocation of departed souls. With such works the names of Dee and Kelley must have been connected at rather an early period.

In the case of the one, necromancy remained a mere accusation by verbal rumor, founded on the company that he kept; with the other, though possibly on no better warrant, it took a final shape in the publication long after of Weever's Funeral Monuments, in which work there is a circumstantial narrative of Edward Kelley's performances—accompanied by a certain Paul Waring—in the churchyard of Walton-le-Dale, Lancashire, for the discovery of a hidden treasure by means of the forbidden necromantic art. It is thus obvious that, considering the feelings of the period, Dee's denials are comprehensible enough, but there seems evidence otherwise that he was over pliant and an opportunist in respect of less strenuous convictions; if, on the one hand, he showed some signs of unobtrusive adherence to the Reformed Church in the days of Queen Mary, if he did not embrace overtly the Roman interest, it is certain, on the other, not merely that he conformed to Roman ritual and observance on the Continent but made the fact observable.

EDWARD KELLEY EVOKING SPIRIT OF A DEPARTED PERSON.

There are indications also that he was in sympathy with Latin doc-trine on certain points, though there is no evidence that he was express-ly disposed towards any official communion. I believe, however, that in his halting, anxious and curious manner he meant to be a devout man, who was also good naturally, and even pious after the ceremonial and arid manner of a magus. What stands out in his life conspicuously is, however, the hunger and thirst after knowledge, seeking to get it hon-estly if he could, but, somehow, to get it resolved. In other words, his aspiration was apart from that true and inward sanctity, which is the only title to a safe possession of secret science. If he is an instance far excellence of the magus by calling who took art magic so far sanely and seriously that he never tampered willingly with the evil side, he was not less undone by his credulity, which accepted most spirits for angels and his seer-in-chief, Edward Kelley, as the lip of truth concerning their ex-ceedingly composite, not to say mendacious, messages. As the scandal-ous life of this man did not make a shipwreck of Dee's confidence, so the spurious prophecies of the spirits may have distressed indeed but did not crumple up his faith. All this, notwithstanding, it remains that the True and Faithful Relation—once published in folio—of Dee's dealings with spirits is, for us and for our consanguinities, the deed of his exon-eration in respect of occult sciences—from all but the root of its follies and the fatal issues thereof.

His other interest was, as I have said, alchemy; but seeing that I do not find in his history any token that he was a chemist, even for his pe-riod, much less a "philosopher by fire" according to the canons of the adepts, I conclude that it was not so much by vocation as out of the hun-ger and thirst which I have also mentioned, increased in respect of the medicine of metals by the eternal straits of his finances and in respect of the greater elixir by a desire to prolong his life that he might protract research therein. And the direction of the hope was characteristic of the incentives and of him; forlorn indeed for us but for him perhaps substantial, it was a hope that Kelley, who claimed proficiency in the art, did not utterly deceive him, while it rested also in a faith still more blind, being the covenants of his world of spirits. That which was donum Dei altissimi for adepts of all the ages might, to him in particular, after years of invocation and response, come down direct from heaven, restoring his fallen estate and effacing the ravage of his years.

That he had vague doubts occasionally as to the warrants of the min-istering intelligences—this the records exhibit; that he questioned Kelley—except in respect of his little moral worth—this they do not show; it might have been all devilry, but as to common chicanery—no. We are without a canon of criticism to determine on our part as to the second alternative, but that the dealings were mendacious and evil, if they were spirit-communion at all—this stands naked on the surface. The communications, however, followed a system concerning which a reserve of judgment as to their ultimate design is a tolerable counsel, for more remains to be said of it than can be set down in this place. I refer to the so-called Tablets of Enoch, an account of which will be found in the Faithful Relation, but it is not entirely clear whether they originated with Dee, through the skrying of Kelley, or from another source. On that question depends the bibliographical history of a certain Sloane MS., which contains a very full account of ceremonial evocations of putative angels on the basis of the Enochian system. The MS. does not pretend that the intelligences with which it is concerned are other than an admixture, but the powers by which they are summoned are those of white magic, one test being the absence of blood-sacrifice. Here, the matter rests for the ordinary world of students; but in certain occult societies the Enochian system has been developed further, and as regards my own reserve of judgment, it is actuated by the fact that an examination of cognate systems has led me to discern, beneath the surface sense, the occasional presence of another intention, and to see that things which are of magic externally are sometimes theosophic within. It remains that the Enochian system has never been investigated in the root-matter thereof, but the work could scarcely be done by an unaffiliated student; it depends upon several considerations which cannot be adduced here.

The next point for our reflection involves another aspect of the John Dee tradition, and I suppose that it arises in part from the speculative tendencies of occult historians in the past. There is not so very much, after all, in the ascertainable life of Dee to indicate that he came into conspicuous relation with numerous occult personages, either at home or abroad. He was thinly acquainted with the kabalist and fantasiast William Postel, and the alchemical pretensions of Kelley brought him at Prague into some communication with Nicholas Barnaud; but he was rather an associate of ordinary learned men than of mystics and adepts. He was able to interest many in his own thaumaturgic subjects, but he did not often encounter those who were versed therein. The Latin life is useful because it makes this plain unintentionally, and it does further good service by its account of the unpublished Dee Diary, which covered the period preceding the Faithful Relation; we see that these almost unexamined MSS. do not differ therefrom; they are memorials of ceremonial seership which embody, by way of accident, certain facts of life. Now, Dr. Dee passed into an unblessed and indeed very troubled retirement at Manchester, having been appointed Warden of the College; but, from that city as a center, imagination has credited him with the invention in secret of the Rosicrucian mystery, meaning that he was the actual founder of the unknown brotherhood. The chief ground of this hypothesis is that a certain tract entitled Secretions philosophies brevis Consideratio, 1616, published under the name of Philippus d Gabello, is bound up, as if by way of introduction, with the first issue in Latin of the Confessio Fraternitatis R.C., and the said Consideratio has been regarded as a new recension of Dee's Monas Hieroglyphica. At that period and in that language, nothing, or very little, would depend from the fact if it proved on examination to be true. Independent works were frequently collected into a single volume by the inchoate methods of primitive publishing, and this is the first point; the second is that in 1616 Dee had been dead for eight years; he had doubtless ceased to be even a name in Germany, and to rob him by reproducing one of his tracts under a thin veil might seem a safe speculation.

But on a slight study of the later work, it is found that the analogies lie chiefly in the fact that it is a commentary on the special symbols which are the subject-matter of Dee's Monas Hieroglyphica, and though I do not doubt that Philippus a Gabella had a full acquaintance with the thesis of his precursor and founded his remarks thereon, he produced neither a new recension nor a slavish imitation. On the contrary, he devised therefrom a hypothesis concerning the universal medicine, philosophical gold, the Mercury of the Philosophers, and the first matter of metals, on which subjects—alchemist though he was—Dee says practically nothing in the place referred to herein; he deals rather with the prime Monad, the mortal and immortal Adam, and the horizon of eternity, though one of his schedules seems to indicate vaguely the various preparations which ex hypothesi preceded the confection of the alchemical stone. The possibility that the Mortlake philosopher had a hand in the initiation of the Rosicrucian mystery rests, therefore, on clouds, so far as this question is concerned. Philippus Gabella terms himself Philemon Philadelphia R. C., which proves nothing; he makes one reference to the order in his dedicatory remarks, which also comes to nothing. It remains that the Confession of the Fraternity is attached to his discourse, but he shows no knowledge of its claims and no real concern therein. It is unlikely that he was himself a member; it signifies little if he was; it is utterly certain that he is no veil for John Dee, and the fact that the latter was imitated, at some far distance, or his work extended, a few years after his death can carry no consequence to any reasonable mind.

Independently of Monas Hieroglyphica, there have been other inventions and legends working in the same direction, and among them there is a forged treatise in manuscript belonging to the eighteenth century; it pretends that Dee was a Rosicrucian and the author of the brotherhood's laws and statutes. Devices of this kind are numerous; I have met recently with yet another manuscript, transcribed perhaps from some earlier copy and giving a very curious account of the sodality, all put forward under the name of Thomas Vaughan, an English Royalist mystic of the seventeenth century. This pretense is referable to circa 1869. Like several other departments of occult literature, the canon of criticism regarding Rosicrucian books still remains to be established; few departments are more important at their root, but few have a wider environment of external fraud and false seeming; it is, therefore, a matter for temperate satisfaction to have disposed here of one question of pretense.

Many personalities of the late sixteenth and early seventeenth centuries have been sifted in search of the true author of early Rosicrucian documents and the possible headship of the fraternity at that period—the latter, of course, by those who had decided that the whole mystery was not a mere matter of pretense and of jeux d'esprit; an alternative explanation which once at least was favored. The theologian of Wurtemberg, Johann Valentin Andreas, still appears as a possible solution, and he confesses in his autobiography that he was responsible for the Chemical Nuptials of Christian Rosy Cross. He terms it a ludibrium, or jest, and ridicules the grave commentaries which it occasioned; but supposing that he had originated the whole scheme, either as a hoax or an experiment, his reserve subsequently may have been scarcely a matter of choice. I do not believe that the allegorical romance in question was a ludibrixim at all; 1 do not believe that, as stated, he wrote it at the age of sixteen or earlier. It is by no means the work of a boy; and at the period of its publication, in 1616, he was thirty years old, a man of travel and experience, who would not be likely to issue juvenilia which were already of the far past. Moreover, the document in question is the last of a trilogy, and he does not confess to the anterior tracts, namely, the Fama and Confessio Fraternitatis R. C. I think, on the contrary, that he was once at least connected with another secret theosophical society in which we should look for the root-matter of the whole Rosicrucian scheme. It was actually in session within measurable distance of his home at the very period when he claims to have been writing, using its own terminology and reflecting its own subjects. Ibis is as far as it is possible to take a question which, interesting as it is and important not only for the history of esoteric societies but for that of the general secret tradition in Christian times, is a little extrinsic to the purposes of a biographical memorial. It remains only to say that the Latin life of Dee is a memorial of curious admixture; it is by way of being seemingly the work of an austere and critical mind, considering the period, but it is full of uncertain notes and curious confusions. It is dubious but hostile on the claims of astrology; dubious but a little impressed on those of alchemy, and as regards the prolific seership recorded in The Faithful Relation, it challenges this more especially in respect of the angelic source. Mr. Ebenezer Sibley, in his astrological Key to the Occult Sciences, took much the same point of view; and perhaps it is nearer the truth than a gratuitous hypothesis of undiluted imposture based on the common sense which characterizes the crowd. This judges as it best can, but always wrongly, on matters which do not lie outside the immediate contact of the five senses.

SVFFICIT.

N.
MDLX
XXVI
AVG
XVII

O
MDC

IOH VALENTINVS
ANDREÆ

PORTRAIT OF ANDREÆ.

THE TAROT: A WHEEL OF FORTUNE

December, 1909

THIS is not, for once in a way—though it may seem certainly for once only—a study in withdrawn areas of mystical philosophy, nor precisely an investigation of root-matters of symbolism, nor is it even exclusively an account of divination, which in itself would suggest a sufficiently wide departure from my known and admitted concerns. Having thus stated a fact rather than opened out an apologia, I will take up the matter in hand and complete the circle, if necessary, by reverting at the end to the point at which I begin. To the great majority of my readers, I suppose that it will be scarcely necessary to answer, by way of precaution, the hypothetical question: What then is the Tarot? Everyone knows that it is a method of divination by cards, but that the cards which are used for the purpose differ in some important respects from those ordinary playing kinds which are perhaps a good deal more familiar in most homes than the things which used to be called household words. These cards also are used for fortune-telling, and the publishers of The Occult Review have recently issued a certain Manual of Cartomancy, which gives one of the modes of operation among a hundred and one curiosities for the delectation of people with occult predispositions and perhaps some intuitive faculties. The writer of this Manual, who has sufficient grace in his heart to speak of trifles only with becoming seriousness and of grave things as if he knew that strange worlds lie occasionally behind them, has included in his budget of paradoxes a long and recollected section on this very subject of the Tarot. I have myself still more recently prefaced and revised a new edition of The Tarot of the Bohemians, translated into English from the French of Dr. Papus, the head of the school of Martinism at Paris. There is thus once more available a work which had become scarce, and for which many have been looking there and here in the catalogues.

EIGHT OF PENTACLES. (Actual size of Cards.)

It follows that the Tarot is, as people say, in the air; but there is one difficulty with which we have had all to contend in England. It is easy to read about the subject, and if people have the mind, they may become quite learned respecting it, more especially if they are familiar with French; but the cards themselves are not too easily obtainable. They are imported from the continent, which usually produces very indifferent versions in these our modern days, and has just now nothing to offer us but a very inferior Italian pack, which anyone who can be called a student would do well to avoid. A little further afield some pains may secure one of the Etteilla sets, in which, however, the symbolism has been confused by the reveries of the editor, who was firstly a professional cartomancist of his period—being the end of the eighteenth century—but secondly a virtuoso in general occult arts whose zeal was in advance of his discretion and out of all measure in respect of his learning. The Marseilles pack is very much better, but this also is not at the corner of the streets, either in the city which has given it an imprint or in the great center of Paris. Bolognese and Venetian Tarots are mentioned rather than seen.

This being the case, and recurring for a moment to the fact that the Tarot, as I have said, is in the air, while many people who divine—and a substantial minority who are students rather than dippers at random into the chances of fortune—are all in want of the cards, I have embraced an opportunity which has been somewhat of the unexpected kind and have interested a very skillful and original artist in the proposal to design a set. Miss Pamela Coleman Smith, in addition to her obvious gifts, has some knowledge of Tarot values; she has lent a sympathetic ear to my proposal to rectify the symbolism by reference to channels of knowledge which are not in the open day; and we have had other help from one who is deeply versed in the subject. The result, and for the first time on record, is a marriage of art and symbolism for the production of a true Tarot under one of its aspects; it should be understood that there are others, but whatever has transpired about them or is likely to be related hereafter is and can be only concerned with a part of the hidden system and will mislead rather than direct.

The version with which I am concerned is on the eve of publication; this is therefore an advertisement concerning it, and that it may not want for boldness I produce here in their order certain specimen cards, which, on the artistic side, will—I think—speak for themselves. About their meanings a word must be said presently, and to this I will lead up by a few preliminary remarks on the debated origin of the Tarot. It has been referred to India, China, Egypt, which allocations are speculative, and, though presented in the terminology of certitude, they are so much fantasia. No one knows whence it came, unless, by a great dispensation, he happens to have been born in France, where there are high grades of conviction in all that belongs to the province of occultism and its history. It is in this way that the Tarot is called The Book of Thoth, the Book of Thrice Great Hermes, and because the cards themselves did not support the attribution, they have been perfected by late editors and adorned with Egyptian characteristics. The truth is that the intimations of mystery abiding behind the Tarot have suggested too readily the conventional places of mystery; but seeing that secret doctrine—admittedly concealed therein—is of all ages and peoples and climes, remoteness of origin in time and the farthest Orient in place are not indispensable assumptions.

Now, the Tarot has twenty-two Trump-Major cards, which have no analogy with playing cards, and from these I have selected four specimens taken direct from the drawings and naturally much larger than they will appear in the color-printed set. I will speak of these in respect of their higher symbolism. Last or first, as you please, in its own series, is the card which represents Zero and is entitled The Fool. It is in no sense, though it has been so called, a type of humanity as the blind slave of matter, though in the common traffic of fortune-telling it may, and does, stand for extravagance or even for enthusiasm and the folly which its name implies. It is said by Eliphas Levi to signify eternal life; it is a card of the joy of life before it has been embittered by experience on the material plane. On the spiritual plane it is the soul, also at the beginning of its experience, aspiring towards the higher things before it has attained thereto. The first numbered Trump Major, called the Magician, is he on whom "the spark from heaven" has fallen, who draws from above and derives thence to below. Levi says that it is God in His unity and man as a reflection of God; others describe it as the Divine World and the Absolute. It is the card of illumination, and so looks the Fool when he has seen God. The second numbered Trump is the High Priestess, here beautifully depicted, with all her symbolical attributes. She has the solar cross on her breast and the lunar crescent on her head. She is called the House of God, the Sanctuary and even the Kabalah, or secret tradition. She is really the Great Mother and the Secret Church. The last of the Trumps Major which I present here is the nineteenth in the series, and is called the Sun as the symbol of light and revelation. It is the glory of all the worlds. The naked child mounted on the great horse is the complement by antithesis of the thirteenth card—which is Death, also mounted.

My smaller cards are designed to illustrate the Minor Arcana, and I will refer to their divinatory meanings. The King of Wands—ardent, equitable, noble— represents goodness blended with severity. The Queen of Cups signifies love and devotion, the images of which she sees like visions in her vessel. The Knight of Swords is even as Galahad on the Quest, dispersing the enemies thereof. The Page of Pentacles—a youthful figure looking at a talisman, which hovers over his raised hands—really typifies the scholar, but he is also one who bears news. I can hardly mention the remaining numbered cards—the Six of Wands, crowned with hope and confidence; the Five of Cups, which is the card of heritage diverted and life emptied of joy; the Eight of Swords, which means disquietude, conflict, crisis, sometimes fatality; the Nine of Swords, which should be compared with the former; it is the card of disappointment, well-illustrated by the picture.

The meanings attributed to the Trumps Major, or Greater Arcana, when taken, as they usually are, apart from the ordinary numbered and court cards, depend upon the worlds or spheres of consciousness to which particular interpretations have referred them. When they are combined with the Lesser Arcana for purposes of divination, and when thus the pack forms one sequence of seventy-eight cards, each cartomancist has followed his own intuition and observation of results. The gift of second sight overrides conventions and precedents, but for those who do not possess it, or in whom it has not been developed, a summary of accepted meanings is desirable, and this I have sought to supply in the little interpretative work which accompanies the set of cards. The question remains whether there is an integral connection between the Greater and Lesser Arcana, and in this case how to establish their respective offices in higher Tarot symbolism. If, however, their connection is arbitrary, a separation should be effected, the Lesser Arcana being allocated to their proper place in cartomancy and the Trumps Major to their own, which is to seership of another order.

The compiler of the Manual of Cartomancy calls the Tarot the higher way to fortune, and—between the Major and Minor Arcana—if anyone can so interpret it—as he and I do—let me say unto him with the Psalmist: Intende, prospere procede et regna. And so, I return to the question of an apologia, but only to conclude that after all, the Tarot is a research in symbolism; its study is a mystic experiment; and though it has been, is and will be used for divination, it belongs to another realm and began therein. Those who desire to go further will learn how and why in my short Key to the Tarot, which accompanies the set of cards.

WOMAN AND MYSTIC DOCTRINE

December 1910

THE appearance in recent days of a brief but brilliant book on Modern Woman: Her Intentions (Palmer, London, 1910) offers an opportunity to put forward, perhaps for the first time, some considerations which are not of less moment because, legitimately or otherwise, they may scarcely arise therefrom. They are rather an illustration of how certain burning questions strike a contemporary in his detachment. If it should happen that they are in the region of complete antithesis, it may be so much the better for the subject at large. I should make it plain at the beginning, however, that I am not writing a counter thesis, an argument in contradiction, or anything that can be called by way of rejoinder and criticism. Miss Florence Farr's latest work, in its light touch and its paradoxical manner, will remind a good many of the Dancing Faun, published in those days when the Keynote Series spelled the highest expression of advanced thought, and it has attracted a good deal of pleased attention, including something on the part of those who, for all that I know to the contrary, may have a right to speak on the subject. I have no such right, for which reason, but more especially as it is (a) rather necessary to my point of view and (b) something of the matter of duty, I shall begin by presenting in summary the heads of the writer's own considerations, so far as it is possible without direct quotation. Against this I confess to a prejudice, because of its literal nature. In case I should do injustice unwittingly, I recommend the book to at least two classes of readers: (1) to those who being modem women confess to intentions, whether in correspondence or not with those which are understood by Miss Florence Farr; and (2) to those who would like to be instructed by the entertainment which she offers on the subject, though by sex or otherwise they may not enter into the previous category. Fortunately, or the reverse, I suppose that I am in neither class, and I have tried to make it plain otherwise that I am not in the seat of judgment.

The thesis is then as follows. This is to be the woman century, when she is to awake from her sleep and come into her kingdom, being firstly emancipated from the position created for her by Semitic religion and its reflections, the root-matter of which is the story of Adam and Eve and the Fall of Man. The modem woman has for this reason a long score to settle with Jews, Mohammedans and even the Christian dispensation itself. The fact that she has already awakened is shewn by the question of the vote; and the further fact that the vote has been refused is to bring about a great social revolution. The path of her redemption is by independence of the caprice of individual man; in respect of what is called love, it is by the removal of the stigma which now attaches to those who are not capable of lifelong fidelity; it is by the improvement in the marriage state which will follow the realization that it is not respectable for men and women to live together when their tempers are incompatible; it is by the simplification of divorce, when this is wanted on both sides; it is by some amelioration in the financial aspect of married life, by education in the laws of sexual health, and by making the care of mothers a national question. I have not specified every head of the thesis, because some of them might be difficult to discuss in this place, but what I have given is, I think, representative enough.

No one knows better than Miss Farr that her program is quite incommensurate; no one, perhaps in a sense, may take it less seriously than herself. It has given her an opportunity to write a bundle of short papers which are full of clever things. Perhaps she is most serious when she affirms that the whole object of modem civilization is to conceal the fact that we are animals. On the contrary, its whole process has served to cloud and overlay the fact that we are divine, and my own thesis is that until we take this as the point of departure our processes of amelioration for man or woman are foredoomed to failure because they begin at the wrong end.

At the head of her book Miss Farr puts a quotation from W.B. Yeats, who says that "another fire has come into the harp" and that "it has begun to cry out to the eagles." The point is that the eagles do not answer—no, not even in the last resource. But having taken all mysticism for my province, I know that the fire which has come into the harp has begun to cry out to God, as deep unto deep crieth, and I know also that God answers. The hope of womanhood and manhood, the awakening, the redemption and the kingdom do not depend on the simplification of divorce—which, for all that I see or care, may be desirable enough in the world of things as they are. They do not depend on the legitimation of license or the freedom of all the cities of Belial to all the inclinations of sex, though till marriages begin in God, the lesser evil may as well be recognized with the greater. They do not, in fine, depend on the encouragement of incompatibility of temper as a path of escape for distaste. They do depend on the mystic recognition of the sacramental nature and sanctity of that intercourse, which is the outward expression of love within the sexes.

For all that I can advance to the contrary, it may be true that Semitic influence has been a barrier to the liberation of womanhood, but it is just as well that we should know what is the Secret Doctrine of Israel on this exotic subject. I proceed to recite it as follows:

(1) The union which is manifested in Nature is the symbol of a more perfect union. It is designed to build the spiritual palace of love, wherein is the integration of all beings by their attachment to the Mystery of Mysteries. It is the sacrament of the union of all spirits with the Supreme Spirit. It should therefore be fulfilled only in the light of the Mystery of Faith.

(2) The marriages celebrated on earth should be enacted in the likeness of the celestial espousals, wherein the bride is adorned with crowns of light. They are then in the school of illumination; they confer and produce light. They make possible a union which is more than that of the earthly body, and in this sense they are eternal.

(3) When God said, Let there be Light, the word Light signified perfect love, and this is the Divine counsel to those who enter into the wedded state according to the law and the order.

(4) The work is one of continence and purity in the greater understanding of these terms. It is on such continence that the world is based. Happy is the man who guards this quality of purity, for therein he is united to the Holy One.

(5) Marriage is for harmony in the world. The birth of children is thus a work of sanctification, and the Shekinah dwells in the house of a man who is married in this sense.

(6) The mystery of sex is a part of the Great Mystery, but it is inaccessible to ordinary understanding and is therefore called the Mystery of Faith. It is in other words that mystery of love which constitutes the likeness of man to God.

(7) Hence also it is said (a) that the male and female principles must never be separated; (b) that the Holy One chooses not that abode where the male is apart from the female; and (c) that no male is worthy of the name of a man until he is united with the female.

(8) There is another great mystery in the Secret Doctrine concerning the union of man's higher spirit with the Shekinah or Indwelling Glory, of which the union below is an image. When man has in view the Shek-

inah at the moment of his conjugal relations, that which the experiences is meritorious and it redounds to the glory of his celestial companion.

(9) I will add one point more. It is understood throughout in the doctrine that the union of married people must be continued as it is begun by mutual consent, by affection and tenderness, without which it is unsanctified. And as regards the question of equality, or otherwise, between male and female, man is compared to the written word of Scripture and woman to the Secret Doctrine. The doctrine comes out of the written word and does not subsist alone, but the external sense apart from the inward meaning is the body without the life.

It remains to say that the theosophy of Israel is at one with the theosophy of Christian Mysticism as to the deep things implied in the wedded state, and this is why I have cited it at some length.

These things are by way of intimation only, for again, by the necessity of the subject and a certain sacred frankness in the old Zoharic texts, it is difficult to give it full expression in the present place. If, therefore, we compare these rough and undigested notes with the catholic doctrine of marriage, understood mystically, some of my readers may see in what direction the path of redemption lies. It is in the consecration of desire, the exaltation of love to its true place as the manifestation of the Divine in Nature. And if ever the time should come when there can be schools of truly higher thought, where our young men and women can be instructed in the sanctity of human love, I think, in the words of Miss Florence Farr, that the social world will indeed be melted down and remodeled "nearer to the heart's desire." We shall be able to burn Nietsche and the other quackeries about the revaluation of all values; we shall forget Mr. Harold Gorst and his Philosophy of Love—if anyone happens to remember it; and we shall not require the nostrums of someone called Mr. Havelock Ellis, who is probably quite famous, as most people are of whom I refuse to have heard. We shall take part in the nuptial mystery as we take part in the other sacraments, and for ever and ever the outward signs will be transmuted from high to higher by their inward grace. Until then, there are many ways in which the counsels of this little book on Modern Woman may possibly tend to alleviate a situation which they cannot remedy. We have turned the greatest of God's manifest gifts into what proves too often a curse because we have misunderstood its office, and until we recur to the root and begin there, we may go on altering and seeking for betterment, but it will continue to be a curse all the same. For the rest, the intentions of modem woman do not explicitly appear, for which Miss Florence Farr may be felicitated; nor does she tell us what that kingdom is into which woman will come this century. If it is another kingdom of misrule, the change may be welcome; man is sick of the old one as well as woman, and having been done well by now on his one side over the gridiron of things as they are, it may perhaps be a relief to be tinned completely round and done as effectively on the other. It must, of course, be idle to suggest that any especial good is coming out of the woman of the twentieth century until she has been rooted in God; but Miss Farr is much too wise, much too entertaining and too disenchanted by many degrees to hint that there is any particular good in anything. I do not know whether this can be counted to her for righteousness, but it makes her good reading, and that is the chief point about books when their subject does not matter in the ultimate and when the writer has the grace to know it.

This is how it strikes a contemporary in spiritu humilitatis and with a certain sense of dismay at having strayed so far from his proper subjects.

COUNT CAGLIOSTRO AND FREEMASONRY

January, 1911

SO considerable a space was allotted last month in the editorial Notes of the Month to the subject of Joseph Balsamo versus Count Cagliostro that it might be regarded as fairly exhausted at least for the time being. On the question of distinction or identity between the two figures on the stage of history there is no doubt that we have reached a point at which it must be concluded to pause, unless by a happy accident of research we should come upon some further knowledge. There are certain matters, however, which remain over, and it seems desirable to deal with them while the interest is fresh in the memory of readers. They have been enabled to appreciate in a plenary sense the high value which attaches to the recent monograph of Mr. Trowbridge, so far as the personality and adventures of the founder of Egyptian Masonry are concerned. It is now nearly a quarter of a century since, in my edition of the Lives of Alchemistical Philosophers, I published what I believe to have been until the present moment the most extended current biography of Cagliostro in the English language. This was, so to speak, in the days of my youth; it does not happen to have come within the knowledge of Mr. Trowbridge, which signifies nothing, as, if I remember, it was utterly hostile and was based on the authorities till now accepted implicitly. I mention it only because it enables me to add that—then and always—I have regarded the communication or invention of the system called Egyptian Masonry as the point of a new departure in the life of the Magus. When the ultimate verdict is pronounced on the "master of magic," I believe that this part of it, so clearly exhibited by Mr. Trowbridge, will not prove subject to mutation. It was, of course, the opinion of Louis Figuier, whose extended notice of Cagliostro in the Histoire du Merveilleux dans les Temps Modernes has perhaps been taken otherwise somewhat too seriously in the present memoir, as indeed by myself long ago. It is little better than a romantic narrative and might be comparable as such to the work of the Marquis de Luchet rather than that of Mr. Trowbridge. As I am dealing in a sufficiently extended section with the so-called system of Masonic and Egyptian initiation, which claimed to come down from the prophets Enoch and Elias, in my Secret Tradition in Freemasonry, I do not propose to refer to it especially in the present place. It has been misjudged by previous critics, and although it was in no sense Masonic, it had points of decorative interest whereby it may suffer comparison with other occult movements enrolled under the banner of Freemasonry at the close of the eighteenth century.

Well, there are limits to special knowledge and first-hand research in nearly all the departments, and considering the real contribution to our acquaintance with Cagliostro contained in the volume under notice, I suppose that the author will be excused beforehand if in the accessory matters, he remains open to correction. He will also understand the spirit in which I approach his work from this point of view. It has been indicated that his familiarity with occultism in the eighteenth century leaves much to be said and something here and there which calls for restatement. A few of the more important points I ask leave to specify. Mr. Trowbridge, in the first place, is evidently not a Freemason, and he does not seem to realize the absurdity of the Courier de l'Europe when it spoke of Cagliostro's initiation in London by the alleged Espérance Lodge together with his wife. Whether such a Lodge existed at the period I do not know; that, if so, it was affiliated with the Rite of the Strict Observance I do not believe; but there neither was then nor is now any warranted Lodge in England which would have received a woman, and the Strict Observance was the last Masonic obedience in the universe against which the accusation could be brought. From other sources

Mr. Trowbridge has derived many errors of fact in respect of L.C. de Saint-Martin, and should question whether he has consulted any authority posterior to Matter. He can never have seen Des Erreurs et de la Vérité, the first work of the mystic, published in two vols., demy 8vo, pp. 230 and 236, or he could scarcely describe it as "a strange little book." He can neither have seen nor read Saint Martin's later writings, or he could not have seriously said that Liberty, Equality and Fraternity were the sacred triad of the mystic. He can know nothing of his life or his attitude towards external secret societies, or be would not have perpetuated the old illusion that Saint-Martin established a Masonic Rite and above all a Rite of Swedenborg, about whom he has left a very definite statement of opinion. He would not in fine have called him the founder of the Martinists; that is another fiction which has been exploded long ago.

Similar exception must be taken to every Rosicrucian reference which occurs in the memoir. The adepts of this dubious brotherhood did not revolutionize belief in the supernatural; their first manifesto did not claim to have been found in the tomb of Christian Rosenkreutz; the so-called doctrine of elementary spirits was the least part of their concern, the Abbé de Villars being responsible in the Comte de Gabalis for the importance ascribed to it a century and a half later; they did not regard the Philosopher's Stone as signifying contentment; and their alleged impostures in no sense led up to the Masonic Convention of Willhemsbad. At that period, they were working under a Masonic aegis and their secret Rituals are in my possession.

Lastly, in respect of Alchemy, if Mr. Trowbridge in his brief review and in his casual references to this subject had made his starting-point the collection of Byzantine, Syriac and Arabian Alchemists, published by Berthelot, he would have given us a more informed account, and the allusion to Gebir would not have appeared in its present form. The fact that there was a mystical as well as a physical school in Alchemy would still have escaped him, but this is an involved subject and beyond the scope when a consideration is so wholly inexpress.

I have indicated already that these things, and others like them, are by the way and without prejudice to the major interest -of the memoir. Mr. Trowbridge does not, perhaps, claim to have determined once and for all that Cagliostro was not Joseph Balsamo, and, accepting the distinction between them, he does not present his subject in a better light than that of an impostor with a cast of seriousness, some elementary psychic powers, and several good qualities with which he has not been credited previously. We have to thank him for a book which has cleared the issues substantially, and though I hold no brief except for the condemnation of all things included by the conventional name of Magic, it is satisfactory to know that one of its most celebrated masters was by no means so black as he has been painted.

WILLIAM SHARP AND FIONA MACLEOD: TWO ASPECTS OF PERSONALITY

February, 1911

I N the life of William Sharp, written by the one person—for there is indeed no other—who could tell it from first to last, there is for my present purpose scarcely anything to extract of the formal biographical kind. He was born in 1855 and died in his fifty-first year at the end of 1905. Fiona Macleod came into manifestation within him in 1893. I shall assume that my readers are less or more acquainted with his literary career on the acknowledged side and with the fact that the true authorship of Pharais and the Dominion of Dreams, with other books which are dear to the hearts of many, became public only after his death.

The distinction of his two literary sides is that of the man and the woman in literature, but it so happens that in the present instance, the feminine was the greater and more real side. There is therefore more to explain than arises from, and is explicable by, the recognized truth that the poet, psychically speaking, has the two senses within him.

When William Sharp became Fiona Macleod, it is clear to those who have eyes that he did not assume a pseudonym as one takes up and puts down a mask, or adopts, after considerable toil, a concealed style of handwriting. When I say that he became her I think that the essence of truth escapes in the expression, though for want of a better form I have put it tentatively like this. One alternative is to speak of dual personality, but I am more certain that this is untrue and, from my point of view, as a mystic is not short of mischievous. The case is not to be explained by the crude experiences, which are called spirit control; by the obscure embryonic state recognized in the so-called reincarnation of Kabalism; by the inspirations of an angel guide; or by the notion of a feminine complement on another plane. The fact is that we are in the presence of a problem which in one sense is psychic and in another lies deeper than the psychic nature. It is a question of the opening of a door in consciousness, as a result of which another side of the one nature may occasionally manifest. We have most of us met with this in certain individuals and up to a certain point, but we have not found it previously in literature. The case of William Sharp seems to standalone therein, and he has an abiding interest on this account. It offers in literature a very curious illustration of the psychic life, but there is very little to account for it along ordinary lines of psychology. In his childhood he was dreamy, imaginative, with a love of wandering, and there was a wild part of him, as if he were a pilgrim from the sun striving to escape the restraint of earthly conventions. I saw him at his middle period, when he was writing against time for his life and leading the ordinary life of literary journalism, qualified by occasional literature. But it was not under this aspect that one got to know him really, because, as I have said, it was his lesser part. The other side of him was greater, because it had not been with him except sub-consciously in the mill of his daily life. There is a part in all of us which stands outside the diurnal round and has not been wearied thereby, but a few only enter into the realization concerning it.

It is evident that William Sharp thought in his heart that Fiona Macleod was in some sense "the true inward self." The intimation was in no sense correct, and of this he was in part aware. He spoke alternatively of something that had breathed to him or had awakened him, of something that he remembered or that was lurking within him. None of the descriptions satisfied him, and this is why they are rather numerous. Mrs. Sharp, speaking her own language, recognizes a third self which lay behind the dual expression, but she calls it the "psychic quality of seership," and this is also incorrect. The inner self which lies behind all our forms of expression is the part which watches them all and is yet none of them. It is neither male nor female; it is the part which knows. It is that which can and does say to us in certain high mystic states: I am the resurrection and the life; I am Alpha and Omega; behold I am alive for evermore. In his later life, William Sharp passed through periods of illness which took him into cosmic states. He who had been on the hills of heather lay on his bed of sickness, but was "in the greater and freer universe," or rather that universe had opened up some part of itself within him. Nature had also nourished him in many ways, and he had been nourished on the food of the faerie. He had the sense of the infinite and realized the conscious presence of the eternal Goodness. He had also the inner life of dream and vision; he saw the white ladies and the nature spirits. The sense of these things was put to sleep in the working world of literature till it awakened to a fuller being in Fiona Macleod. Of this awakening, I should have no space to speak, supposing that the need arose; most of us are acquainted with the books and the eloquent messages therein. It is as if all that was best in the Celtic spirit had entered into a new life; it was as if the voice of womanhood were being heard after a new manner. The response to it was immediate and wide.

WILLIAM SHARP.

As Fiona Macleod of necessity dwelt in a world of mystery, being heard but not seen, the speculations were great concerning her, and she was identified many times by people who thought that they knew, but it was never dreamed that her veil concealed the personality of a man.

The idle chorus of reviewers thought that Fiona Macleod was wondrous till they found at the end of all that she was also William Sharp. They said then: after all; it is only Sharp. They had proved to be wrong at the beginning, which made the idle chorus not unnaturally angry. They were much more wrong afterwards, but this time they will not know Fiona Macleod was not the William Sharp who wrote for The Academy and something called The Athenæum, or for that Young Folks' Budget which first enabled Stevenson to testify concerning himself. It is just this that the chorus is not qualified to understand. But there are some of us who, on our part, do know exactly why Fiona Macleod was not William Sharp and why, which is for the same reason, when we remember William Sharp, we shall say always: Yes, he was Fiona Macleod. God keeps green among us the memory of the man who had so much of such a woman within him.

Let me add in conclusion one word of cordial recognition in respect of Elizabeth Sharp, who has done her labor of love in a manner which is excellent from all points of view. Her reward will no doubt be with her in many ways.

THE VEIL OF ALCHEMY

March, 1911

I SHOULD perhaps begin by saying that the Veil with which I am concerned is not only one of the most deeply inwoven of those which have been held to cover the mysteries of secret knowledge, but that it is also triple in its character. In other terms, the records of the literature present Alchemy under three analogical aspects. One of them embodies the Hermetic doctrine concerning the macrocosm and its development. It is therefore a department of transcendental philosophy and does not as such pass into experience with the adept, except in so far as the physical work of Alchemy in the transmutation of metals is, by the hypothesis, an exact pattern and reproduction of the unfoldment from within which took place in the work of creation. The so-called Hermes Trismegistos, saluted as father of sages, affirms in The Emerald Table that the art is true, without any shadow of falsehood, is true indeed above all things, and that after the self-same manner the world was made. The fundamental correspondence is developed curiously by numerous writers and might be extended still further than the adepts seem to have carried it. It rests literally on the text of Genesis, which opens, however, by affirming the creation or making of heaven and earth—thus presupposing an antecedence when these were not—and it is obvious therefore at the beginning that the strict correspondence is stultified, because the First Matter—which constitutes the initial mystery in Alchemy—is not of the adept's making.

PORTRAIT OF HENRY KHUNRATH.

The knowledge concerning it is either the gift of God by a sudden illumination, as the reward of toil and the zeal of a right spirit, or it is transmitted by one who knows. Among the cryptic doctrines concerning it, there is the affirmation of its identity with the primordial matter out of which the world was formed. The authority in chief is the text already quoted, which says that all things whatsoever have come forth from One by the mediation of one, according to the mode of adaptation. If I may somewhat interpret the analogy, it follows therefore that on the threshold of adeptship God created in the elect alchemist that knowledge of the First Matter which is necessary to the work of the wise, and the alchemist perceived at once that it was an earth which was without form and void, immersed also as if in the primeval waters. Having few concerns as an exponent of the physical side, I do not attempt to indicate at what stage he assumed on his own part a species of demiurgic work, so that his experimental spirit moved like that of God over the face of the waters and his operations became as a formulation of light in the darkness. Nor does the process which took place in his vessel itself concern us. It is enough that the analog followed the path indicated till the cosmos was produced in that vessel as it was produced at the term of creation in the greater world—a perfect work of Nature and of Art. It is thus summarized in part by the rare Latin tract entitled Cato Chemicus: (a) In creation there was firstly the confused chaos, without distinction of anything, and a similar confusion in the philosophical work hinders the discernment of the matter; (6) But as there were earth and water in the greater world, so there are dry and humid in the chaos of adepts; (c) There is also a night of great darkness in the vessel, the appearance of which is, however, a cause of joy, as a sign of progress in the work; (d) After such darkness there came light in creation, which answers to the White State of the Stone supervening after the Black State; (e) But the sun was in fine created, to which corresponds the Red State of the Stone, and this is the desire of our eyes.

I have described here two analogical veils of the Hermetic subject. The third is that of the microcosm, understood as the human being, and to discern the nature of this veil, we must approach another form of the symbolism, forgetting our analogy between the work on metals and the work in creation. It is now the question of a medicine which can be administered to metals and to man. This medicine is the same at the root but not in the mode of production, though the loose terminology of the literature seems often to identify them too closely. The philosophical analogy is found, under a certain distinction, in the traditional doctrine of the Fall. This is not to say that the inferior metals, which it is the design of Alchemy to transmute, were once gold and have degenerated from that state of perfection. The intent of Nature was always to produce gold, but owing to imperfection in the media through which Nature works, it has often failed in the design. The operation of the Fall of man corresponds roughly to the imperfection of media in the metallic kingdom. Again, the relation is fantastic, but it serves a certain purpose. There is a way of saving the metals and raising them to a perfect state, and this kind of medicine signifies the successive operations in the performance of the Great Work. There is the Medicine of the First Order, which is the separation and purification of the elements; it is followed by that of the Second Order, which is a process of fermentation and conjunction; there is lastly the Medicine of the Third Order, which is a method of multiplication. The first is a work of Nature, the second of Art and the third of Art and Nature in the marriage thereof. There is a tract entitled Libellus de Alchymia which may be consulted for the process of the work; it is attributed to Albertus Magnus, the great master of the greater St. Thomas Aquinas, and is actually included in the collected edition of his works which was published in the seventeenth century. Its authenticity is, of course, doubted and is indeed dubious enough.

PORTRAIT OF ST. THOMAS AQUINAS.

To his pupil, the angel of the schools, there is also ascribed a Thesaurus Alchymice, which is certainly spurious, but it is interesting as a summary memorial respecting the transmutation of metals and maintains that the work of their redemption is accomplished in a single vessel, by one mode and with one substance. According to the Hermetic doctrine, the body of man also can be saved from disease and raised to a state of perfection which corresponds to that of gold in the metallic kingdom. The Medicine in this form is called Elixir par excellence, Potable Gold, and Medicine of the Superior Order. It prolongs life to the furthest limits, but the true adepts do not say that it confers immortality. This is rather the intervention of romanticism extending the horizon of the texts for its own objects. It is also the claim attributed to adventurers like Cagliostro and to mysterious personalities after the manner of Comte de Saint-Germain. It is inconceivable and yet true that there are persons at the present day who take these claims seriously.

Now, it is out of this hypothesis concerning the Medicine of Men that the mystical side of Alchemy more especially arises. The new life of the body, the youth renewal, the suggestion of immortality in the physical part are phases of a dream on the external side and a reflection of that which takes place within as a result of those processes with which transcendental religion is concerned. This consanguinity is recognized indifferently by the physical alchemists and by those who seem to have been concerned only with the spiritual work. The preparation of the philosophical Magistery is in analogy with the work of regeneration, and the state of divine beatitude in the arch-natural part of man, with the vision and the union therein, is symbolized by the perfect Stone. This also in the metallic region corresponds to the office of the Holy Eucharist, which imparts a Divine tincture to the spirit of man as the tingeing Stone of Alchemy multiplies the gold of the sages and communicates its glorious state to all prepared substances. Hence, it is said that the operation of the Stone is "a certain metaphysical work, not a work of words but real, not doctrinal but experimental." And this is the truth concerning it on the mystical side—a work of experience in the spirit of man for the attainment—at the end of our separation as individual beings—of a Divine Union with the one and eternal nature. Some of the most curious intimations concerning mystical Alchemy are in The Amphitheatre of Eternal Wisdom, by Henry Khunrath, a poor and obscure student who died in 1601, aged about forty-five years, leaving his work unfinished, so far as the description of the plates is concerned, and these unfortunately are the most important part of the work. As an exponent of the Hermetic doctrine of analogy, he believed in the physical Stone but was concerned with the mystic side. He delineates the process as follows:—(a) Purification of the personal part, that we may come to see God. (b) The closing of the avenues of sense, stillness of soul, sanctification, illumination, tincture by the Divine Fire, (c) Hereof is the path of attainment for the Stone of the Philosophers, (d) which Stone is the living Spirit of the Elohim and (e) the out-breaking of Jehovah, the Divine Power, the Word of God in Nature. (f) That Word is made flesh, so to speak, in the virginal womb of the greater world and (g) is manifested as Jesus, in the virginal womb of Mary, but also (h) in the soul of man as a light super-added to that of Nature; hereby the knowledge of God and His Christ is communicated. I have spoken very briefly here of a great and important literature.

I may add that it is a matter for satisfaction that Alchemy on the external or material side has been taken over of recent days by a practical chemist, Mr. H. S. Redgrove, who has given us a sane and enlightened review of the subject in his work entitled Alchemy, Ancient and Modern. He is alive to the main issues, including the mystical aspect, and it is by collaboration of this kind that the desired canon of criticism in respect of the literature will be established ultimately. I do not know much of the outlook otherwise, save in respect of France, where there is an Alchemical Society, the efforts of which were once mentioned courteously by Berthelot. To judge, however, by the work of its Secretary-General, F. Jollivet de Castelot, there is no especial encouragement. He establishes a ridiculous program, some heads of which may be given for the entertainment of my readers. It is entitled Comment on devient Alchimiste, and the postulant in the path of Hermeticism is invited to take notice— on the assumption that he is also a Frenchman—that the true adept, as the son of Hermes, is always a royalist, while the Fleur de-lys, which is the apanage of Mgr. le duc d'Orléans, expresses (a) the doctrine of analogy and (b) the relation between macrocosm and microcosm. Qualified after this manner in the political sense, he may begin the study of the Tarot, which throws great light on chemical combinations. He must cultivate a certain status of the moral kind, but it is conveniently relaxed in respect of the sixth commandment and does not insist on marriage. He should cultivate the psychic faculties and practice magic, for he must be a magus before an alchemist. He should also play the violin, but I am not sure that this counsel is peremptory. A study of the texts is not unnaturally enjoined, but those which are most recommended are the work of contemporary writers belonging to the same school. They do not know the First Matter or the process of the Art—these Marinist's and Rosicrucian's of Paris—but they testify one of another; they cleave one to another, and they have a stock of admiration in common which belongs to the heroic degree.

PORTRAIT OF ALBERTUS MAGNUS.

LAMPS OF CHRISTIAN MYSTICISM

May, 1911

JOHN RUSKIN recognized seven Lamps of Christian Architecture; very sacred and wonderful things he wrote under this title concerning shrines of the western world built to the glory of God in the highest. The lesser lights of homes and temples and palaces are as the sands of the sea and beautiful as the names of God. So also, there are great Lamps of Christian Mysticism, but I should assume that they are twelve at least, rather than seven—twelve signs of grace and sanctity, with that Sun which is Christ in the center. So again, there are lesser Lamps of Mysticism, and yet are they great beacons, shining over the pure heights of the written word, and thereby are we led to the deep meanings of the unspoken word within. Between the greater and lesser, the path of the higher salvation can be missed as little in the dark night of the soul as it can in the summer solstice; and for those who can see in the heart there seems scarcely an undisclosed secret concerning the life which is hidden with Christ in God. I know not whether I am called in the present place to enumerate by name those twelve apostles of the splendor who have walked in the light of experience rather than that of faith. The personalities in the long line of illumination and consummate sanctity are passing before me as I write, and now it seems that such a numbering is arbitrary, or that it speaks with eloquence only of special predilection. If I did myself better justice, perhaps I should rather say that I can classify only as the lights have shone to myself: to others there might be another shining, another appealing list—which I should be the last to disparage. To me the Divine brilliance seems to shine more especially above and within the following talismanic names: Dionysius, Erigena Johannes, St. Bernard, St. Thomas Aquinas, Ruysbroeck, Hugo of St. Victor, his successor and pupil, Richard of the same chapel, St. Francis of Assisi, the English author of The Cloud of Unknowing, Suso, St. Bonaventure, and—no, the twelfth shall be, for the time being at least, an undeclared quality of efficacious grace. I had nearly written the great Chancellor Gerson, but he did not understand Ruysbroeck, and there was the burning of John Huss. There shall be no one integrated in the line of the Christ-tradition, according to my numbering, who has caused or suffered the persecution of others, whether for justice' sake or for something called right thinking in the matter of official doctrine. And, by God's grace, this reminds me that as there are sheep which are not of this fold, so there are lights of Christian Mysticism which are called false in the institutes of orthodox theology: Eckart, Molinos—I will not give another list—but the Master knows where His lamps are hung in the wilderness, and so do those who have seen in the light of their shining. There is a string of lamps in my hand at the present moment, which have been trimmed up anew and honorably by Mr. Thomas Baker, and I am writing these words that those who should know may learn how they are ready to their need in a fair form, or even as a garland of light. John Ruysbroeck, admirable and divine doctor, shines among my greater names, and is of such quality that he can be put for a moment in apposition with Santa Teresa, the "undaunted daughter of desire." There is something in Ruysbroeck which we can find elsewhere only with great rareness. He is on the side of white light—calm and clear and steady—while St. Teresa is on the side of fire. As he draws very little from authorities outside Scripture itself, so he seems to speak and write with no enchaining sense of an external and official rule, to which he must ever defer. He is humility and submission and obedience, as if these virtues had taken flesh beneath his monastic gown, but they are things implied or presupposed: they are not, so to speak, enforced; they are not paraded. But I am telling of him at his best and highest. The characteristic of St. Teresa is so much in the other scale, that if in ways so divine as those which were trodden by her it can be said that the soul grows tired, then her iterations of submission are wearisome. She has written her life with her own consecrated hands, but she is afraid that her nuns will not be permitted to see it, so she writes thereafter immediately The Way of Perfection, and is no more certain of its fate. Her directors, her advisors, her censors, her ecclesiastical enemies at need, are men of learning and sanctity whom she does not tire of praising.

THE BLESSED JOHN RUYSBROECK.

Arthur Edward Waite - Forgotten Essays: Book First

Their names spell nothing to me, and by explicit intention I shall never learn concerning them; but one is haunted by a rebellious conviction that not one of them was worthy to loose the latchet of her shoe. When, however, she rises out of these clouds of a time terrible in Spain, you begin to see after what manner her way of perfection is a most sure and perfect way.

Saint Teresa

It was written for her cloistered nuns in a convent of St. Joseph; but here is a school in which we can all be nuns, my readers, whether we are male or female, in, virginity, espousals or widow¬hood; whether we are men on change—perchance as one and more of you—or a Writer—like me—of essays and books without end, in which I have forgotten for a moment if the grace of God and His union are not mentioned on every page. It does not matter if some or most must read her at this day from another standpoint than that of her own exactly, and so retell her thesis in their language; we may come notwithstanding to be as those who, having received divine favors, do "desire to be where they will no longer taste of them by sips." It is remarkable how much the treatise contains for any and all the followers of the inward life, including those who are outside the Latin communion. I must not, however, be misconstrued; it is for beginners with a good intent rather than for those who are advanced; it is somewhat hindered by the saint's perpetual self-depreciation; it is not perhaps to be characterized as a great spiritual work, though perfect after its own manner. It is what the old writers would have called "exceeding profitable" for those who stand at the gate of the life of God in the soul. The editorial work of Father Francis Zimmerman has been done with admirable and zealous care.

Of the Admirable Ruysbroeck, it was said by Dionysius the Carthusian: (a) that he was the Divine Doctor; and (b) that he had no teacher but the Holy Ghost. And Surius, who translated Ruysbroeck into flowing, too intelligible Latin of the schools, bore witness that every word was a work of salvation: it was God alone who spoke, said Surius. Now he who was thus glorified by generations near to his own is held up to our contemplation in Reflections from the Mirror of a Mystic almost through a glass and darkly. The little book is rendered from the French of Ernest Hello, who was a mystic of his own day, being somewhere midwise or later in the nineteenth century. His compilation was based on the Latin of Surius, not on the Flemish originals, and that which is offered to us in English represents the wisdom of Ruysbroeck when it has passed through successive alembics of three languages. I am no Flemish scholar and have, therefore, no right to speak, except by the way of inference on the bare question of likelihood. But Maeterlinck said of Hello's selection that it had been disfigured by the operation of even the second alembic, and that, albeit admirable in its way, it did not contain more than three or four passages reproduced in their entirety. We must conclude that in the form before us it gives only intimations of Ruysbroeck, but they are beautiful and arresting. If it could be shown that the Flemish mystic had evaporated utterly, seeing that he remains elsewhere, I should still cleave to this little Mirror on its own merits. I do not care what saint is shining therein so that it is, what it is truly, a pure and high light of sanctity.

Let it be read, therefore, by the postulants of the beautiful house and the mystic temple, and they will find that their reward is with them. They shall hear therein concerning the most holy and unsearchable life; of integration in the abyss of Divinity, by contemplation of the royal road, which is that of the most perfect resemblance and most blissful union; of the possession of our own essence in the depths of our own being; of the individual spirit's enjoyment of God in that depth of very ownness; of the liberty of the naked spirit, which is above reason; and further, concerning that liberty, when the simple eye beholds, in the Divine Light, whatever God is; of the knowledge therein, which is without mode or form; of the state that is beyond this state and is the free ascent of the infinite heights of God, in a naked love; but further concerning the state of naked love, wherein the spirit is united to God above reason and virtue, beyond all forms and images.

Whether this should be called truly the essence and marrow of Ruysbroeck could be shown at a later time, did the need arise, by reference to his proper writings. Meanwhile, in a Medieval Mystic, those who would know of his life can learn at large. The writer of this interesting memorial has forgotten or ignored the translation of Maeterlinck, which appeared in English long before the selection published under the name of Mr. Earle Baillie. The point is not important; as to the narrative, it is, of course, delightful from the subject and has merit in its own simplicity; but the account of Ruysbroeck's writings has been done to better purpose by Maeterlinck and, as I have intimated, is available otherwise.

There are shining names in English Christian Mysticism, but in that which can be said of them at their highest, they do not emerge at the highest except in a single case. The Unknown Lamp, who is the author of The Divine Cloud stands at the apex of the literature, and there is a distance almost immeasurable between his light and the beacons set up by Richard Rolle of Hampole or Juliana of Norwich. Both are in the annals of holiness, and The Form of Perfect Living has many memorable utterances—as, for example, regarding some vanities of the ascetic way; the middle path therein; and the ascent to the Spouse. It is also a wise counsel that we should not be worse than we seem; and it is truth of very truth that He Who is Ordainer of all things suffers, not that our sleep be without reward to us, if we "dress our life to His will." This is the sense in which it is divinely said that He giveth His beloved sleep. That sleep is love: give us, therefore, the sweetness in the heart of the love without end, that we may sleep in Him.

Hereof are the lights which I have drawn from my cluster of Lamps at a special moment and in a certain mood of records, but I have touched here and there only, as one who dips his fingertips in a well of water; it is a free water of life; I should end, for those who can hear me, with: Taste and see.

ST. CATHERINE OF SIENA

August, 1911

I SUPPOSE that there is no form of verbal symbolism which is so profound and so full of pitfalls as that which describes (a) the union between Christ and the Church in terms of the bond in wedlock between Bridegroom and Bride; (b) the union between. Christ and the individual soul in the imagery of earthly espousals; and (c) the Divine Union, which is the term of mystic life, as the mystic marriage par excellence. The latest biographer of St. Catherine of Siena has elected to salute the great character-in-chief of her narrative as the Mystic Bride; the title is correct, and this perfectly, according to the mind of that Church which keeps the records of the experience and of its analogues without number; to myself, it is also useful, by the accident of things, as it provides an opportunity to offer certain reflections which may not be without practical interest as a clearance of issues on the general subject.

Catherine Benincasa, who was born in 1347 and died in 1380, had two especial experiences, one of which was the marriage in question, and the other her reception of the stigmata. Both furnish points of difference from recurring instances well known to everyone in the annals of sanctity. Of the second I shall not speak, partly because it was an episode of purely inward vision, partly because it has little relation to the mystic subject. As regards the espousals, it is necessary to make a distinction before considering the case in point, and for this purpose I must be permitted to vary the tabulation which, following the authorities, I have just made above. For the school of which I am a spokesman there are two mystic marriages, one of which is celebrated in this life, while the other may be begun here but is only completed hereafter. To make use of accepted terminology, the first is the union of our psychic and spiritual part, and is a state of consciousness irradiated by the light and grace of the Christ-life. This description must be understood, however, as approximate to the truth rather than truth exact; it would require a considerable thesis to justify a less simple but more precise form of expression. The second is the ineffable union of the spirit with God; it is the only real and eternal mystic marriage. That of St. Catherine belongs to neither class; it was a matter of psychic vision, and it took place at the beginning of her spiritual life. What it secured to her was the presence of a teacher at need, of a guide in the likeness of Christ, who said that he was the Eternal Truth. He came to confirm her in the faith to which she belonged, and for her better assurance he appeared in the vestments and carrying the other insignia of that sovereign pontiff at Rome who was for her, in express terminology, the Christ on earth. He was that no less when—in virtue of the warrants which she held direct from her Divine Master—she was offering him religious and even moral instruction; when she was denouncing his worldly policy; when she was recommending his retirement from the papacy because his hesitation and delay imperiled the cause which she championed. He was that no less when he or his successor used her as the tool of his statecraft and closed the public side of her mission in comparative failure.

Let us look, however, somewhat more closely into the question of the marriage. Mrs. Aubrey Richardson has a few quickening sympathies with the spiritual side of a nature like that of St. Catherine, some little hindrance of worldly wisdom and shrewd sense notwithstanding; but she has nothing of the mystic consciousness, and the distinctions with which I am concerned are quite outside her categories. She understands—perhaps for this reason—and has expressed exactly the particular set of sentiments which led her heroine to insist on a celibate life. The root of it was that Catherine was "in rebellion against the notion of her personality being butchered to make a sultan-bridegroom's holiday." The feeling went back far into her life, for, at the age of six years, getting to know in some unrealized way that there was the bride of heaven and also the bride of earth, she had prayed to the Virgin that her Son might be the Spouse of her soul and had promised on her own part that she would receive none but Him.

The experience of her spiritual bridal took place at the close of a certain time of carnival. In answer to her prayers, fasting and other austerities, the Lord Christ appeared to her and said that, because of her denials and macerations—but not explicitly, be it observed, because she had renounced earthly marriage—He had determined to espouse her soul to Him in faith. It was a ceremony of great pomp, performed amidst a concourse of the blessed, including Mary the Mother of God, St. John of Patmos and—somewhat out of expectation—David the king and psalmist. A ring set with earthly gems was placed on her finger by the Bridegroom, with the words: "Behold I have espoused thee to Me, thy Maker and Savior, in faith, which shall continue in thee from this time forward, evermore unchanged, until the time shall come of a blissful consummation in the joys of heaven."

THE ECSTASY OF ST. CATHERINE.
By Domenico Beccafumi. Preserved in the Accademia Siena.

Mrs. Richardson says, with the best simplicity: "The vision disappeared and the ring also," but the maid always "beheld the sacred emblem on her finger," though it was only discerned spiritually.

It would serve no purpose to examine alternative hypotheses concerning the nature of this experience. I register my personal conclusion that, in the more inward world, it was true and real after its own kind, for St. Catherine was, all things considered, the sanest saint on earth. She appears to have distinguished roughly, among her many psychic happenings, those which were merely the formulated images of her own thoughts. This was of another order, and, as I have intimated, her Guide, her Teacher, her Friend, was thenceforward continually near her. With her He paced the cell, with her He recited the psalms, and at a later stage, in reply to her prayer that He should create a clean heart within her, He removed it altogether and two days later substituted His own in its place.

But now as to the tests of value in respect of the teaching which she received. As an example, in the doctrinal order—and I think that this will suffice—she was told that the smallest offence against Him Who is the Infinite Good—being the speaker, ex hypothesi—calls for an infinite satisfaction. Here is the old stereotyped theological argument for eternal punishment, but carried to its final issue, since it swallows up the distinction between venial and mortal sin. As regards the Church and its ministers, it was impressed upon her (a) that those in religion have been placed where they are "to announce My word" in doctrine and in truth; (b) that the Religious Orders have been founded by the Holy Spirit; (c) that "I do not wish any temporal lord to be their judge"; (d) that they are the "anointed ones" appointed "to serve Me, the Eternal God." It is too easy to see from what recesses of Catherine's nature this voice issued. It was not, in my judgment, hallucination; it was not arch-deception; it was of those who speak at the psychic gates, who utter great things on occasion—even high things and holy—but for some reason are always in mask. The channel of the recipient's personality may be itself the veil.

It should be mentioned, as another illustration, that after the exchange of hearts—after and not before—St. Catherine entered upon that public and, so to speak, political life in which her capacity was shown so strongly. Here I can only glance at it to establish a single point. The mission was two-fold: (a) the removal of the papacy from Avignon to Rome, and (b) the consolidation of the temporal power by another Crusade. That these projects were near to the heart of Christ let those affirm who dare. She secured the one, but that which she most hoped for did not follow therefrom. The other scheme came, as it deserved, to nothing, and in the alternative event it would not have encompassed its object. In the course of her activities, the Divine Heart which she carried—by the assumption—within her, fell into a few errors of extravagance, of duplicity even, of believing that the end justified the means; but as it follows that what dictated such policy was only the eager, too zealous, human heart of Catherine, there is no need to dwell on these things.

'. CATHERINE IN ECSTASY, AFTER RECEIVING THE STIGMATA.
From Razzi's Fresco, San Domenico, Siena. Lent by Mr. Y. Werner Laurie.

Arthur Edward Waite - Forgotten Essays: Book First

Of her native purity of intention, utterly impersonal detachment and singleness of purpose, there is and can be no question. There can be none also that she was an important political figure for a few years, and one of great astuteness. That which followed in failure did follow not by fault of hers, but because there was greed, insincerity and the craft which is not statesmanship on the other side.

And now in recurrence towards the chief point with which I am concerned in this notice; from any study of the life of St. Catherine, it is clear that she was a most holy woman in herself, and deservedly a popular saint; but she was not a mystic, and she had little conception as to the real nature of the Divine Union. She was a true daughter of the Church of power temporal, and she made the grave mistake of believing that the kingdoms of this world were the rightful appanage of him who claimed to hold the keys of the Kingdom of Heaven. Perhaps if she had served less zealously the power, spiritual and otherwise, of the papacy, she might have been more truly the bride of Christ. She was a woman on occasion of high, clear and convincing insight belonging to the spiritual-intellectual order; she was also a woman of psychic visions and communications, which were characteristic of her period. Her literary remains are of unimpeachable value as records of greatness in womanhood, and this statement is with especial reference to her correspondence. The belief that earthly marriage is inimical to the mystic marriage is another characteristic of her place and time: the first should be a path to the second. Whether she herself might have become a spouse of heaven had she been a wedded wife on earth is another question; but it does not really arise because she was not on the path of the union. She was on that of the joys of Paradise or of the Beatific Vision in its secondary sense. There is for this reason, a specific misconception about her title of the Mystic Bride, but it must be condoned because it is inevitable. Presumably I need not add that the nuptial state on earth is seldom entered now, and was perhaps more seldom then, in the spirit which may lead to realization on the planes within. Had Catherine met with a man like unto herself as a woman, there might have been one of those marriages over which earth and heaven would have rejoiced.

I conclude that a holy maiden in the early ecstasies of prayer and the ascetic life does not attain to the true mystic espousals, nor does bachelor, wife or husband. It is a high prize at the end of a long journey. But there are certain substitutes, and some also of these are in the path of sanctity.

FINIS

AUTHOR AND MANAGING EDITOR

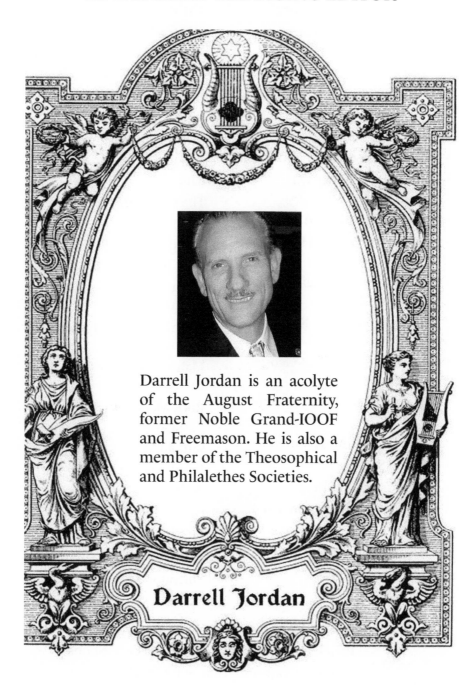

Darrell Jordan is an acolyte of the August Fraternity, former Noble Grand-IOOF and Freemason. He is also a member of the Theosophical and Philalethes Societies.

Darrell Jordan

BOOKS BY THE AUTHOR

- Illustrations of Masonry
- Surviving Document of the Widow's Son
- The Undiscovered Teachings of Jesus
- The Initiates
- Jefferson's Bible
- Master Masons Handbook
- Forgotten Essays - W.L. Wilmshurst
- Forgotten Essays - A. E. Waite
- Forgotten Essays - H. Stanley Redgrove
- The Writings of Sigismond Bacstrom M.D.
- Forgotten Essays – Reincarnation
- Masonic Writings of George Oliver
- Masonic Lectures by Wellins Calcott
- The Fellowcraft Handbook
- Secret Societies
- Vibration and Life
- Key to the Rosicrucian Characters
- The Revelation of John
- Life and the Ideal
- The Mystic Key
- The Philosophical History of Freemasonry
- The Magic of the Middle Ages
- Musings of a Chinese Mystic
- The Life of the Soul
- Christian Mysticism
- Krishna and Orpheus
- The Eleusinian Mysteries & Rites
- The Crucifixion Letter
- You Paid What?
- The Illustrated Pioneer History of the America
- Montana Freemasons 19th Century
- Washington Freemasons 19th Century
- Idaho Freemasons 19th Century
- Rock Metaphysics
- Emblems: Jean Jacque Boissard and Otto van Veen
- Emblems: Nicholas M. Meerfeldt
- Alchemy Art: Manly P. Hall
- Emblems: Manly P. Hall
- Alchemy Art & Symbols
- Splendor Solis

For the latest information, please visit author's site:
Parallel47North.com/collections/esoteric-books
If you have any question or feedback, please contact:
info@Parallel47North.com

Hand-drawn Illustration of Book Cover Art by Jessica Naomi.

The Artist Portfolio: JessicaNaomiDesigns.com

For those interested in Rosicrucian or similar Esoteric teaching.

Soul.org

Theosophical.org

Whiteaglelodge.org

PTTHfoundation.com